What Ought I to Do?

What Ought

CORNELL UNIVERSITY PRESS   *Ithaca and London*

CATHERINE CHALIER

I to Do?

Morality in Kant and Levinas

Translated from the French by Jane Marie Todd

This translation was prepared with the generous assistance of
the French Ministry of Culture—Centre National du Livre.

Original French edition, *Pour une morale au-delá du savior: Kant et
Levinas*, copyright © 1998 by Editions Albin Michel, Paris.
All rights reserved.

English translation copyright © 2002 by Cornell University

English translation first published 2002 by Cornell University Press

First printing, Cornell Paperbacks, 2002

Printed in the United States of America

Library of Congress Cataloging-in-Publication Data
Chalier, Catherine
    [Pour une morale au-dela du savoir. English]
    What ought I to do? : morality in Kant and Levinas / Catherine
Chalier ; translated from the French by Jane Marie Todd.
        p. cm.
    Includes bibliographical references and index.
    ISBN 0-8014-3709-1 (cloth : alk. paper) — ISBN 0-8014-8794-3 (pbk.:
alk. paper)
        1. Kant, Immanuel, 1724-1804—Ethics.   2. Levinas,
Emmanuel—Ethics.   3. Ethics, Modern.   I. Title.
    B2799.E8 C4613 2002
    170'.92'2—dc21   2001006789

Cornell University Press strives to use environmentally responsible
suppliers and materials to the fullest extent possible in the publishing
of its books. Such materials include vegetable-based, low-VOC inks
and acid-free papers that are recycled, totally chlorine-free, or partly
composed of nonwood fibers. For further information, visit our
website at www.cornellpress.cornell.edu.

Cloth printing   10 9 8 7 6 5 4 3 2 1

Paperback printing   10 9 8 7 6 5 4 3 2 1

contents

What Ought I to Do?

Introduction

The crisis of the subject, precipitated by the modern suspicion surrounding metaphysics, is causing man to lose all certainty about his being. The cogito no longer constitutes the certain and unquestionable "Archimedean point" that Descartes hoped would serve as a basis on which to reconstruct the order of truths.[1] The *I*, denounced as an illusion, fails to *posit itself* and leaves confusion about the self in its wake. The subject is no longer what it is conscious of being. It no longer finds its identity "within" and must often be content to play a role in a private, social, and historical drama whose author and stakes no one really knows. The *I*—forgetful of the infinite, which, according to Descartes, dwells within the subject and confers permanence on its self-certainty, and incapable of finding the law that governs its thoughts and acts in the innermost depths of its finitude—reaches the point where it expects the sense of its being to come from a social or historical exteriority, where it hopes to be recognized by others, and at the same time demands that recognition with a violence commensurate with its own precariousness. But the riddle of the question *Who?* seems to have become pointless, given the chasm opened by the rise of the human sciences, which eliminate the very idea of the subject from their conception of causality, as if that idea were a fiction or a humanist and spiritualist nostalgia. And even the authority of the human sciences has now been overtaken, shaken as a matter of fact, by certain claims of biology and by the reductionism of "neuroscience."[2] In the name of reason, of which these sciences claim to be the sole guarantors, they sometimes do not hesitate to heap scorn on philosophy, literature, and the arts. They then proclaim themselves in possession of the only true human "science" and denounce the metaphysical character of the alleged separation between the human and the animal.

Must the subject succumb to these attacks? In any case, if we agree that its sovereignty has been called into question by the various hermeneutics—psychoanalytic, sociological, historical, or biological—from which it undeniably stems, is that the same thing as consenting to deride it in order to better assure oneself of its futility and death? Clearly, that question assumes a primordial importance in relation to moral thought. In fact, if the radicality of a flawless determinism were to replace the illusion of the subject grounded in itself, the latter would become an epiphenomenon whose word would no longer be credible, since that word would have to conform to structures that govern the subject unbeknownst to itself. As a result, moral notions as a whole—particularly those of responsibility and freedom—would be open to the charge of inconsistency. A subject's recognition that its acts, and, should the occasion arise, its transgressions, are imputable to itself would become meaningless. In spite of everything, however, alienation does not constitute an alibi or a justification in the eyes of society, or even (enigmatically for anyone who assimilates the subject to a fiction) in one's own eyes. Therefore, one often bears the burden of one's misdeeds, real or supposed, in a different way. "Man no longer confesses his sins, but rather acquiesces to the accusations." It is as if human beings, rather than being schooled to respect themselves, were instead stripped of any moral responsibility and left to cling to a vain pride; as if they were finally, in spite of everything and in many circumstances, called upon to surrender to the inaccurate and evil image that other people happen to impose on them. Nevertheless, with freedom and responsibility disappearing under the weight of countless "microscopic mechanisms" to be studied scientifically, human life might no longer have recourse to the notion of the subject. The moral and political consequences of that disappearance ought to command our utmost attention. How can we characterize our battles for human honor and freedom if the subject disappears under the sway of determinism, and if freedom and responsibility are absurd concepts, superseded by scientific discoveries?

From that "scientific" perspective, and with respect to historical development, interlocutors are also not unique and irreplaceable people but rather "moments" in the universal discourse of an impersonal reason.[3] Philosophies of history have certainly attempted to show that such alienation could someday be overcome, but the tragedies of the twentieth century have continued to contradict their hopes. Anxiety is growing, therefore: "It stems from the experience of revolutions that have become mired in bureaucracy, and of totalitarian repression and violence that pass themselves off as revolutions."[4] The end of that distress is, in itself, not enough to give humans the sense of a life as responsible subjects. But, in spite of everything, the resistance of men and women who, living under oppression and persecution, sometimes in extreme isolation, did not resign themselves to becoming dead souls, still brightens the human horizon.

The moral subject is now looking for itself in a world where many have decreed—in the name of science or ideology—that it is decidedly out-of-date. It is looking for itself in a world deserted by the hope for sense. Often, it seems that to speak of sense is purely and simply to confess one's incapacity to take on the burden of nihilism, which, since Nietzsche, it is said, has paralyzed every value. But the moral subject is also looking for itself in a world still marked on a daily basis by the human resistance to humiliation, oppression, and death. That resistance does not wait for tyranny and terror to take root before it manifests itself: it has already begun, on the most ordinary days, when a person, with head held high, confronts the subtle or brutal denial of freedom that afflicts so many lives. That resistance comes about every time people, whatever their familial, social, historical, or even biological antecedents, refuse to give in to the glamour of death and the intimidation of one person by another, when they choose life and act in a just manner. That resistance prevails, finally, whenever a person remembers that every act—positive or negative—has repercussions beyond the appearance of its immediate effects,[5] when, that is, wherever that person happens to be, out of circumstance or necessity, he or she acknowledges responsibility for the fate of the world.

From that viewpoint, my reflection on the moral subject with Kant and Levinas is a contribution to an understanding of the significance of the moral imperative—its connection to freedom and responsibility—within the context of modernity. Given that its traditional foundations—nature, cosmos, being, and God—have, along with the subject itself, been shaken by the scientific and philosophical critique, what can still justify the idea of such an imperative? I would like to demonstrate that a philosophy of the subject is, in fact, indispensable for replying to that question, despite the level of suspicion weighing on the subject and despite the often peremptory declarations regarding the closure of the metaphysical field and the disappearance of the referential schema. For many people, in fact, moral conduct, if it is not to be self-contradictory and to veer toward submission, cannot be dependent on any reference to the authority of religious or social tradition. But it also cannot depend on conformity to a nature or a history, without attending to and looking kindly on human singularity. Does that mean that such conduct no longer makes any sense? Does it mean that the ideas of good and evil, freedom and responsibility, are henceforth null and void or absurd?

I am not recommending some "return" to the subject, now that it has gone through the ordeal of being called into question. That questioning is still pertinent, and the idea of a return is complex and problematic, given the irreversibility of time and history. I will simply attempt to show that a philosophy of the moral subject remains possible and necessary.

Kant and Levinas point in that direction. Nevertheless, these philosophers do not have a high opinion of human beings' actual moral behavior. On many occasions, Kant confesses his agnosticism in that regard, and Levinas has to admit that men have shown themselves capable of "little good." As a result, ethics requires a philosophy commensurate with that fragility or with the "little good" that, incomprehensibly in terms of the cult of perseverance-in-being at all cost, nevertheless introduces a dimension of hope into history, sometimes even at moments of the most extreme wickedness. But does the act of seeking the source of ethics in the subject—divorced from the support of a reference to God, being, or the natural order—suffice to give sense to that fragility and, hence, to that hope? Does it suffice to redeem such notions? Kant and Levinas respond with a shared admiration for practical reason's aptitude to exceed the bounds of speculative reason. Kant writes: "We cannot consider without admiration how great an advantage the practical faculty of appraising has over the theoretical in common human understanding."[6] Levinas recognizes his proximity to that philosophy, since, "beside the theoretical access to the being of the phenomenon," Kant's reflections examine how the implications of moral action can be explained by the existence of a reasonable subject "without becoming the object of any knowledge of being."[7] That view corroborates his preoccupation with an ethics that is not based on an ontology. Nevertheless, in spite of the profound complicity between them, there is not *one* philosophy of the moral subject common to the two philosophers. Their analyses differ on many points, and the major issue, it seems, has to do with the moral subject's relation to finitude and to the infinite.

Kant adopts the point of view of the subject's radical finitude, whereas Levinas, closer to Descartes, analyzes how the infinite dwells within the subject's finitude. The moral philosophy resulting from each of these two approaches obviously bears the mark of that difference. Kant seeks to discover how the moral law makes itself heard to a finite subject, irremediably limited in terms of speculative knowledge to the intuitions of time and space. Levinas wishes to show how the infinite, without leading to any speculative or dogmatic proposition, occurs within the subject itself, how the idea of infinity is introduced into the subject through an ethical relationship to the other. The Kantian subject knows it is finite, particularly by virtue of the respect that the presence of the moral law within it inspires. The Levinassian subject conceives of the infinite—which is not the same as conceiving of an object—when it responds to the appeal of the other's transcendence.

By comparing these two philosophies of the moral subject, I intend to analyze and evaluate the meaning and the stakes—especially regarding the significance of the word *human*, so present in both bodies of work—of their similarities and differences. I wish to examine their common interest in conceiving of a moral obligation beyond any possible theoretical knowledge and the difficulties, even the aporias, of their analyses in relation to one another. In fact, if, despite the Enlightenment, Kant is distrustful of the capacity of knowledge to make people moral; a fortiori Levinas, living in the twentieth century, can only note the persistence of the somber connection between culture and barbarism, can only share Kant's disheartening bitterness. The two philosophers therefore seek to emancipate ethics from the level of a person's knowledge and education, even while refusing to rely on feelings or spontaneity to redeem moral behavior. They know, clearly, that an ethics founded on these principles would remain at the mercy of their precariousness and partiality. Nevertheless, whereas Kant, faithful to the great tradition of reflexive philosophy, responds to that terrible fact with the analysis of the moral subject's good will, Levinas departs from that tradition, seeking what awakens the subject to morality in an exteriority and not in its own self-reflection *(retour sur soi)*. His analysis of the human face dislocates the source of morality: moral obligation does not come from the self, from the decision to act out of good will, but from an awakening in oneself of that obligation by the other.

Nevertheless, Kant and Levinas immediately encounter difficulties internal to their analyses: How can one explain ill will and deafness to the appeal of the face? Neither philosopher fails to appreciate the threat of evil; each knows that its implacable burden is felt in every life, even the life concerned with morality. And yet, faced with these questions internal to their philosophies, they respond similarly: evil is formidable—radical, says Kant; insurmountably ambiguous, says Levinas—but it is not absolute. Good is anterior to it. That nonchronological anteriority—an anteriority of principle for Kant, an anarchical anteriority for Levinas—prevents them from placing good and evil on a symmetrical plane and explains why good will and the act of heeding the appeal of the face remain possible, despite the devastating grip evil has on the subject.

The great dividing line—the fracture even—between the two philosophies is already drawn: Kant's position in relation to moral ipseity leads him to defend moral autonomy without fail; Levinas's position cannot possibly accept it. Kant asserts that every form of heteronomy without exception leads to the destruction of ethics, whereas Levinas does not hesitate to reconsider the case. Even as he clearly challenges the alienating forms of heteronomy—submission to the tyrant, for example—he defends the idea of a moral heteronomy. Is freedom a lost cause, then? No, says Levinas. Unlike Kant, he distinguishes the concept of freedom from that of autonomy, conceiving of the former as the subject's accession to its irreplaceable uniqueness or as election. For Kant, the moral law appeals to the self as lawmaker—hence the constitutive autonomy of ipseity. Conversely, for Levinas, it entails the imperative of an exteriority—hence heteronomy. And these different views lead to consequences regarding the idea each philosopher forms of the human and its universality. To understand the human, must one start from the self and the decision to submit one's maxims to the universal form prescribed by law? Or must one concede that the consciousness of human universality is awakened in the subject at the instant of its response to a singular appeal that decenters it?

What, then, is the status of sensibility in relation to reason in these two philosophies? The pride of asserting one's autonomy—something approaching the self's positing of itself—would have the subject obey practical reason without being affected by anything else. The Kantian reflection on respect and on the sublime, however, shows that things do not happen in that way: affect belongs to pathology and contradicts autonomy, but respect and the sublime are exceptions. Levinas does not share that distrust of sensibility. Even though, like Kant, he rejects the influence of egoism over the moral subject, he does so to better envision sensibility in a different way, as an unavoidable condition of the ethical. In fact, the moral subject is not autonomous, and the way alterity inhabits it needs to be described, which requires conceiving of how it is exposed to the other, how the moral subject is, in its passivity, vulnerable to the other's suffering. Levinas, then, maintains that the moral self is the object of affects. But these affects are not the opposite of ethics, as they are for Kant. On the contrary, they are constitutive of ethics.

These analyses lead Kant and Levinas to different assessments of the connection between freedom and responsibility. The Kantian idea of a transcendental freedom and of a timeless choice defends, to the limit of the conceivable, the idea that freedom is primary and foundational. The subject's responsibility is deduced from it, whatever the chance events of its existence. In supporting the thesis of the moral subject's election, Levinas displaces the axis of that mode of thought. Only the response to election or to the appeal—responsibility—gives man a sense of freedom. In discovering that it alone is capable of responding, the subject discovers its uniqueness and only then its freedom. The subject—free, unique, and capable of response—knows it is solicited from time immemorial.

These philosophers require a great deal of people. Do they promise us anything? Must the moral subject act in a disinterested manner, to the point of ignoring the very idea of its own happiness? Although Kant criticizes eudaemonism for its incapacity to conceive of moral autonomy, he nevertheless claims that the subject can make itself "worthy of being happy." The virtuous person can hope that his or her efforts will lead to happiness. But the highest good—the union of virtue and happiness—presupposes the immortality of the soul and the existence of a God. Such are the assumptions of practical reason: God will see to it that the efforts of the virtuous person will not remain without reward. Does Levinas share that hope? He does not say it in that way. Like Kant, he dissociates the idea of happiness from a knowledge of the absolute, but he does not speak of the ultimate hope. Conversely, he evokes an eschatology without hope within the time of the ego. Finally, he maintains that the desire for God does not subside in the happiness of contemplation but is lived as an infinite obligation.

Why does the word "God" occur in the analyses of the two philosophers, given that neither of them bases ethics on any religious belief? What sense are we to make of Kant's references to Christianity and Levinas's to Judaism? Since they are not proposing a theology, we might well wonder why, in their works, the reflection on the moral subject leads us to the trace of the word "God."

o n e   **The Critique of Intellectualism**

The tragic events of the twentieth century were not the result of the barbarism and savagery of uncivilized people, denied education, driven by instinct, faithless and lawless. A highly civilized country produced the Shoah; the hope for a fraternal and just society gave way to the Gulag. "Art, intellectual pursuits, the development of the natural sciences, many branches of scholarship flourished in close spatial, temporal proximity to massacre and the death camps."[1] Even now, the suffering and premature deaths of so many individuals victimized by history and the needs of the moment, but also by the immorality of daily life, cannot be attributed to a general lack of education and cultural refinement. That proximity between culture and horror makes the hope of seeing men bettered by education appear futile. It seems to sound the death knell of any idea of moral and spiritual progress through intellectual enlightenment. "When we were in the camp," writes Zoran Music, "we often told ourselves that this sort of thing could never occur again: 'we were the last' to whom it would happen. . . . As time went on, I saw that the same sort of thing was beginning to occur everywhere in the world. . . . The truth is, *we are not the last.*"[2] People do, of course, learn from the history books. They know the evil that prevails on earth, but that knowledge does not change them; it does not seem to give them the desire and the strength to become better people.

The gulf that separates culture and morality has been pointed out since ancient times. At the dawn of philosophy, Socrates was already telling the Athenians that moral failings threaten the life of a man, whatever his level of education and respectability, because moral conduct, the care of his soul, does not rest on knowledge.[3] Kant laments this fact as well: "To a high degree we are, through art and science, *cultured.* We are *civilized*—perhaps too much for our own good—in all sorts of social grace and decorum. But to consider ourselves as having reached *morality*—for that, much is lacking."[4] As for Levinas, he is horrified by the tragedy of a century more concerned with science and technology than with attention to particular lives, a century inclined to believe in the relativity, even the equivalence, of values and cultures. Clearly, these philosophers do not conclude that education is futile and ethics impossible; on the contrary, they seek to understand the significance and timelessness of the moral imperative, even if that imperative must be acted upon without the aid of knowledge.

Kant tells us that the few manifestations of particular wisdom he has observed "on the great world-stage" do not dispel the dark mood that comes over him when observing "everything in the large[,] woven together from folly, childish vanity, even from childish malice and destructiveness"—that is, human behavior as a whole. The philosopher wonders whether that situation will remain, whether it will, in the end, produce "a hell of evils, however civilized we may now be, by annihilating civilization and all cultural progress through barbarous devastation"; or whether, on the contrary, we must embrace the hope that the human race will one day escape its chaotic situation. Of course, Kant favors the latter hypothesis, which requires every political community to endeavor to shape the hearts and minds of its citizenry. He believes that such a hope is legitimate, because, he says, *the age of enlightenment* dawns gradually, "with intermittent folly and caprice," giving us "a consoling view of the future." Someday, we will no longer be "forced to turn our eyes from [the history of mankind] in disgust." But, Kant concludes, the concern is to know "how our descendants will begin to grasp the burden of the history we shall leave to them after a few centuries."[5]

Those descendants now know how well founded that concern was. "The hell of evils" feared by Kant has come about, and people of culture were powerless to check its advance; indeed, they were often compromised by it. Levinas knows this, and he does not share the Kantian hope in an *age of enlightenment;* he clings to the few manifestations of particular wisdom that, for Kant, did not counterbalance the folly. These manifestations, says Levinas, such as one person's ethical behavior or a humble gesture of kindness even in the midst of historical tragedy, allow us to continue to place some hope in humanity.

The two philosophers thus begin their moral reflections by observing the gulf between culture and morality. What is the significance of that gulf? Given that neither philosopher gives up the possibility of constructing an ethics, how and from what perspective does each analyze the reasons that ideas are powerless to induce moral behavior?

Culture and Immorality

Love of the arts, of literature, philosophy, or science, like religious concerns, does not prevent an individual from being compromised by immorality and barbarism. Particularly in the twentieth century, many examples point to the monstrous alliance between intellectual qualities, aesthetic taste, or spiritual concerns on the one hand and inhumanity on the other. "A fair proportion of the intelligentsia and of the institutions of European civilization—letters, the academy, the performing arts—met inhumanity with varying degrees of welcome."[6] In the death camps themselves, some of the guards had an appreciation for music, and orchestras existed there.

> But the same Kramer who wept listening to Schumann, and who had been a bookseller before becoming a Commandant at Birkenau, was capable of smashing in an inmate's skull with his club because she was not walking fast enough; in Struthof, where he had previously worked, he personally pushed the naked women into the gas chamber and observed their agony through a window installed for that purpose. At his trial,

he declared: "I felt no emotion in carrying out those acts." Why did music make him weep and not the deaths of human beings who resembled him?[7]

Clearly, that terrible fact might lead us to conclude that, though some men and women acted with courage, often at the cost of their lives—like the young people in the "White Rose" group in Germany, who felt certain it would be a sin to break ranks with the victims or simply confine themselves to a vague pity—ethics is not learned in books or in academic or religious institutions. No book, no institution, required Sophia Scholl, her brother, and their friends to denounce the murder of the Jews as "the most frightful crime against human dignity."[8] In their tragic solitude, these young Catholics knew that it is only by listening to one's inner voice that one can find the strength to resist when, all around, even educated and religious people are making their peace with the extermination orders.

But what does "inner voice" mean? Why is it not accessible through knowledge? How are we to understand what it is?

The intelligence is in the service of ideas, and this often makes it possible to construct an ideal, sometimes with universal moral or political implications; but that ideal remains without impact on the concrete commitments of the person professing it. Ignorance of *particular facts* and *persons* in favor of the reverence due to *notions* and *causes* justifies the worst compromises. In that respect, Hegel detected an attitude typical of German intellectuals, always ready to give a distorted explanation of the situation in the name of their *notions*.[9]

That attitude is not the monopoly of German intellectuals, of course; it is the result of the very desire to seek universality through abstraction rather than concrete singularity. Yet abstraction is the very essence of knowledge, and "philosophy itself," which concerns itself with knowledge, "is characterized by the substitution of ideas for persons, of the theme for the interlocutor, of the interiority of the logical relationship for the exteriority of the act of questioning. Beings are reduced to the neutrality *[le Neutre]* of the idea, being, the concept."[10] And yet, how are we to deal with individuals, how are we to conceive of morality, in such abstract terms?

Kant encountered that difficulty early on. "There was a time," he writes, "when I believed this [thirst for knowledge] constituted the honor of humanity, and I despised the people, who know nothing. Rousseau corrected me in this. This binding prejudice disappeared. I learned to honor man."[11] Levinas observes that culture and its magnificent institutions—those of a Europe marked by centuries of Christianity and by the Enlightenment—offered almost no resistance to Nazi barbarism. Both philosophers, then, observe that ideas, even beautiful ones taken from humanism, are power-less to steer a person toward the good, the true, and the just, as soon as one judges, rightly or wrongly, that one's own self-interest may be at stake. Thought, in this view, incurs no consequences in real life, and an intel-lectual, to avoid suffering, might alter his ideas or forget what he professes. The intellectual will then often feel contempt, jealousy, and hatred toward those who tremble in fear when a beautiful thought is expressed if their own behavior is not consistent with it. But what value does a philosophy have if it vanishes when it is put to the test? What value do ideas about ethics have if human beings do not place the fear of transgressing them above their articulation?

Kant and Levinas obviously do not abandon philosophy, but they re-mind us that thought transcends knowledge and is not an act of mastery tending to banish uncertainties, shortcomings, and threats from the out-side. And it is precisely that dimension of humility—that consent at the limit of theoretical reason—that allows these philosophers to point the way toward a moral philosophy not dependent upon theoretical knowl-edge and to keep alive the quest for the good. To do so, they seek the source of morality *in the subject* and not in its level of knowledge.

Both Kant and Levinas note that moral conduct sometimes prevails un-expectedly in one person or another. Hence, in the tragic twentieth cen-tury, "the memory of Jews and non-Jews, who, in the midst of the chaos, without even knowing or seeing one another, knew how to behave as if the world had not disintegrated," attests to the fact that ethics transcends in-stitutions, since even those institutions called upon to educate people and ensure moral and political progress were compromised by the nihilist dev-astation. Ethics, says Levinas, thus resides entirely "in the obligation to lodge all the humanity of man in the ramshackle house of the conscience, exposed to the elements."[12] From that point of view, ethics makes it im-possible to remain content with abstractions when we are confronted with a being of flesh and blood, but it also commits us to ask how we are to con-ceive of and transmit that obligation. In fact, although it is true that no system of ideas can adequately account for such an obligation, Levinas's statement does not serve to praise simple, uneducated people, since prejudices and the absence of thought are more likely to encourage brutality and hatred than they are to encourage a responsible attitude toward the weak. The ideologies of hatred go hand in hand with a lack of reflection.

When Kant, taking his cue from Rousseau, remembers the honor residing in the ignorant and uncivilized people, he does not do so to praise ignorance in matters of morality. When Levinas evokes the solitary conscience capable of behaving morally even when reason has broken down, he does not do so to champion the obliteration of culture. But both philosophers challenge us to understand how and why *the moral subject* transcends the limits assigned to theoretical thought.

The Quest for Principles

Is ethics derived from reason or from feeling? Kant's and then Levinas's philosophy gives us a new way to reflect on that very old alternative. The question had attracted the attention of many thinkers before them. Hume, for example, lamented the confusion surrounding the subject. He noted that some thinkers claimed that "virtue is nothing but conformity to reason" but believed that it drew its existence "from taste and sentiment"; others evoked the beauty of virtue and the deformity of vice but explained these distinctions with "metaphysical reasonings, and by deductions from the most abstract principles of the understanding."[13] Hume remarked that no act of reasoning has the power to incite a feeling or an action: "the truths" discovered by the inferences and conclusions of the understanding "are indifferent and beget no desire or aversion, they can have no influence on conduct and behavior."[14] Without feelings—without the attraction to virtue and the repugnance for vice—moral ideas could not possibly lead to moral behavior. "Reason is wholly inactive and can never be the source of so active a principle as conscience, a sense of morals."[15] Astonishment at education's incapacity to make men moral would thus be unjustified, since ideas have no power over the passions and the feelings.

Since moral behavior exists and cannot be deduced from ideas, however, it depends, according to Hume, "on some internal sense or feeling, which nature has made universal in the whole species." The distinctions and conclusions of reasoned argument serve only to point the way. In addition, Hume rejects the idea that *all* moral qualities can come about through coercion—the fear of punishment and the hope of some reward—and he concludes that feelings are the most important source of ethics. The feeling of *benevolence* confers the highest merit on man, and *sympathy*, so natural to human beings, "can alone be the foundation of morality."[16]

Kant seems close to Hume and the other English empiricists in his *Observations on the Feeling of the Beautiful and Sublime*. He notes, in fact, that the principles on which "true virtue" rests "are not speculative rules, but the consciousness of a feeling that lives in every human breast and extends itself much further than over the particular grounds of compassion and complaisance."[17] And he believes that that feeling—irreducible to a "moral sense," however, which he will denounce as false[18]—is particularly well-demonstrated by Rousseau. Kant pays tribute to him for having discovered, "in the diversity of conventional human forms, the nature of man where it had lain buried."[19] Like Newton seeking the laws nature obeys, Rousseau, in this view, demonstrated a unity hidden behind the multiplicity of human behaviors. Kant is delighted by this, since he is not satisfied with the *particular* cause of compassion or complaisance but wants a *universal principle* of morality.

The charitable impulse and the spontaneous gesture of benevolence are not enough. In fact, despite their goodness and beauty, they are often partial, even blind, and forgetful of the justice due the species. True virtue cannot be founded on sympathy, as Hume would like, because the human heart is incapable of having that feeling for "every human being," which makes sympathy unjust. Charity toward an indigent individual, if it is to remain virtuous and sublime, must therefore be subordinated to principles that take "the human species" into account. "True virtue can be grafted only upon principles such that the more general they are, the more sublime and noble it becomes." In morality, these principles, or these first propositions from which particular judgments are derived, are thus the result of the consciousness of a universal feeling—and not from a speculation—present in "every human breast." But what is that feeling? Since Hume's sympathy and Rousseau's compassion do not meet the criterion for indispensable universality, Kant does not embrace them. For him, only the feeling of "the beauty and dignity of human nature"[20] appears to meet the requirement of universality and, consequently, of virtue.

That feeling therefore constitutes the principle of virtue, even though, because of "the weakness of human nature," it does not always take root.

That is why providence bestowed "assisting drives" on human beings that propel them toward generosity, compassion, or complaisance. But these "adoptive virtues" do not rest on principles. They do not suffice, moreover, and often, concern for the opinion of others must come to counterbalance people's "coarser selfishness" and "common sensuality."[21] Frequently, individuals accept sacrifice, not on principle or out of sympathy, but to save appearances and hold on to other people's respect.

Only the presence within a person of the feeling of the beauty and dignity of human nature justifies one's conduct being called virtuous. Many people act courageously, justly, or generously as a result of circumstance and for self-interested motives. In spite of the appearances, it is impossible to defend their morality. Conversely, the truly good person subordinates his spontaneous impulses and personal emotions, his own interests and self-love, to the feeling of the beauty and dignity of human nature; he makes all his actions conform to that principle. In addition, the good person is aware of the difficulty of the task and knows that he must exercise self-control, check his spontaneous benevolence or aversion, and limit his egoism. Kant even maintains that, for this reason, true virtue is akin to a *melancholy* frame of mind.[22] The virtuous person has a keen sense of sinfulness. The feeling of the beauty of human nature incites one toward a general benevolence, but, to that end, one must struggle against one's personal inclinations; the sense of the dignity of human nature leads one to a general respect for human beings, but that respect is not a matter of course, in the case, for example, of people who have committed an offense against oneself, or who, quite simply, have no respect for themselves.

The sciences and arts tolerate immorality. Scientists, artists, and philosophers, despite their distinguished education, make their peace with immoral behavior. This observation by Kant leads him to seek a moral principle that admits no exception, and he says he finds it in a feeling—and not in a knowledge—that is not addressed to a particular person but to "human nature." That feeling does not belong to the particular sensibility of each individual; it stands apart from the partiality of the emotions and excepts no one. Beyond all the singularities and all social or cultural differences, its aim is the beauty and dignity of "human nature." Therefore, it is not dependent on the impressions of the moment. It is, in fact, a principle valid for all places and all times. Kant seeks a way for ethics to transcend all particularities—otherwise, the relativism of opinion will prevail in this realm as well, giving free rein to the worst deficiencies. In his *Observations on the Feeling of the Beautiful and Sublime*, Kant finds the universal principle of morality in the feeling—and not in the idea—that "human nature" is, as such, worthy of respect.

The reality of that feeling is not a matter of course, however. Kant admits this and attributes that fact to the weakness of the very human nature whose dignity he simultaneously asserts. Yet, if dignity can be characterized as what is priceless, what admits of no equivalent, what has an intrinsic value,[23] we must wonder what the feeling of the dignity of human nature can mean in relation to individual human beings, whom Kant sees as fundamentally weak, mediocre, and egoistic. The philosopher, in fact, never evokes the dignity of man *(Würde des Menschen)* or human dignity *(menschliche Würde)* but embraces only the dignity of humanity *(Würde der Menschheit)*. That expression, however, does not refer to the concrete individual but rather to the species capable of progressing toward a better future.[24]

Nevertheless, despite Kant's assertion of its universality and its character as principle, a feeling relating to an idea—the species or human nature—and not to a concrete singularity—*this* person—cannot fail to raise a difficulty, especially since the philosopher, in his concrete descriptions of human beings, seems to perceive nothing dignified about them, noting above all their wretchedness. What becomes of the principle of morality, despite its universality, when it is confronted with an individual at a particular moment in his or her life? It is truly at that moment, when the progress of the human race is still unknown, and in the presence of individuals who share that moment with oneself, that moral behavior has a meaning. Can a universal principle that applies to an abstraction—nature or the human race—awaken the concrete gestures of moral behavior toward a particular person? Can it do so *even if* its source resides in good will, as Kant will explain,[25] and not in knowledge, which, as such, is incapable of making people moral? Can it awaken toward that particular other, who cannot wait for the time to be ripe, as Kant says, to be consoled of his present historical misfortune, a misfortune endured by flesh-and-blood victims and not by human nature? The concern for universality is indispensable for an ethics interested in moving beyond the relativism of values proper to each culture; that is, it is necessary if we are to recognize the human being in humanity. But can that concern be posited as a principle on the basis of which the singularity of persons will be respected, or must it emerge (and how so?) from a sensible[26] encounter with these individuals?

This dilemma can be expressed another way: Does the source of moral behavior toward the other lie in a subject's principles, independent of any encounter the subject might have with the sensible and concrete exteriority of individuals, or is it in fact produced by that encounter, independent of preexistent principles?

The dialogue between Levinas and Kant begins with that question. Therefore, we might well wonder why, despite their common critique of intellectualism, the two philosophers do not share the same confidence in the notion of "principle." Levinas does not posit any principle as a guide to moral behavior toward the other; he does not approach the other with a preexistent idea or feeling of his dignity but in a *"breathlessness of the spirit"*[27] that suspends knowledge. More precisely, according to him it is the encounter with a person's singularity that obliges one to think anarchically, and which, without any prior reference to the ideas of nature or of the human race, gives a human being his or her "highest dignity" as a unique individual.[28] It is as if it were necessary to reach the universal via singularities rather than attempt—in vain, as history teaches us—to rediscover these singularities on the basis of a universal principle, even that of the dignity of human nature. It is on the basis of an "anarchical situation," "more ancient than the beginning and the principle,"[29] that the dignity of humanity—of *this* human, fragile and unique, living at this moment with oneself—comes to mind.

How are we to understand this anarchy that defies knowledge?

The Voice of the Ethical Conscience

The extreme urgency of morality defers speculative labor which, via deduction, would lead back to the universal principles that are supposed to guide action. That urgency does not lend itself to an intellectual receptivity concerned to evaluate behavior in terms of a prior theoretical knowledge in order to be sure of its validity. No original idea of human nature comes to enlighten the subject faced with that urgency. Ethics, says Levinas, does not begin with the will applying what is said or taught—even if it is also appropriate to do so—but with a decision to allow oneself to be assailed by the moral imperative without reflecting on principles. Feeding the hungry, hiding the persecuted, and finding the resources to save them are not the result of a reflection conducted with complete independence of mind, even if it were guided by the fine principle of the dignity of human nature. The swiftness of the gestures to be made does not allow time to examine the ins and outs of the situation or to weigh the consequences to oneself. Hence, says the historian R. Hilberg, during World War II, the people who saved Jews "had to make their decisions instantaneously. . . . Finally, they had to have the inner flexibility to alter or abandon personal routines."[30] Is moral conduct, inseparable from an obedience to what the uniqueness of a situation dictates, an obedience subject to no condition and to no principle, therefore merely spontaneity deprived of thought?

Levinas criticizes the idea of the priority of knowledge over action as something that tempts us toward a perpetual disengagement "within universal compromise."[31] The adult ego weighs the pros and cons before taking any action and criticizes the generous but unreflective impulses of youth. Yet, in the end, that ego also often abstains from acting on the pretext that things are too complex. For Levinas, however, to call that temptation into question is not the same thing as to justify spontaneity or the "spirit of childhood," much less to refuse the rights of thought. Like Kant, Levinas remarks that people are not spontaneously inclined to behave in a disinterested manner, but, unlike Kant, he does not posit a *principle* of morality but seeks to hear "the *voice* of the ethical conscience."[32]

What is the meaning of that voice irreducible to any principle? What does it allow us to hear? Whereas the principle—which Kant presents as a given of sensibility or, in a later formulation, as a "fact of reason"[33]—implies a stopping point, a point of certainty within reflection, the "voice" surprises the subject who hears it. The person who has moral principles—the principle of the dignity of human nature, for example—probably knows nothing about that human nature, since the principle has no objective and gnoseological value, but that person does have a solid, albeit subjective, basis for his or her moral judgments. As Kant says, that person can "orient himself in thought." In contrast, whoever hears "the voice of the ethical conscience" is confronted by a strangeness irreducible to the firmness of a principle, an always-disconcerting strangeness. What is its significance?

When Levinas evokes that voice, he associates it with an idea harshly criticized by Kant: that of inspiration. In fact, he says, that voice irreducible to a principle depends neither on the intentionality of a cogito, a thinking self, which would then retain the privilege of judging the merits of what he hears, nor on an innate instinct or feeling. It is "inspired by an unknown God," who compels the individual "to bear nontransferable responsibilities."[34] That "transcendence of inspiration," or the ethical conscience's act of hearing a voice that exceeds its capacity to know, is not, however, to be confused with the enthusiasm Kant denounces as the rejection of thought and the source of the worst kind of illusions. *Schwärmerei* does not appeal to Levinas, who is very concerned to move beyond pathos to the "sobering up" of the conscience, particularly when the word "God" is uttered.[35] For Kant, *Schwärmerei* is evil in philosophy because it overturns principles and opens the door to extravagance, superstition, and "even the mania of atheism," on the pretext of an exalted intuition called faith.[36] For Levinas, however, it remains irrelevant, given the transcendence of inspiration as he understands it. In fact, that inspiration does not suspend thought and does not justify abandoning oneself to so-called divine impulses. As Levinas explains, it is experienced in the confrontation of the subject with the paradox of the idea of the infinite. It is Descartes, and not some enthusiastic thinker, who explains the significance of that paradox, when, in his third metaphysical meditation, he discovers the presence of an idea in his mind—the idea of the infinite—for which he cannot be the cause, since the finite and imperfect subject, despite its lofty thoughts, remains incapable of containing it.[37]

According to Levinas, many other philosophers, though wary of the imagination and anxious to hold onto reason, are open to that philosophy of excess. Aristotle's "theory of the active intellect" and the "winged thought" evoked by Plato in *Phaedrus* attest to this. In the latter case, Plato does not hesitate to use the word "delirium"; yet, for him, this word has no "irrationalist sense." That delirium "is only a shattering, divine in its essence, of custom and rule." It is "reason itself, rising up to the ideas," or "the end of solitary thought."[38] Therefore, it is not an exaltation unamenable to reason and unable to be shared but rather the opening up of that reason that prevents it from resting on principles, even very rigorous ones. That opening up—to the idea of the infinite in man, as Descartes says—troubles the subject. Levinas then wonders whether a reason that determines its own laws, and obeys no other, truly constitutes, in a privileged manner, "the final touchstone of the judgment," as Kant would have it.[39] In that case, reason would truly have the strength and solidity of a stone but also its opacity; no encounter with alterity would be able to affect it and call the firmness of its principles into question. No voice would trouble it since, thanks to these principles, it would know from the outset how to respond. It would not let itself be surprised since the only aspect of alterity it would hold on to is that which can be measured by the yardstick of its principles.

When Levinas evokes "the voice of the ethical conscience," he is not referring to any principle (arche), since a principle would block the intrusion of that voice within oneself. Contrary to Kant, who denounces "the anarchical use of reason,"[40] Levinas does not shrink from the word "anarchy." But that word does not mean, as it does for Kant, an audacious, lawless, and supposedly inspired impulse but suggests an obedience to a command that is formulated "in the voice of the very person who obeys it."[41] That obedience leaves no time to consult one's list of principles.

That anarchical ethics, an ethics that does not result from putting into practice previously known or posited principles, is, in fact, very constraining. Yet, despite Levinas's references to Plato and Descartes, who, according to him, had a sense for what exceeds principles, Levinas looks above all to the Jewish tradition for the moral implications of anarchy. He looks for the way to understand, without naivete, the expression, "we will do and we will hear" (naase venishma), uttered by the children of Israel at the foot of Mount Sinai (Exodus 24:7).[42] In terms of common sense, these words sound strange, since they imply a commitment without a prior examination of the content of what is to be done and with no reflection on the merits of the acts required. Even though Levinas never demonstrates any particular taste for a carefree or negligent attitude, he nevertheless praises these words. According to him, they do not mean simply that understanding comes through doing, as Aristotle asserts with respect to virtuous actions (hence, by acting courageously or justly, man would become courageous or just and would better understand the essence of these virtues). In Aristotle's example, the act precedes the potential and would therefore reveal to man what he did not know beforehand in a theoretical manner. But the Israelites' assent to do and to hear means something else; it attests to an original obedience—in this case, to God's word—which unveils a certain secret. What is at issue?

For a free mind intent on thinking for itself, that obedience is absurd and dangerous, since it may lead to acts whose import the subject does not properly assess. Nevertheless, Levinas says, it is characteristic "of any inspired action, even an artistic one, whereby the act simply makes the form rise up, and where, in that form, the act recognizes its model, never glimpsed before that moment."[43] An action that manifests the presence of spirit—and not merely reference to principles—surprises its author. Hence, just as the artist often discovers his or her work while creating it, without referring back to a knowledge or plan well established in advance, and may even stand astonished before it, the moral subject discovers, through action, what the spirit inspires in it. It discovers this spirit and, at that moment, it understands, in the solitude of its conscience, unable to call on the support of an external authority, that it was precisely that word of support, that act of justice, that commitment to make amends, that the good required of the subject. Ethics, in this view, does not begin with the establishment of universal principles but with the consent to let the good take hold of you at that moment, when you are confronted with an individual who requires it. The urgency of the situation would not allow time to look into yourself and consider whether the action is consistent with one principle or another. Rather, it would reveal a fundamental structure of the human subject, an enigma to which Kant takes exception: the subject's anarchical alliance with the good.

Obedience to the voice of the ethical conscience does not mean, however, that Levinas is listening to an "oracle within [him]self"[44]—Kant's reproach to those who adopt a superior tone in philosophy and believe in the possibility of knowing the supersensible. Levinas merely points out that ethics is a "way of *actualizing without beginning from the possible*," a way "of knowing without examining, of placing oneself outside violence without that act being the privilege of a free choice." According to Levinas, that obedience demonstrates the structure of an unimpeachable alliance between the subject and "the good, anterior to the alternative between good and evil."[45] Even before the moral subject wished or decided it, without assessing its validity by the yardstick of some universal principle, that alliance has placed its mark on the subject. That alliance does not posit a universal and abstract principle on the basis of which the moral subject will turn toward individuals but makes the subject destined to be responsible, without equivocation, for every living individual. The words of the Israelites at Sinai—We will do and we will hear—would be the expression par excellence of that moral obligation.

Understood from that point of view, the act of hearing the voice of the ethical conscience does not presuppose any doctrinal content regarding the essence of the good or of God. It does not claim to abolish the distance between the idea of the infinite and the mind that conceives of it but only to give meaning to that idea in concrete situations, when a person is summoned to act morally. It is as if the words "infinite," "good," or "God" made sense only at the instant of obedience to that voice, which, without revealing the nature of God, compels one to be good, here and now, toward every individual.

Kant challenges any idea of "rational inspiration"; according to him, the expression is a contradiction in terms. Although he nevertheless admits the idea of a "rational faith" necessary for the practical use of reason, that faith does not imply any inspiration from a God. It does not correspond to any knowledge or presentiment of the divine but only to the quest for an unshakable foundation for morality—outside the field of theoretical knowledge—in order to "make human beings morally *better.*"[46] That quest begins with the establishment of principles that mark out the moral terrain in an unshakable manner. It is these principles that found morality. Their "adamant voice"[47] dictates to the trembling man and tells him what he ought to do, but it is not necessary to link that voice to an unknown authority. "The veiled goddess before whom we of both parties bend our knees is the moral law in us, in its inviolable majesty." Everyone perceives its voice and hears its commands, and that ought to suffice. Often, however, a person doubts that this voice actually comes from the self, and begins to believe that an unknown God—a "veiled Isis," Kant says ironically[48]—transmits these orders to him, something a philosopher anxious to link the moral imperative to principles and clear concepts cannot accept.

The voice of the ethical conscience described by Levinas is not governed by preestablished principles; it points to an inspiration from something that exceeds their bounds and transcends concepts. In *The Critique of Pure Reason*, Kant, having shown the powerlessness of reason to know the infinite, gives a moral—and not theoretical—meaning to the ideas of reason but requires that the human being not be limited by the infinite. In this area as well, Levinas—more faithful to Descartes on this point—continues to conceive of finitude in the light of the infinite and precisely in ethics.

Kant and Levinas abandon the illusion of grounding ethics in knowledge and seek the source of morality in the subject. Nevertheless, their approaches to this subject differ: Kant begins with the finite, Levinas with the infinite. In fact, Kant at first disregards the infinite and the concrete presence of the other man, in order to draw out the moral element in its purity and discover its a priori conditions. He establishes its groundwork *(Grundlegung)* with the help of the idea of principle, and its condition, as we shall see, with the idea of good will. This does not mean that morality exists in actuality. Conversely, Levinas thinks that the ethical dimension of the subject reveals itself only on the condition that one start from the infinite and from what is required by the particular presence of the other person standing before the subject. That modality presupposes that the subject abandon any quest for a groundwork. It entails a relation with the infinite irreducible to a knowledge, a paradoxical relation with something that signifies without revealing itself, something Levinas calls the "face."

t w o   **Good Will and the Face**

K ant's and Levinas's reprobation of knowledge, which is powerless to make people better, does not lead to any attempt to substitute a praise of feelings as the vector of morality. Both, in fact, are reluctant to trust efforts to defend man's spontaneous compassion or sympathy toward others. Nothing is less sure, they say, and no ethics can rely on the partiality of individual impulses, even generous ones, without running the risk of injustice. But these philosophers also do not seek an external order—the cosmos, being, or even society—as the objective groundwork of morality. The laws that govern natural processes remain alien to moral concerns; they tell people nothing about how they should conduct themselves. To conceive of ethics, it is thus not enough to internalize these laws, as the ancient Stoics taught, and to bring one's will into line with what is.

The principle of ethics, according to Kant, is found neither in nature nor in being; no certainty regarding the order of the world or of society guides human beings toward virtue. No submission to the necessity of what is via he progression of adequate ideas, as in Spinoza's *Ethics*, instructs a person on what he or she has to do. That principle, says Kant, is not found in nature but in the subject. It does not stem either from an act of speculation that would reserve its privilege for intelligent people or from experience, which is always partial, but rather from an internal disposition he calls "good will."

Levinas agrees with the idea that the question, "What ought I to do?" does not stem from a cognitive approach to being or to nature but rather from an obligation that extends beyond theoretical knowledge. He also maintains that a reflection on the subject is indispensable for responding to that question. Unlike Kant, however, he does not think that a principle *(arche)*, even a categorical one, is a satisfactory guide. He dares use the vocabulary of anarchy to describe the subject sensitive to "the voice of the ethical conscience." This means that the origin or beginning *(arche)* of such a subject is not within itself, and that no guideline, not even one established by the subject, marks out the terrain of its morality in advance. The moral subject described by Levinas cannot rely on any great, universally valid principle that would dictate its conduct in the individual situations it faces. Man's spiritual adventure in philosophy is never dangerous, Levinas says, because "anything unknown that can happen to him is revealed, open, manifest, in advance; it is shaped by the known and could never be absolutely surprising."[1] For Kant, the principle of morality has no ontological import, but it nevertheless reassures the subject about what it has to do, even before it acts. That principle avoids the surprising and disturbing aspect of the encounter with exteriority. Yet, according to Levinas, it is precisely when that disturbing aspect affects the subject, in spite of itself and in spite of its principles, that the subject catches a glimpse of the sense of morality. The encounter with the face stems precisely from that anarchy.

What, then, do the imperative of good will and the imperative emanating from the face tell the person anxious not to be compromised by the mockery that so often engulfs the moral idea, on the pretext that such an idea is constantly and tragically betrayed?

The Inner Disposition

Kant seeks to identify the "supreme principle" of morality in its purity, without referring to anthropological data or the circumstances of life. That approach implies that one set aside desire and the emotions, self-interest and even concrete efficacy, since true ethics begins at the point where confusing and random particularities cease to interfere. In fact, says Kant, the moral principle never depends on empirical factors; it remains universally valid for every time and place, even if no one ever puts it into practice. But what is it? Intelligence and skill do not make the subject moral, nor does the successful completion of acts reputed to be virtuous, since their author's motivations are rarely exempt from ulterior motives; therefore, the intention that governs the action still needs to be examined.

Only the person who is animated by good will, that is, by the fundamental intention to do his or her duty whatever happens, disregarding any other consideration, achieves morality. Kant writes: "It is impossible to think of anything at all in the world, or indeed even beyond it, that could be considered good without limitation except a good will *(ein guter Wille)*."[2] He also assumes that this principle is accepted by every sincere person. Everyone, whatever his degree of education and intelligence, shares that self-evident belief in the absolute value of good will, a will that, refusing to take spontaneity or self-interest as motives for action, subordinates them without reservation to duty.

But what is the source of good will, which is supposed to constitute the morality of an act? Kant tells us it is found in the reason as a practical potentiality, that is, as a potentiality that must have an influence over our will: "Nature . . . assign[ed] reason to our will as its governor."[3] Yet, since the purity of that practical reason is guaranteed by, among other things, its independence in relation to the ability to construct arguments, everyone, even someone who is not well educated and who has no particular taste for daring speculations, understands from the outset the meaning of the concept of good will. "It already dwells in natural sound understanding,"[4] Kant adds. He does not argue the merits of that postulate but immediately assimilates it to a self-evident fact. All people, he asserts—accepting not the slightest discussion on this point—provided that they reflect without hedging, are well aware that the definition of morality lies in the purity of intention.

Of course, the fundamental intention governing behavior almost always eludes the clear conscience, but that changes nothing. It hardly matters, Kant says, whether a person knows how to discern that intention. In spite of everything, it—and not the result obtained—is what constitutes the morality of the act. In every circumstance, only the person who acts with the pure intention of doing his duty, without giving in to his inclinations, and solely out of respect for what duty commands, can be deemed moral. Nevertheless, the examples offered in Kant's *Groundwork of the Metaphysics of Morals* exacerbate the difficulty. For how are we to know if the unhappy person preserves his life out of duty—hence out of morality—and not out of a secret inner hope that better days are ahead, hence out of self-interest? How are we to know if a person's love for his or her neighbor stems from pure good will and not from some inclination, that is, in Kant's vocabulary, from the *pathological?*

Kant responds by asking the subject to examine the maxims—the subjective principles of the will—behind its actions. Would the subject want those maxims to become a universal practical law? If someone proposes to end his life, would he wish that the right to commit suicide when overcome by unhappiness be erected into a universal practical law? In preparing to tell a lie to get out of a difficulty, can anyone wish, without contradiction, for everyone to accept lying as a universal law? No, says Kant, these maxims cannot "fit as a principle into a possible giving of universal law":[5] the behavior of the desperate person who gives in to the temptation of suicide, or that of the liar who tells tales, even to save another person's life, is immoral. In the same way, it seems, despite diametrically opposed results—one life is lost, the other saved—both people fall short of their duty. Both subordinate the moral imperative to private motives incompatible with ethics; they thus want an exception to be made to the principle of the imperative's universality—in their favor or in that of others—which is contradictory.

Kant claims that "reason issues its precepts unremittingly, without thereby promising anything to the inclinations."[6] That is why, although the desire to save a life through a lie is understandable in terms of pathological love, it constitutes an attitude alien to practical love. In ethics, it is imperative to tell the truth because no one would want lying to become a universal and objective law, that is, valid for every reasonable being. The purity of moral law tolerates no exception. In his famous dispute with Benjamin Constant, set out in "On a Supposed Right to Lie from Philanthropy,"[7] Kant maintains that the right to lie would make any society impossible. Whatever the potential harm to others, the moral subject cannot want to lie, since that would be an injustice against humanity in general.

In fact, in addition to requiring that the maxim behind one's action be universal, Kant asks the person seeking to be moral to act in such a way that he treats "*humanity*" both in his own person and in that of others "*always at the same time as an end, never simply as a means.*"[8] But how can the moral subject treat a person who intends to murder as a means—by lying to him to protect the fugitive he wants to kill—and, *at the same time*, as an end—by telling him the truth out of respect for his humanity, despite his evil intention? Since he cannot do both *at the same time*, the principle of respect for humanity in his person must prevail. By definition, practical principles do not rest on casuistry; they thus suffer no exceptions, "for exceptions would nullify the universality on account of which alone they are called principles."[9] Hence the subject remains moral only if it tells the truth in every circumstance, even when a third party suffers as a result.

In a letter to Maria von Herbert, Kant does admit that a person who is "sincere but reserved" always tells the truth but may not "tell all the truth,"[10] for example, to a dying man; but, all the same, Kant does not deduce from that any *right* to lie. He also does not accept the idea of conflicts between duties—that of always telling the truth and that of protecting a stranger, for example—since there is no higher principle able to decide between the two. Thus, the potential murderer, like any human being, has a *right* to the truth, since that truth is addressed to the humanity in him, not to his singularity as a wicked person. There is no right to lie, then, even out of compassion for a third party, and even if that third party must perish as a result of that respect for humanity in the person of the potential murderer to whom the moral subject has told the truth.

There have been vehement protests against that duty to be absolutely truthful because of its sometimes disastrous consequences. V. Jankélévitch maintains that Kant is wrong because "cannibals have no right to truth." The moral subject, if it is not to consent to violence, must know how "to render wicked people powerless to cause harm."[11] It is necessary, says Jankélévitch, to introduce the variables of time and circumstance—that is, impurity in Kant's terms—into the principles of moral conduct or risk committing horrendous misdeeds. "The will that wills purity from the outset is not a *serious* will; what is serious is to take on the composite, soul and body united."[12] A fragile body must not be placed at the mercy of the murderer, on the pretext that I owe him—like any other person—the truth.

Otherwise, the person who wishes to respect the principles of ethics without fail runs the risk of producing disaster for himself or others.

Clearly, similar objections can be raised for each of the duties Kant examines. Hence, in his view, the desperate person has no right to put an end to his life, and a third party has even less the right to help that person carry out his plan—the third party runs the risk of not respecting "the principle of humanity" in the suicidal person; but the introduction of impure variables, such as the fact of an intolerable and irremediable suffering, makes that assertion murky. Kant, however, would not admit that this very real murkiness implies a *right* to die or to help others die. "The *contemplative* right to one's own death, as it is consistent with human dignity,"[13] in H. Jonas's words, a right that goes hand in hand with a patient's permission to die without fearing legal reprisals against anyone who assists that patient, would, according to Kant, destroy the principle of morality. To claim that "the cry that asks for the relief of suffering stifles the prohibition to destroy life, or even to shorten it" and must therefore be heeded[14] undermines universality, the sole guarantor of morality. Despite its apparent humanity, the proposition of a *right* to die is morally inadmissible.

Can a philosophy that erects respect for universality and humanity—and not the singularity of every human person—into an absolute principle of morality allow for these objections, all of which introduce casuistry into ethics? The moral subject's conduct must be consistent with "the idea of humanity as an end in itself," not with the idea of other people—unique, finite, and vulnerable—as ends in themselves.[15] Yet that principle of humanity, which, according to Kant, is derived from pure reason, dissolves immediately as soon as it allows empirical situations to be taken into account. Therefore, the will remains good only on the condition that it respect the principle in absolute terms. That is why "the adamant voice" of duty must speak louder than the powerless voice of the person who asks the subject to lie so that his life might be spared, or of the one who, tormented by suffering, pleas—albeit silently—that he be allowed to die.

As his commentators have noted, Kant does not propose a new system of ethics, an ethics destined to take the place of other systems, on the pretext that the latter are weak. He formulates "what life knows to be a commandment," and "examines and establishes" the supreme moral principle. But that formulation, "in order to make sense, essentially presupposes the living relationship to moral law."[16] It presupposes that, without external pressures, a person is concerned about his own morality. Hence the subject animated by good will wants to "act in accordance with maxims that can *at the same time have as their object themselves as universal laws of nature.*"[17] As a result, even if the person knows that nature will not disappear with his suicide, the desperate person, imagining a nature governed by his maxim, posits that it would be destroyed. Out of good will, that person therefore abandons his plan.

If self-love impelled people to destroy themselves rather than suffer, if the love of others led them to lie to reduce the risks incurred in life, a nature constituted by these laws would disappear very quickly. The moral subject's effort to imagine its maxim as a universal law of nature thus reveals that the subject was blinded "by the illusion of passion."[18] A world governed by such maxims would sink into anarchy; it would no longer constitute a nature. Yet the moral subject must, according to Kant, work to regard the human world *as if* it constituted a nature, even if that is not the case. "That anticipation is a moral project of ends unconditioned by the sensible world,"[19] a plan that does not take the empirical facts of life into account and which, in that sense, falls within the realm of utopian thinking: one does not find oneself in that nature but one must find oneself there or risk immorality.

The good will at the root of morality leaves open the question of the concrete and singular urgency of situations. That impure element would disrupt practical reason and would add an immoral coefficient to it. A principle admits of no exceptions, even for noble reasons; it is not concerned with singularities. Hence, the moral subject does not directly perceive the humanity in the person it respects, but its respect is nevertheless addressed to that humanity and not to a person bearing a singular name and face.

Levinas is not content to introduce a casuistry, as opposed to a moral principle; he raises a more decisive question, since he wonders whether the road to moral universality must necessarily be built on an abstract principle. He envisions an anarchical ethics, an ethics sensitive to the singular names and faces of people, whom he refuses to sacrifice on the altar of principles, even the principle of respect—sublime for Kant—for the humanity in every person. What does that respect mean, Levinas asks, if the unique and irreplaceable person must perish as a result? What does universality mean if the vulnerable flesh of every person has less value than the respect for the person's humanity?

The aim of these questions is not to bring about a return in force of the finer feelings dismissed by Kant or to defend some sort of moral intuition more decisive than a principle. These questions express the rejection of "the alienation of man by universality itself, which, from the dawn of our civilization, was supposed to guarantee the humanity of man." They express the certainty that no universality is valid if it disregards "the uniqueness" of individuals, the uniqueness "of a hunger, a need, a love."[20] To satisfy the hunger of the starving, here and now, even without good will, without seeking to know whether that maxim is in harmony with the universality of the respect for humanity, would, according to Levinas, attest to the subject's morality.

The objection will be made that Levinas, by holding good will in scorn, bankrupts the morality he intends to defend. Where does the moral subject's concern for the present uniqueness of people come from, if it is not the result of an emotional or altruistic attitude, which Levinas challenges just as surely as Kant?

Morality and Legality

The subject of good will, says Kant, refuses to let its particular, sensible inclinations determine its maxims. It acts out of pure respect for duty, even if the latter contradicts its sympathies and enjoyment. The principle that governs such a subject consists of making universality and the idea of humanity supreme guides of its behavior. Nevertheless, to remain moral, the subject of good will must really want that principle to be the discriminating criterion of its maxims and must not be satisfied with mimicking its consequences through behavior that actually rests on various, but all self-interested, motivations. The moral subject can act with sympathy but not out of sympathy—good will supposes no friendly feelings toward the individual, even though it does not rule them out. It acts out of duty. Legality—conformity to the requisite duty—is thus not sufficient and does not make it possible to pronounce a verdict on the subject's morality. Hence the kindly man who spreads joy around him and delights in the contentment of others undoubtedly acts in a manner consistent with duty, but is he moral? Kant writes: "I assert that in such a case an action of this kind, however it may conform with duty and however amiable it may be, has nevertheless no true moral worth." It often rests on a personal motivation, which, even "if it fortunately lights upon what is in fact in the common interest and in conformity with duty,"[21] does not entail morality.

The intention that guides behavior—to act out of respect for universality and humanity—is the sole determinant of the morality of the act, even if the consequences go counter to one's sympathies, even if, in the view of the average person in particular, that is, the person who does not have an understanding for the sense of universality and humanity, these consequences turn out to be harmful to the uniqueness of individuals.

Is it philosophically irrelevant, however, to ask whether it is truly appropriate for ethics to *begin* with respect for universality and humanity rather than with concern for singularities? Levinas asks: must "the time of universal Law, which is always the *dura lex*, and the time of citizens equal before the law"[22] be the time of morality? Do universal principles, indispensable for institutions, and especially for legal institutions, constitute morality? Does not *good will* fail to appreciate "the cruelty"[23] of these principles, which oblige you to divert your eyes from individuals on the pretext of respect for universality and humanity? Hence, when Kant writes that "the mere dignity of humanity as rational nature, without any other end or advantage to be attained by it . . . is yet to serve as an inflexible precept of the will,"[24] does he not fail to appreciate the dignity of *each* human face?

The examples of moral behavior, as Kant describes them, disregard that parameter, which, however, does not give way to the rule of affect. Can the moral subject, anxious about that prospect, imagine a different outcome to the case of the man with evil intentions to whom it is appropriate—out of respect for his humanity, according to Kant—to tell the truth, even if that means handing over the fugitive hiding in the moral subject's home? As soon as the moral subject accepts the dignity of *each* human face, that subject must ask itself the following question: "Is not one the persecutor of the other?" The response to that question tells the subject, without its abandoning itself to some spontaneous compassion, "which of the two comes first."[25]

But, clearly, that question implies a different access route to morality than that which consists of making a strict respect for universality and humanity, on the basis of good will, the principle of one's acts. It relies on the notion that this principle must remain secondary in relation to the concern for each human person. It is not appropriate, says Levinas, to begin with universality; one must rather move toward it, beginning with the moral uneasiness elicited by individual lives, precarious lives always at the mercy of the violence of principles, even those that are generous and worthy of respect. According to him, moral obligation is not tethered to the awareness of a universal principle; it arises as a response to the vulnerability of every man. Nevertheless, since the other is never alone with the moral subject, the latter must take human universality into consideration, as Kant requires. "I do not live in the world where there is only one 'anybody'; there is always a third party in the world."[26] As a result, the universal *dura lex* intervenes but remains secondary in relation to the concern with the weakness characteristic of every person, a concern that awakens in the subject when it encounters a face.

It is not appropriate to hasten, out of good will, to consider that face as exemplary of the human race; one must rather dwell on its uniqueness, even if, as Levinas emphasizes, it is also all of humanity that looks at the subject through that face. "The epiphany of the face, as it bears witness to the presence of the third party, of humanity as a whole, in the eyes that look at me,"[27] does not imply that one abandon universality. Nevertheless, universality does not result from a principle accepted by each person but rather from that epiphany, and, above all, it does not make the epiphany disappear. The face that suddenly appears in the subject's world is also exposed to others, which might oppress and persecute it. Sometimes it is that face that makes other faces suffer. In encountering the face, the subject thus finds itself in a relation with the person of everyone else, and must then "judge and decide," compare situations, "determine justice within a logic of genus and species."[28] The subject then introduces universal categories to guide its behavior rather than give in to compassion or an ill-considered leniency toward one person or another. Universality prevents the injustice of emotional preferences, which are never neutral but necessarily inflict suffering on innocent people.

This moment of comparing people represents the moment of universal law, but, Levinas insists, it is neither at the beginning nor at the end of ethics. "There are necessities that are terrible because they stem precisely from the need for the reasonable order. There are, if you like, tears that a functionary cannot see: the tears of the Other. . . . One must defend subjectivity, put right a certain disorder resulting from the Order of univer-⟩ sal reason."[29] It is precisely the moral subject's role to watch over the uniqueness of individuals, in spite of the need for universal law, which the subject must also take into account, or risk injustice.

The concept of legality, then, does not have the same sense for Kant and for Levinas. For Kant, legality consists of behaving in a manner consistent with duty but without the inner intention of respecting that duty because it is duty. It resides in the lack of respect for the categorical aspect of the moral imperative and in the submission to external pressures. The person concerned with legality is afraid of "trouble"; that person is preoccupied with the opinion of others and wants their respect. That person fears authority and obeys it, not out of respect for the law, but because he lacks audacity and courage. *Religion within the Boundaries of Mere Reason* cites Judaism as an example of that conduct. "The Ten Commandments . . . in that legislation . . . are given with no claim at all on the *moral disposition* in following them." And yet, Kant concludes, "a God who wills only obedience to commands for which absolutely no improvement of moral disposition is required cannot truly be that moral being whose concept we find necessary for a religion."[30] Kant therefore privileges Christianity, which, according to him, has placed the emphasis on the intention within the heart. "Blessed are the pure in heart: for they shall see God," Jesus said in the Sermon on the Mount (Matthew 5:8). Hence Christianity is closer to the idea of good will as the sole and pure criterion for morality, even if, as Kant emphasizes, that access to morality is not spontaneous and implies a conversion, and even if it is never achieved once and for all and requires continual progress.[31]

The relevance of Kant's assessment of the Decalogue is very debatable, however, since nothing in the wording indicates that the intention of the subject that hears the commandment does not count. Does not the author of the Psalms (in the Hebrew Bible therefore) also speak of a "pure heart" (Psalm 24:4)? Nevertheless, the words of the Decalogue do not come from the subject itself but from an exteriority, and, for Kant, that is what poses the greatest difficulty in terms of ethics. In fact, the words "Thou shalt not kill" do not result from the impossibility of wanting a universal maxim prescribing murder but from an absolute command to be respected whatever the heart's disposition or the will's intention might be. Kant does not take into consideration the fact that, in Judaism, that prescription—like all the others—must educate the heart, not release it from responsibility. As a result, Judaism for Kant remains exemplary of a legality alien to ethics, because even if a subject, out of concern for the Decalogue, abstains from lying or stealing, for example, its conduct is dictated by an external source—which it probably fears—and not by its own will. Kant denigrates what he calls the subject's "servile faith" and prefers the "moral faith" introduced by the "teacher of the Gospel."[32] Finally, to avoid all discussion on this matter, he asserts with calm self-assurance, that "whatever moral additions were *appended* to it, whether originally or only later, do not in any way belong to Judaism as such."[33] Judaism remains the example par excellence of a legality from which the moral person liberates himself already through the teachings of the gospel but particularly thanks to his own good will. Kant will not hesitate to evoke the need for "the euthanasia of Judaism" in pure moral religion and to ask Christians to eliminate Judaism from their faith.[34]

Clearly, Levinas does not agree with that analysis of the concept of legality or that assignment of the term "legal" to Judaism and "moral" to Christianity. Nevertheless, since no one has the monopoly on the moral good news, he also does not reverse the terms.

Legality, he says, represents the second moment of morality. It is not, as Kant claims, the moment when good will is caught red-handed in a self-interested submission to an external authority—without any intention of its own to have respect for the imperatives—but the moment when human universality is taken into account. Ethics awakens in the subject as a result of the subject's concern for the singular and irreplaceable person of the other and not out of voluntary submission to abstract principles. The latter, despite their consideration for humanity, and often in the name of it, inevitably entail the risk of forgetting the unique, fragile, and unsubstitutable character of individuals. But, Levinas explains, since the other is never alone with the moral subject, that subject must also weigh and compare, that is, must introduce a universal measure: that is the moment of legality. It alone makes choice possible within situations of conflict, it alone makes it possible to judge individuals. The moral subject cannot do without a universal measure; if it does, it runs the risk of committing an injustice toward the third party. Nevertheless, that universal measure—the law that disregards singularities—constitutes neither the first nor the final moment of morality. As an awakening to the vulnerable singularity of every person, morality precedes legality and also judges its assumptions. In fact, on the pretext of founding an ethics and of respecting equality among men, universal norms too often entail a dismissal of singular faces.

Levinas, to be precise, does not seek to "found" an ethics but to understand how concern for the fate of one's neighbor might arise in man, often unbeknownst to him, without good will on his part. On the contrary, he says, the subject forced to awaken to ethical concerns would nearly always prefer to turn its back on the imperatives they entail. No one becomes moral out of good will, out of the decision to universalize the maxims behind his actions, but rather as a response to a command emanating from the encounter with the face.

That difference in the access to morality in Kant and Levinas is explained by the fact that Kant first conceives of the *finitude* of the subject and seeks the principle of all intelligibility in it, whereas Levinas begins with the idea of the *infinite* as an original discourse and analyzes how that "miracle" dwells within the subject's finitude from the outset. "It is the welcome of the Other, the beginning of the moral conscience,"[35] that reveals its meaning to the subject. "The Other, or the idea of Infinity,"[36] says Levinas.

Unlike the "Kantian notion of the infinite [which] posits itself as an ideal of reason, as the projection of its imperatives into the beyond, as the ideal completion of what presents itself as incomplete, without that incomplete entity confronting a privileged *experience* of the infinite, without it drawing the limits of its finitude from that confrontation" (since the finite subject "no longer conceives of itself in relation to the infinite"), Levinas thinks that "the idea of the infinite does not come from within ourselves a priori," and that it even constitutes "experience par excellence."[37]

That, in any case, is how the epiphany of the face presents itself.

The Ethical Awakening

To speak of awakening rather than good will is to suppose there is a lethargy to shake off, a sleep to disturb. Man is not spontaneously moral and no natural benevolence or altruistic inclination explains the sense of that awakening. It is, moreover, incommensurate with the purely legal behavior of conformity to the law and to duty, a behavior the Talmud—without referring to the Gospel and before Kant—already condemns, mocking the sort of Pharisee who declares: "Define my duty and I will do it." That person sees himself as beyond reproach, the rabbis say (Babylonian Talmud, Sotah 122b); but is morality the same thing as placing oneself beyond the reach of any possible reprobation? The question remains: how does that awakening come about, since it results neither from a movement—spontaneous or willful—proper to the subject, nor from a pure and simple submission to a code of duties?

Levinas says that such an awakening is produced by the Desire for the other [*le Désir d'autrui*, also "the other's Desire"—trans.]. Desire differs from need, since need "opens onto a world that is *for me*—it returns to oneself," and points to "the Ego's concern for itself, egoism."[38] The Desire for the other, by contrast, comes into being within a satisfied and complete subject, a subject with no essential lack and which probably wishes to persevere in its being and in its enjoyment of things. But now an other stands before the subject and turns the order of the world upside down; this other introduces a new orientation into the world, independent of the familial, social, or cultural context of the encounter. This other's face appeals to the subject, takes aim at it without leaving it time to get hold of itself and, as they say, to compose itself. On the contrary, this other empties the subject of its self and obliges it to give.

What does the face mean, then? How are we to understand the fact that it is the living source—and not the principle—of the ethical awakening?

Levinas describes the face as "a misery," a vulnerability and a destitution that, in itself, without explicit words, entreats the subject. "But that entreaty is a demand" for a response, a demand for support and aid. "The face foists itself on me and I am unable to cease being responsible for its misery. Consciousness loses its first place,"[39] stands aside.

Levinas's analysis departs decisively from Kantianism. The Kantian subject never loses that first place. Hence, in a similar situation, that subject asks *itself* if it can disregard the misery of the other, if it can want its egoism to become a universal law of nature. It then realizes, Kant says, that, if its will were to make that choice, it would be contradicting itself, since, in spite of everything, "many cases could occur in which one would need the love and sympathy of others and in which by such a law of nature arisen from his own will, he would rob himself of all hope of the assistance he wishes for himself."[40] That argument—which is self-interested in spite of everything—does not intervene in Levinas's analysis: the shock produced by the epiphany of misery is in itself an imperative that does not suffer the shilly-shallying of a reflection on the possibility or impossibility of desiring the universality of one's maxims.

When it encounters the face, the moral subject is stripped of the primacy of its being, is unseated and called into question, without any consent on its part. When it encounters the face, Levinas says, "Desire reveals itself as goodness."[41] It reveals itself as such even to a subject that has fulfilled all its duties assiduously and with good will, by surprising it and causing a shock. The encounter with the other goes hand in hand with a suffering inflicted on this subject: an imperative to respond to the misery of the face is inflicted upon the subject, an imperative it did not choose, an imperative it did not wish for. The other beseeches "it" and, as a result, whatever the cost, the subject cannot pass by indifferent to the other's fate—even while being concerned for that of humanity.

Clearly, Levinas is not describing a state of affairs; he is analyzing how the encounter with the other is likely to bring to light—that is, to reveal—a level of the psyche irreducible to a resolute and willful act or a spontaneous gesture. The face *compels* the subject looking at it to ask of itself: what will happen to that singular other, vulnerable and threatened with violence, if I—also a singular subject—fail to act? The revelation lies in that obligation, in that order made by the face, which makes the subject lose its sovereign place while obliging it to accept the welcome and humility proper to any service. When the ego encounters the other, it discovers the Infinite that dwells within itself, discovers it in the mode of a responsibility it did not choose but that prevails upon it. "The Other that produces that ethical movement in the conscience, that shakes the good conscience loose from the Same coincident with itself, entails a surplus incommensurate with intentionality."[42] That surplus or overabundance, beyond the reach of reflection, orients moral life as a whole and places it under the sign of the Infinite.

"The *conscience* of the philosophers is essentially self-reflective [*réfléchissante*],"[43] Levinas remarks. Yet the ethical encounter makes it necessary to depart from that model. Kant grasps the subject in its finitude, at the moment when it returns to itself, but "the extreme urgency" of the encounter with the face makes the subject unavailable for that return. In that encounter, the Infinite reveals to the subject its profound complicity with the Infinite. The other pits the infiniteness of his transcendence against the subject, since he resists every grasp, every understanding. Even murder, which annihilates the other, does not put an end to his transcendence; it makes that transcendence disappear in violence and abandonment but does not comprehend it. In addition, Levinas insists, the infiniteness of that transcendence entails, precisely, a prohibition on killing. The other "paralyzes power by his infinite resistance to murder, a resistance that, hard and insurmountable, glimmers in the face of the other, in the complete nakedness of his defenseless eyes, in the nakedness of the absolute opening of the Transcendent."[44] That prohibition on murder is also understood, positively this time, as an obligation to serve the other, to do everything possible to see that the other will live.

The subject cannot flee that obligation through deafness, silence, or indifference. In the face of an individual's distress, it cannot be content at having done its duty by respecting universal principles. In an unimpeachable manner, the subject hears the demand resonate in its psyche. It is as if, unbeknownst to itself, the subject were confirming the words of Rabbi Yohanan, quoted by Levinas: "To leave men without food is a sin that no circumstance extenuates; the distinction between the voluntary and the involuntary does not apply to it." Levinas concludes: "The face opens the original discourse, the first word of which is an obligation that no 'interiority' allows you to avoid. A discourse that obliges you to enter discourse."[45] And that discourse obliges you to respond rather than to speak up and have the first and, often, the last word. It does not allow you to glory in "being right," it obliges you to cede the first place.

According to that analysis, the relation to the Other reveals the infinite to man, not as an idea alien to his psyche, or as an extravagance characteristic of a few fanatics, but as the intimate, albeit unknown, structure of his clear and lucid conscience. The subject then discovers its morality.

Levinas's ethical interpretation of the idea of the infinite implies calling into question all the transcendental models of the conscience as the first and adequate guide toward morality. It goes hand in hand with an urgency that justifies no return to oneself, no withdrawal to a safe hiding place. The moral subject enters into an infinitely demanding relation, loses its naivete and its dogmatism. It can no longer rest on a knowledge.

Despite their differences, however, do not Kant and Levinas share one idea: the possibility that a person may be touched by the good? And do they not also have to respond to a common difficulty: the refusal to conduct oneself with good will or the callousness when one is confronted with the face of the other?

three   **Good Precedes Evil**

T he reality of the failure of good will—so often found lacking, as Kant acknowledges, admitting it is impossible to establish with absolute certainty "a single case in which the maxim of an action . . . rested simply on moral grounds and on the representation of one's duty"[1]—does not imply that one is resigned to moral impurity or that the wicked man is irremediably condemned to wickedness. To be sure, the criminal is not tormented by "the inner reproach" of his conscience, as the virtuous man imagines him to be because he attributes to the criminal "the characteristic of his own constitution";[2] nevertheless, that conscience can awaken in the criminal at any moment. Neither pleasures nor distractions are a permanent guarantee against the "terrible voice" of the conscience: the wicked person can obviously go through life not worrying about it, making fun of it, and even committing devastating misdeeds, but, says Kant, "he cannot help *hearing* it."[3]

The possibility of hearing that voice represents, precisely, the most remarkable point of moral reflection. It implies a predisposition toward goodness in human nature, a disposition that no evil succeeds in erasing completely, and which alone explains how a person can become good or can repent after going morally astray. It is a given, Kant says, a real, albeit not empirical, given, and not the result of a project. It is a "fact" of pure practical reason, a fact to be drawn from the subject's finitude and located within that finitude. Given this fact, evil thus becomes secondary, even if it rules a person's every act and thought. And furthermore, given this fact, evil, as deep-seated as it might be, can never be assured that it has had the last word.

Despite different premises, since Levinas does not use the language of the subject's original finitude, he, like Kant, maintains that good and evil are not symmetrical. The connection to the good, he says, is anterior to the rule of evil. That obviously does not mean that, in people's lives, the good can in some way "glory in being." On the contrary, the idea of the good, "paralyzed and trembling" and constantly facing "the nihilist desolation" to which so many people and institutions consent, is very often condemned to shrivel up "in the depth" of the subject. But, precisely, that fragile dwelling place, always at the mercy of the insanity of the extermination order, bears witness to an origin of ethics independent of any civilization. That "precarious and divine" dwelling place, in Levinas's terms, represents the true "matrix" of human ethics.[4] Even when history and people's daily behavior belie morality—that is, almost always—the voice that makes itself heard in that dwelling place persists. It does not, however, have the "terrible" character Kant attributes to it. Most often, it remains inaudible, since it carries no weight when confronted with the noise and power of persuasion—that is, the seduction—produced by the heralds of the major ideologies. It is powerless and has a closer resemblance to the "still small voice" *(qol demama daka)* heard by Elijah (I Kings 19:12) than it does to the violence of an imperative issued from an objective social order. These "whispers of a subjective voice,"[5] powerless to reverse the dark course of history, are nevertheless the only rampart against barbarism. They attest to the influence of the good on the human psyche, an influence anterior to any reflection and to any concern for a groundwork—a preoriginary influence.

How, then, do Kant and Levinas analyze that anteriority of the good? On what basis do they speak of it, since neither empirical data nor onology account for it? And why, finally, do they both, despite their lucidity about the seductiveness and the depths of evil, never, in spite of everything, lose their *confidence* in that anteriority?

The Predisposition for Good and the Propensity for Evil

Despite the dark portrait of man's corruption and misdeeds, Kant refuses to condemn him and to decree human nature evil. If that were the case, he remarks, no one could become good *on his own*, since a bad tree never bears good fruit. The wicked man can always *come back* to the good after being separated from it by his preference for the murky path of complacency with evil, but how could he *come* to it if his nature were evil? Moreover, despite the immorality of so many, good fruit ripens: some respond positively to the voice of duty, and virtue comes to light in the world, even if it does not counterbalance egoism, iniquity, and cynicism. To be sure, it is an astonishing exception, compared to the rule of evil over human hearts; it exists in spite of everything, and that would be incomprehensible if people were evil by nature. Nevertheless, even when repentance, virtue, and the submission to duty are thus taken into account, it does not follow that the human being is good by nature. More strictly, and in a manner never established once and for all, the implication is that he "has been created for the *good*" and that the "original *predisposition* in him" is good.[6]

The keen admiration Kant claims to feel for "that original moral predisposition in us"[7] is clearly understandable. Without it, it would be absurd to order people to do their duty and to improve themselves, since, quite simply, they would be unable to do so. Yet it must be possible, since that is precisely what moral law requires of everyone, without discrimination regarding temperament, culture, or social position. The empirical arguments cited by Kant do not demonstrate the existence of that good moral disposition; they assume it.

As a result, that disposition explains why the fundamental law of ethics takes root in the conscience as "a fact" or "a given" and not as a project, remarkable to be sure, on the subject's part. Kant writes: "Consciousness of this fundamental law may be called a fact of reason because one cannot reason it out from antecedent data of reason . . . and because it instead forces itself upon us of itself as a synthetic a priori proposition that is not based on any intuition, either pure or empirical."[8] This fact, he explains, is "indisputable": every man recognizes moral obligation, even if he disputes it or rejects it, and he needs no particular subtlety to do so. A child of eight or nine already knows that a man ought to return a deposit entrusted to him by a person who has just died, even if, thanks to the deposit, that man could end his poverty, and even if the heirs of the deceased owner possess great wealth and do not know of the existence of the deposit. The child knows it would be *unjust* to keep the deposit for himself; he knows it would go "against duty." Kant concludes that moral distinctions are written in the human soul "in the broadest and most legible characters" imaginable.[9] The prescriptions of duty are "inscribed in the heart by reason."[10] And, according to Kant, despite the depths of evil, that inscription is ineffaceable.

The meaning of the Kantian subject's finitude begins to take shape: that finitude does not stem from the limited life span accorded each person, in an unequal and incomprehensible manner moreover; it does not result from any meditation on death as the final horizon. "The decisive reason for man's finitude is not . . . death, it is moral obedience to the unconditional commandment." It is related to the idea of "moral law as fact."[11] In fact, the "writing" of moral law in the heart or soul, in Kant's two formulations, presupposes no transcendence, no experience of the infinite. It is a "fact" independent of any idea of God or any religious belief. Hence, no exteriority—not even biblical teachings—constitutes a moral authority for reason. The Bible, says Kant, must be interpreted consistent with that "fact" of moral reason, rather than ethics being extracted from the Bible, since the latter would entail a corruption of the finitude of the subject, which would be receiving a lesson from the outside. Kant criticizes the Jews on this point, for having misunderstood the greatness of the moral subject's finitude.[12]

Consciousness of the moral law thus represents an indisputable fact of reason. Its unconditional obligation is imposed on everyone, whatever his or her age and level of education. It is the single fact of reason. It is worth emphasizing that theoretical reason knows nothing of a fact of this kind; only practical reason encounters it, as an inescapable given, thanks to which finitude raises itself up, without external support, without any experience of the infinite.

To be sure, the human being does not always obey moral law; indeed, he often makes decisions that go counter to it. Nevertheless, consciousness of that law takes root in one and one cannot avoid being tormented by it. Hence, the subject, questioned about whether he would bear false witness against an honest man at the risk of immediately losing his own life, may not dare make assurances that he would give up his life, since that life is so dear to him, "but he must admit without hesitation that it would be possible for him." "He judges, therefore, that he can do something because he is aware that he ought to do it."[13] The idea that one must conform to this "fact" of reason, regardless of the empirical and contingent conditions, is itself found in the reason. Even extreme abjection does not exempt a man from that original moral disposition, where he has to answer only to himself, even while feeling the obligation to submit to what the moral predisposition commands.

Does the finitude of the subject suffice, however? Does the shame experienced by a person who has given in to intimidation or to the desire for prestige, and who has chosen to denounce the innocent person for the sake of his career, for example, and to enjoy honors, truly come from the consciousness of the moral law within oneself? In the twentieth century, when denunciation, abandonment, and horror ravaged the world, and when the evildoers did not tremble at their misdeeds, is it truly the moral law in oneself that elicits a feeling of shame, sometimes at least, and only for a moment? Or, as the terrible story of V. Grossman suggests, is it not the experience of the infinite in the form of the innocent condemned man looking at him that, momentarily, troubles the guilty man? Ivan Grigoryevich, in Leningrad after twenty years in the Gulag, meets his denouncer, who, during that time, has prospered. "With alert and sad curiosity Ivan Grigoryevich looked unreproachfully into Pinegin's eyes. And Pinegin for one second only, just one brief second or perhaps two, felt he would gladly sacrifice his country house, his government decorations and honors, his authority and his power, his strength, his beautiful wife, his successful sons engaged in studying the nucleus of the atom—that he would give up every last bit of it, just so as not to feel those eyes resting upon him."[14]

In describing the mute prayer of the face, could Levinas be thinking of anything else? He too leads us to reflect on the need for the subject to be kept alert by the infinite or risk running away from any moral conduct and forgetting the destiny for the good, which Kant describes as inherent in the subject's finitude. Without that experience, without the encounter with the particular face of the other, reason may allow "the adamant voice" of duty to be heard, but, it seems, that voice does not disturb, or no longer disturbs, the subject. Without the violent shock produced by the weakness of the face—and not only that of someone a subject has personally offended or humiliated, denounced or abandoned—that voice runs the risk of becoming inaudible. That voice may continue to forcefully articulate its principles, but can a principle ever convert—that is, incite to repentance and reparation—someone who has given in to the glamour of evil? Does it, as Kant believes, have enough force to compel one to respect and to obey?[15] Levinas does not think so; he doubts that a principle inherent in the subject's finitude, even a sublime principle, could affect the subject in the form of an imperative. To do that, he says, the infinite—irreducible to an idea—must unhinge the subject or call it into question at its very heart, must deal a blow to its self-importance. The infinite must weaken the subject's certainty of its finitude. In fact, even though that finitude is experienced as an ultimate destiny doing battle with the elements and the neutrality of being, struggling with the "faceless gods" of a world to be transformed so that the subject can keep its foothold in being, that finitude loses its meaning when confronted with the other. It then enters into a relation with the infinite, with what exceeds its capacities. It receives the revelation of the infinite within it at the precise moment when the face appeals to finitude from its lofty place and from its humility. In fact, although the honesty of the face-to-face relationship deals a blow to the subject's finitude, which is solicited by the vulnerable and threatened alterity of the person looking at it, that honesty also awakens the subject's experience of the infinite. Through the impossibility of consenting to the evil that burdens the other, and through the need in which the subject finds itself to respond to that appeal even without wanting to do so, the subject discovers the psyche's original affinity with the infinite, discovers it in the form of a commitment to goodness that is prior to the subject's decisions and whose unassailable character depends on no "fact of reason."

Kant, of course, does not disregard the depths of the evil into which anyone may fall. He looks for its cause and observes that none of man's dispositions—to animality, to humanity, and to personality—is evil in itself. Self-love, the desire for recognition by the other, and the aptitude for responsibility to which these dispositions lead do not represent an evil. Sensibility, for example, which many blame for human egoism and amoral spontaneity, often turns out to be contrary to moral law, since that law runs counter to the sensible impulses; nevertheless, says Kant, it is not evil *in itself.* Moral law "thwarts" propensities, it may "humiliate" them at times, or even "strike them down,"[16] but moral evil does not originate in them. It does not lie in inclinations and preferences but in the desire to give in to pressure when they incite a subject to fail to do its duty. In addition, evil cannot result from a corruption of reason, which Kant decrees impossible and unthinkable.[17]

Moral evil, then, comes about through a "certain self-incurred perversity";[18] it does not originate in the human being's dispositions. It consists of granting priority to self-love at the expense of duty, of subordinating the law to one's own interests, and of combining moral and immoral motives. Kant admits that such attitudes tempt everyone, and that it is legitimate to refer to a "propensity for evil," the universality of which he affirms. But, he insists, the original predisposition for good is still anterior to that propensity, and that is what makes the wicked man's repentance possible. One must assume that "there is still a germ of goodness left in its entire purity, a germ that cannot be extirpated or corrupted,"[19] even in people whose lives demonstrate no sense of goodness. Kant also asserts that, even if, hypothetically, all human beings allowed themselves to be seduced by perversion, this germ would still persist, since the anteriority of the predisposition for goodness cannot be effaced, despite the rule of evil.

And yet, does not Kant also say that the human being starts out badly and that his debt remains ineffaceable? Does not Levinas, who agrees with that idea of the anteriority of the good, speak of a debt that accrues even as the subject seeks to acquit itself of it?

Evil and the Debt

Whatever one's conduct, despite one's effort to obey, resolutely and consistently, the voice of duty, the human being *"nevertheless started from evil."*[20] That poses a formidable, even insurmountable, difficulty, even at the end of a life dedicated to the good, because, according to Kant, the debt incurred by that bad start proves to be ineffaceable. Yet, since everyone must wish to be acquitted of it, no one should believe he is authorized to absolve others too quickly, on the pretext of compassion. Kant declares, with extreme harshness, that it is not appropriate, for example, to seek at all cost to appease the conscience of a dying man and to console him. One must rather "sharpen" his consciousness of his sins, so that that he may hold onto the good to be done and the evil to be rectified until his last breath.[21]

Thus, the predisposition for good is flouted in a decisive, and, it seems, irremediable manner. Man always starts out badly, and the burden of his sins must haunt him until his death. Kant maintains, in fact, that human being is evil *by nature* because, he says, the entire "human species," despite its consciousness of moral law, has chosen and still chooses to give priority to self-interested and impure motivations. The idea of "a *radical* innate *evil* in human nature" is the logical consequence, an evil that everyone contracts,[22] that everyone undertakes to commit. That perverse and innate propensity constantly manifests itself in human behavior, but it is not the result of sensibility—since the natural inclinations have no direct connection to evil but rather offer the opportunity to prove one's virtue. All the same, this propensity does not originate in reason, since an *evil* reason, or an absolutely bad will, would transform the subject into a *"diabolical being,"* a possibility Kant dismisses. Despite man's great moral weakness, he never chooses evil as such as the sole principle for his actions. In fact, his reason is not corruptible, and evil, despite its radicality, is not absolute. This radical evil then has to be conceived as a willful perversion of the moral order, an order whereby the universality of the law must judge the merits of particular maxims. Radical evil appears with the inversion of that order; it lies in a usurpation of the first place, in the subordination of universality to the interests of an individual, usually oneself.

The seduction of evil stems from the preference that the subject spontaneously grants to itself, to the point of choosing behaviors abhorrent to others. Kant insists, however, that, despite its natural and often terrible character affecting the entire "human species," that attitude remains secondary in relation to the predisposition for the good. The notion of seduction demonstrates this, since it entails an ordeal endured by that predisposition, a battle waged by it, but not its disappearance. In fact, if the disappearance of that predisposition were possible, there would be no more seduction, no ordeal, no battle: the human being would quite simply have become *"diabolical."* Since that eventuality is rejected—Kant insists that the repentance of the wicked man is always possible, that he may sometimes look upon himself with contempt when he considers his life— one must say that evil *starts*, and *starts again*, every time a subject agrees to forfeit universality and give preference to itself, but that that evil never effaces the inner predisposition for good. The moment evil starts is not clear, however, since someone who gives in to that seduction, and hence grants preference to self-love or to a singularity—a person or a people—at the expense of universality, does not always know it. He invents noble motivations for himself and lies to himself with such skill that evil seems to vanish. Kant sees sin par excellence in the lie, a sin that, at every instant, allows evil to start and take root in the self. The lie maintains the illusion of the eminently desirable character of the goods of this world and never ceases to make people forget the absolute superiority of moral intentions over any other good. Despite the correct principle, it thus blinds human beings to "the depths of corruption" in which they have found themselves since Adam.

From the beginning of time, Kant says, all human beings have started out badly, all have refused to universalize their maxims and have preferred to lie so as not to face the imperative of reason. As his commentators have noted, however, despite that pessimistic view, Kant does not speak of "original sin." The Enlightenment minimized or denied that sin and the moral depravation it implies, and the Christian apologetics of the era, preoccupied with moral optimism, even appear to have forgotten that dogma. Kant also does not evoke it as such, though he speaks of a "kingdom of evil" to which all the descendants of Adam are subject.[23] "He does not really admit that man has a sinful nature, but speaks rather of a sinful situation, made possible by a propensity and realized through an incomprehensible act of freedom."[24] It is an enigma why every human being since Adam—that is, the "human species" as such—has been disposed to give in to the temptation of evil, since nothing "disposes freedom to lean toward evil,"[25] which it has nevertheless done, inevitably, since the dawn of time. There is something tragic burdening every life, then, since no subject, despite its good will and its resolution to act out of respect for moral law, possesses the nobility sufficient to evade the burden of that legacy. Evil starts with freedom, and yet, it is already there, lying in wait, before any good or bad resolution on the free subject's part, like the misfortune of an unavoidable basic fact, or like a paradoxical legacy that implies that the subject, in freely engaging in an act, necessarily perpetuates a situation that predates it. For Kant, then, evil represents the inscrutable enigma of an act that is simultaneously a habitus, an original event that is also an antecedent.[26]

Kant does not propose to solve that enigma, but he observes that there is evil—and primarily, that every life starts from evil—which, he says, represents a heavy debt for everyone, a formidable, because ineffaceable, debt. Even "the human being [who] strives toward the good" cannot count on acquitting himself of it. In fact, inasmuch as Kant believes that the good done today never effaces even a minor evil committed yesterday, a complete redemption is meaningless. In spite of his merits, the person who has repented of his sins and who chooses the path of the good remains open to condemnation "in a final judgment of his entire life." Absolution for the evil one may have done in the past is not granted that human being on the pretext of his present repentance. Who, in fact, would have the power to absolve him, since reason—the only moral authority recognized by Kant—makes the imperative voice of duty reverberate within individuals but promises them no mercy? Yet everyone must work tirelessly to pay that inexpiable debt and to bear the burden of his sins, without imagining, by way of consolation, that someone else can stand in for him in that task. No one, not even the saint of the Gospel—as Kant calls him—can take on the sins of another and relieve them somewhat. That "original" debt bears the name of every person; every human person is thus destined to assume it on one's own and for one's own account. Each person must answer for the evil he has done and must pay—that is, suffer—for the thoughts, words, and acts that, in this life, have kept him from fulfilling his moral destiny. Despite one's efforts, however, and despite one's willingness to pay that price without seeking to redeem oneself by citing extenuating circumstances—in particular, that of the inexpiable legacy that weighs on the "human species"—the distance that separates the good man from that final goal remains unbridgeable. The sins committed here and now cast an indelible shadow over life; they make the human being's final moral goal inaccessible, despite the possibility of progress allowed by Kant, disconcertingly in fact, since it seems paradoxical to assert both the impossibility of expiation and the possibility of progress.

One hope remains, however, whose "rational" character is asserted by a Kant anxious to avoid the pathos of illusory consolation. Despite every human being's bad start and his sins, the eternal being "who scrutinizes the heart" will one day judge his conduct in terms of the moral intention that determined it and will lighten the burden of his debt. Hence, "a human being can still expect to be *generally* well-pleasing to God, at whatever point in time his existence be cut short."[27] That expectation is founded on the presence within oneself of the principle of the good— anterior to the bad start—which is why the term "rational" applies to it. Despite the obstacles and violations, this principle gives human being the strength to persevere and advance toward his moral destiny, in this life and in the next. Thanks to its presence, even the wicked man can hope to lift himself up and progress. Therefore, no one finds himself definitively and absolutely condemned, in spite of the despair that sometimes overtakes him to the point of making any effort at improvement seem futile. But is not that self-condemnation the supreme temptation of evil, the supreme lie? Kant resists the insinuations of the lie whereby one's conscience is duped into mercilessly condemning oneself. In fact, despite his recognition of the radicality of evil, he rejects the idea that evil is absolute: good retains its anteriority. Hope is therefore possible.

Like Kant, Levinas speaks of evil in terms of temptation and seduction. But he does not call it necessary and does not speak of original sin or of humanity's sinful situation since Adam. He confines himself to evoking the "probability" of evil. Nevertheless, since he immediately adds that that probability stems from "the incarnation of the subject,"[28] it is unclear how it differs from a pure and simple necessity. To locate the origin of the probability of evil in the incarnation of the subject raises a difficulty at least as formidable as the Kantian assertion of an ineluctably evil start of "the human species." If the fact of being incarnated—of having a body—leads to the temptation of evil, who will ever be able to escape that vertigo and seduction? Who will be able to fend off the risk of forgetting the good and of its being relegated to the ideology of moralizing discourses?

For Levinas, as soon as the subject, through its body, is present to being, it experiences the temptation to depart from the rule of the good, to disobey it, and to prefer "seductive and easy evil."[29] This does not mean that the body, the flesh, and sensibility are evil, but rather that they are the corollary of an ego irresistibly inclined to be distracted from the imperative of the good. The ego, even without admitting it to itself, would like to repudiate the influence of the good over it. It seeks to run away—illusorily, in fact—taking the frivolous but ruthless path of egoistic and tragic irresponsibility. "Egoism, or Evil,"[30] says Levinas, in a formulation whose radicality condemns any self-love, even a *reasonable* one, that is, one subordinated to moral law. That love—a love allowed by Kant—is still in excess; it only partly pays the debt of egoism.

Levinas does not think that egoism can disappear by means of a respect for moral principles, the universality of which guarantees that they will make no exceptions for anyone, not even for oneself. Neither good will nor a reasonable decision to subordinate self-love to moral principles stamps out egoism. Only the encounter with the fragility of the other, in driving that egoism to find the resources to help him, forces it—for a little while, in any case—to lay down its weapons. The defeat of egoism does not begin with the subordination of a subject's maxims to the universality of the moral principle but rather in its submission to the appeal of the face. It is experienced in the humility proper to any service, in a humility unaware of itself, since any humility that declares it is so is contradictory. Yet it is precisely because humility bars self-reflection—otherwise, it vanishes—that it liberates the subject from egoism and from evil and allows the subject to begin to acquit itself of its debt. Nevertheless, far from returning the subject's serenity to it, that acquittal is marked by a surplus of concern and scruples. As the subject responds to the appeal of the face, which liberates it from its egoism, it discovers that its liability is growing. It is as if the response continually sharpened the subject's awareness of the evils of its incarnation.

For Levinas, the ego seems to be under the burden of an inexpiable accusation. How will a man have the opportunity to one day acquit himself of his debt if that debt is related to his incarnation? He can, if necessary, ask the offended party to forgive the sins he has committed toward him, can try to rectify the harm that resulted from them, but how can he make amends for the very fact of his presence in being, as an ego? Does not the subject find itself in the grip of an unbearable and terrible accusation, if the fact of being in a body already constitutes a sin, and if, as a result, it is the subject's very existence that needs to be forgiven?[31]

What does the radicality of that accusation mean? And who can claim to have the right to make it, since all people, precisely, are likely—by virtue of their incarnation—to be the object of it?

The ego is held liable on three charges: "the *temptation* of the ease of breaking off, *erotic attraction . . . [or] the* seduction of irresponsibility, and the *probability* of egoism."[32] This terminology, like Kant's, emphasizes the secondary, but powerful and irrefutable, character of evil: the idea of temptation or seduction presupposes an internal struggle, a conflict between two modes of conduct, one of them—from which the ego feels inclined to break off—being anterior to the other. And, despite or because of the harsh imperatives it entails, that mode is described as being better than the second. To give in to temptation and seduction will thus mean falling short of the first mode of conduct. Nevertheless, since the ego, by virtue of its incarnation, inevitably finds itself open to temptation and seduction, there is no doubt that, for Levinas as for Kant, the human person will start out badly. There is no doubt that the originary debt that results will continue to weigh on each person, to haunt each one until death.

Levinas is seeking the conditions for the possibility of evil: he does not proceed to an examination of the vices or concrete sins of people in order to denounce or lament them. For that reason, he turns toward the subject's interiority, as if the secret of evil were to be found there, in the most secret part of every individual; as if, to understand why people are envious of one another, why they so often lie to one another, attack and murder one another, one had to begin by shedding light on a temptation inherent in the very life of the psyche; as if, finally, in order to keep the hope alive that a little good exists among men, the moral subject's psyche had to consent to bear the weight not only of the sins it may have actually committed, but of what makes evil possible for it at every moment, namely, the fact of being an ego. The radicality of the accusation is commensurate with the radicality of the evil made possible by the constant temptation of the psyche: to be an ego, self-important and irresponsible, an ego preoccupied with itself above all, even if it sometimes happens to be preoccupied with the other. That ego, finally, would like—and this is the supreme temptation—to abandon itself to evil while dismissing any scruple or bad conscience, and, as a result, it seeks to posit itself in being, as if it were its own origin, "uncreated—a sovereign principle, a prince."[33] Yet does such an ego, destined for destruction because of its finitude, nevertheless realize the absurdity of its undertaking? "Death makes any concern the Ego would like to take in its existence and destiny senseless," claims Levinas.[34] Unless, of course—as the desire to make oneself into the "sovereign principle" sufficiently demonstrates—the ultimate function of this recurrent concern of every person is precisely to allow the human ego to forget that mortal destiny, to blunt its certainty, for oneself in any case.

Yet, on this point, let us note that the accusation made against the arrogance of the ego, sovereign and preoccupied with the self, does not stem from a reflection founded on a universal and abstract moral principle, as in Kant, but from a shock produced by the encounter with the exteriority of the face. It is as if the ego, having perhaps managed to divert its eyes from its own mortality by asserting its prerogatives in being in order carefully to safeguard its survival day by day, felt accused of consenting to the death to which the other is fated. That accusation would make it feel, for an instant at least, the brutal impact of an offensive question: do I have the right to be? Or, before *having-to-be*, before being this incarnated ego, and in order to be it by rights, must I not let *that* question, stemming from a past resistant to all conscious memory, rise up within me? That question is "repressed most of the time . . . [and] hearkens all the way back to what one sometimes thoughtlessly calls illness,"[35] obviously to defend oneself from it and to keep it far away from oneself. It is as if the uneasiness that arises in oneself when confronted with the suffering of the face denoted a neurosis to be treated and not the emergence of the sharp edges of the subject's humanity, or as if the idea of an accusation without precise guilt—I am of course not the cause of every case of suffering—shattered the ego's identity and had to be denounced for its intolerable and unhealthy character.

According to Levinas, however, even though that accusation, which silently rises up from every face abandoned to its fate, cuts into the pretensions of the ego tempted by self-importance and pride, it does not do so to condemn the subject to neurosis but, in a more demanding manner, to awaken in it the immemorial anteriority of an alliance between the psyche and the good.

The Anarchical Connection to the Good

In Plato's philosophy, it is the encounter with beauty that, by virtue of its brilliance, awakens above all else the desire for the essences that have been glimpsed and then forgotten. Reminiscence, or anamnesis, means that the human soul has the capacity to turn back toward what does not pass away, namely, essences and, beyond them, the Good. In fact, despite change, which carries the human soul along, that soul maintains the sense of eternity. That is precisely what differentiates it from the animal soul, which is wholly at the mercy of change and its own finitude. Nevertheless, the human soul, because it is not divine, cannot turn back toward Being and truth without suffering. For man, truth "is attained only through and in the pain of an ordeal."[36] Hence terror takes hold of the human soul when it encounters beauty, because, as the *Phaedrus* explains (251c), beauty makes "wings sprout," but in feverishness and pain, inscribing fear deep within the trembling for joy.

In Levinas's philosophy, an encounter, a collision with exteriority, is also needed for the sense of the Good, which so often slumbers in the human soul, to awaken within it. Nevertheless, beauty and its brilliance never constitute the parameters of the Good. It is not the splendor of man, radiant and intoxicated with youthfulness, that ravishes the soul and converts it to the good but rather the weakness and misery of one's neighbor. And the terror that seizes the soul when confronted with that nakedness does not apply to oneself, to one's own destiny; it is not the corollary of any "promise of happiness," and, contrary to Plato, it *"does not become eros"* or enthusiasm.[37] That terror wounds the soul because it discovers it is destined for the good for all eternity, even as it remains incapable of responding appropriately to the demands of the good. The extreme fragility of the other threatened by violence and death makes the ego lose its serene innocence as an incarnated soul and subjects it to an infinite anxiety. That encounter reminds it of an anarchical connection that links it to the good. It discovers the infinite within it as a call to service.

Like Kant, Levinas thus alludes to an anteriority of the good that must be reawakened. Nevertheless, his analysis differs from Kant's since he speaks of an "anarchical connection between the subject and the good," adding that this connection—contrary to Kant's teachings—cannot "take shape as the assumption of a principle that would be present as a choice within the subject in any capacity whatsoever," as a will, for example. That connection is not made to the exteriority of a principle but to that of an alliance. All the same, that "exteriority of the alliance"[38] ought not to be confused with the exteriority of a contract, which, for its part, presupposes two partners or two wills who commit themselves to respecting its clauses and principles. The alliance with the Good, anterior to any choice or will, takes root in the soul and destines it to an obedience that reverses its spontaneous tendencies and often its conscious decisions as well. It takes shape in the soul "without the subject having willed it,"[39] before any distinction between freedom and nonfreedom, that is, passively. In the Bible, the alliance *(brit)* resides in the imperious excellence of the "thou" the Lord uses to address man, a "thou," which, as F. Rosenzweig says,[40] incites the human soul to come forth. That alliance, finally, calls for an obedience that is unconditional because not beholden to a reasonable examination by the yardstick of principles. The Good's hold on the psyche does not allow itself to be mastered by an act of knowledge any more than the God of the Bible allows himself to be grasped by concepts that supposedly prove his existence "as if he were part of being or perception." So concludes Levinas, substituting the word "God" for the word "Good."

In spite of man's constant temptation to forget it, the alliance with the Good—a preexisting, prehistoric alliance that was never entered into—governs the possibility of his becoming a moral subject. For Levinas as for Kant, evil, despite the ravages it produces, still occupies the second place. It seems unable to shatter that preexisting subjection even though it obviously seeks continually to erode it, often by mocking it. "Not next to or in front of the Good, but in the second place, below it, lower than the Good,"[41] Levinas says of evil. Obviously, that does not mean he minimizes its power and its calamities. Unlike Kant, he leaves open the possibility of a real rupture with the subjection to the good. Seductive evil, he says, may *"perhaps"* turn out to be unable to break that subjection. But, in delineating the horrifying misdeeds it has perpetrated on some souls, does he not also allow us to doubt this outcome? In becoming enslaved and hardened by evil—the demoniacal according to Kierkegaard—might a person reach a point where he is no longer able to escape it, where he is definitively deaf to the appeal of the good? It appears that Levinas does not absolutely rule out that eventuality: in some souls, the power of evil, in spite of its secondary character, sometimes seems to prevail definitively over the anarchical connection to the Good. But, obviously, no one has the right to assert such a thing since, as the Bible also reminds us, God alone can fathom a human heart. Sometimes, moreover, a person is released, unpredictably and as a reprieve, from the evil that had hardened him, which suggests that the anarchical connection to the good—a fragile connection for anyone prohibited from glorying in being—has not been simply annihilated.

The very idea of an axiological bipolarity is the supreme ruse of evil or of the egoism of the self anxious to claim the title of authorized source of values in order to liberate itself from the ever-so-demanding alliance and to proceed more serenely on the sole path of its own preferences and self-interest. Evil rarely makes its appearance as such; most often, the person seduced by it looks for "good" reasons to act the way he does in order to persevere in his being without feeling troubled or remorseful. Evil, says Levinas, disguises itself "as the twin brother of the good," as equal and contemporaneous to the good. That formidable parody, that "lie," which the philosopher calls "irrefutable" and "Luciferian," blurs the possibility of any distinction, and, in the first place, of the distinction between good and evil itself. Evil, in its perversion, maintains that confusion and, in its most extreme expressions, comes to accuse the good of a fundamental maliciousness. It then makes the suspicion of dissimulated self-interest hang over every human deed, especially when it is just and upright. In a supreme about-turn, the wicked man accuses of arrogance and secret infamy the man who heeds the call of the good and attempts—always inadequately, to be sure—to answer for it with his life. The lie of evil is Luciferian when, out of hatred for the good, it seeks to take its place and lead people to doubt that there is any difference between one and the other. It is victorious if men, sensitive to the power of evil's seduction and terrified by its misdeeds, overlook or scorn the humble resistance of the good—the "small kernel of human kindness" evoked by V. Grossman[42]—as if it were quite simply futile.

Yet is this lie, despite its wicked ambition and its power to destroy, sure to have the last word? Sometimes, the accusations of the wicked man struggling for hegemony, in his unending struggle not to be subordinated to the good, give way before the gaze of the weak, as if that gaze bore the trace of the prehistoric and anarchical pronouncement (dire) of the alliance with the good, or as if it reminded him of the ancient commandment—"Thou shalt not kill"—whereby the excellence of that alliance was established. In any case, Levinas's analyses of the face suggest as much.

Levinas conceives of the moral subject's awakening, or of the emergence of the human in being, as a response to that preoriginary subjection, which is not a happenstance of being. And yet, on that point precisely, he recognizes the importance of Kantianism: "To find a sense for the human without assessing it in terms of ontology, without knowing and without wondering 'what *is* it about . . . ,' and apart from mortality and immortality—such may be the Copernican revolution."[43] According to Levinas, Kant's greatness lies in the role he played in delivering man from the temptation of believing that sense always represents an event of being.

Hence the Kantian idea of rational hope—inherent in the subject's finite reason but irreducible to an object of knowledge—bears witness to the audacity of a philosophy that escapes ontology. Far from responding to some anxious need for survival, it directs thought toward a sense not dictated by a relation to being. "It is not by chance," Levinas maintains, "that this manner of conceiving of a sense beyond being is the corollary of an ethics."[44]

Despite that acknowledgment, however, do not Levinas and Kant disagree on the fundamental question of the source of ethics? Kant continually defends the idea of autonomy as the absolute condition for ethics, whereas Levinas reevaluates the notion of heteronomy.

four **Autonomy and Heteronomy**

Neither Kant nor Levinas believes that the good's anteriority in relation to evil implies that men spontaneously tend toward morality. As a result, both philosophers reflect on the conditions for the efficacy of the good. If man desired the good from the outset, that would imply he was immediately drawn to the universal and impersonal principles of morality (according to Kant), or to the imperative to respond to the other (according to Levinas). Yet, in either case, since such an attitude comes about at the expense of any concern for oneself, for one's own interests, or for one's happiness, it can only be the reverse of spontaneity. Ethics then depends on an education that at every moment attempts to inscribe its demands in the subject's life.

Kant bows to that necessity, remarking that, when a man lives in society, he "requires a master, who will break his will and force him to obey a will that is universally valid."[1] Otherwise, that man will not fail to misuse his freedom against his fellows, even as he desires a law to limit their freedom. But who will be that master? Since he must himself be a man, will he not also have the tendency to exempt himself from the law? Kant says that the difficulty of the question is such that the human species will find a solution to it only in the last instance. To overcome the aporia, that master, even while remaining a man, would have to be "just *on his own*": that is, he would have to behave in a just manner without himself needing a master. In other words, that master would have to be able to set his own moral law without requiring another master to compel him to respect it. Therefore, only *autonomy* provides the solution to the difficulty. And Kant berates the men who, out of laziness, prefer to remain minors all their lives and to obey a master—thus assenting to the opposite principle of *heteronomy*—because they are unable to compel themselves, just as he criticizes the masters who place themselves in the position of guardians to their fellows to keep them in the condition of minors. In politics, as in ethics, only the person who behaves autonomously deserves respect. According to Kant, heteronomy has no value, even if, by virtue of it and the fear it inspires, people respect the precepts of the law and avoid inflicting injury on one another. Kant hopes that an adequate and "rational preparation" will make the human race increasingly suited for autonomy at the political level. But, since the advent of political autonomy depends on respect for moral law—being just on one's own—it seems to be indebted to moral autonomy. Autonomy, the only state compatible with the subject's finitude or with "the *fact* that he does *really* take an interest in moral laws,"[2] leads one to one's highest destiny. But the idea of "destiny" does not imply submission to some form of alterity, human or divine: the subject remains autonomous and finite.

Although he does not want men to bow under the yoke of a master who compels them to obey by intimidating and threatening them, Levinas in no way participates in that praise of autonomy, and he calls into question the pertinence of the Kantian analysis of heteronomy. If, as Levinas maintains, the good has established an alliance with the subject before any choice on its part—before its emergence as a subject—and if that subject is characterized precisely by that openness toward the good or toward the infinite, how could it argue for autonomy without denying what gives it life? Nevertheless, some will maintain that we ought to give credence to Kant when he notes the misdeeds of heteronomy. In a world always at the mercy of the horrors of servitude and the violent acts of alienation perpetrated by one group against another—by the strong against the weak—how could anyone begin to argue for heteronomy? Would that not support such misdeeds and justify the worst injustices? Clearly, Levinas's philosophy does not lead in that direction since his reflection on heteronomy requires that the subject know how to distinguish between the brutal heteronomy of the tyrant—from whom the subject must liberate itself—and the silent heteronomy unknown to itself of the person who does not have the power to impose it. Only the second form of heteronomy could be inscribed in the psyche as something that continually awakens a profound complicity with the good, a complicity that so often slumbers.

What, then, are we to think of autonomy and heteronomy? Do they not ultimately presuppose two different conceptions of freedom?

The Source of the Law

The imperatives of morality cannot be deduced from empirical objects or situations—that is, from a heteronomous source—without immediately becoming hypothetical. "Wherever an object of the will has to be laid down as the basis for prescribing the rule that determines the will, there the rule is none other than heteronomy; the imperative is conditional, namely: *if* or *because* one wills this object, one ought to act in such or such a way; hence it can never command morally, that is, categorically."[3] Kant's argument here anticipates the famous description of the "Copernican revolution" he gives two years later, in the preface to the second edition of *Critique of Pure Reason*. In fact, "just as it is impossible in the epistemological context to explain the possibility of a priori knowledge, if one assumes that our knowledge must conform to objects, so too, in the practical context, one cannot explain the possibility of a categorical imperative, or more generally, an a priori practical principle with the requisite universality and necessity, if one assumes that an object (of the will) must be source of moral requirements."[4] Hence, whatever form it takes, heteronomy inevitably transforms the moral imperative into a hypothetical imperative. Such is, in any case, the first critique Kant addresses to forms of ethics whose source is found outside the subject—in a purpose to be achieved, for example, a purpose Kant places under the common denominator of the desire for happiness—hence to forms of ethics beholden to heteronomy. Without exception, these ethical systems would all be incapable of truly grounding morality since, in various capacities, they always rest on the subject's self-interest—in particular, on self-love and the often illusory idea the subject has of its personal happiness.

But, clearly, that critique is not sufficient to establish positively the need for autonomy. The Kantian analysis of the categorical imperative in fact precedes the elaboration of the idea of autonomy, and we must therefore understand how he establishes what, according to him, represents the only alternatives to the various ethics of heteronomy—all equally rejected for introducing impure and self-interested motives into morality. That alternative is the full autonomy of the will. What does this mean?

An act deserves the qualifier "moral" if it depends on the autonomy of the will, that is, on "the property of the will by which it is a law to itself."[5] That, says Kant, is the sole and supreme principle of morality. The will, or the power to act "in accordance with a priori practical principles,"[6] means, first, in negative terms, that one has the capacity to exempt oneself from the influence of all sensible and empirical causes—psychological, social, or cultural, for example—and that one is not beholden to them when one makes moral decisions and engages in the acts corresponding to them. If one did not have that capacity, the moral quest would quickly prove futile, since all acts would be *pathologically* affected by these determinations. An autonomous will is therefore not beholden to the desires, however respectable they might be, that animate the subject, since, in that case, the subject would be dependent on an empirical coefficient of pleasure or pain that is unrelated to morality. Hence, when the propensities of sensibility seek to rival moral principles, the will must do battle with them to rescue ethics. Kant posits that man certainly has that capacity to keep at a respectful distance the network of determinations that govern him unbeknownst to himself. The fact that the will is autonomous implies, for example, that affective motives do not come to bear on it in an absolute manner and that it can detach itself from them. In fact, autonomy is possible only on that condition, which, as Ricoeur shows, presupposes a gap between will and desire.[7]

Second, the will means, this time in positive terms, that one can decide *on one's own* to act solely on the basis of universal principles. But, clearly, since autonomy is not autocracy, the distance that separates the moral subject from perfect virtue (the transcendence of all obstacles attributable to sensible nature) and a fortiori from holiness (the absence of any temptation to transgress) remains great.

Hence, only the subject endowed with an autonomous will can decide *on its own* to act on the basis of categorical imperatives. It is not enough to articulate the principle of morality—"model the maxims of your deeds on a universal law"—one must also decide *for oneself* to act in accordance with it. That is the moment of morality. It results from the act of setting aside desires, emotions, and self-interest and considering only the form of the deed: is it in conformity with universal law? But since, in spite of everything, that question is not enough to impel a person to act in conformity with what universal law prescribes, Kant admits that, in spite of its "*incomprehensibility*," the unconditioned practical necessity of the moral imperative elicits a "pure self-interest" in man. "It is a *fact*," he says, "that he does really take an interest in moral laws."[8] He *himself* takes an interest—on his own, thanks to his will—in the universality prescribed by moral law. That interest, to the exclusion of all others, can enter the field of morality precisely by reason of its purity, since it depends on no empirical motivation—it depends neither, for example, on a desire for the happiness that would result nor on fear of punishment. In fact, it must enter that moral realm, since otherwise the formulation of the moral imperative would remain without effect on behavior. The *decision* to act morally therefore truly presupposes a motivation that Kant calls "self-interest." Without it, as Bergson notes, it is not clear how an intellectual notion or a rational idea could categorically require its own realization, since Kant has broken the connection between will and desire.[9]

That *fact* makes it possible to understand that the will is predetermined to act in accordance with moral law. Nevertheless, moral law is valid not *because it is in the interest* of the subject (in that case, it would be heteronomous because beholden to particular interests); rather, it elicits "a lively interest"[10] in the subject because it is valid for every person inasmuch as its source lies in the will, that is, in oneself. That is truly the principle of autonomy: moral law is not alien to the subject, it is not imposed on the subject by an external source. The subject establishes that law for itself. "The moral law expresses nothing other than the *autonomy* of pure practical reason, that is, freedom."[11] That alone is a matter of interest to the subject or, as Kant also says, it elicits the subject's *respect*. It must do so in order that the moral law—issued from the rational part of oneself—not remain suspended above the subject's sensible nature. It must do so in order for the will to be truly practical, that is, capable of impelling man to act out of duty, by virtue of his notion of moral law. "In respecting its own rationality, the will *receives* nothing, but spontaneously *produces* in itself that feeling of respect. That is in fact the only case when it produces a feeling."[12]

As a result, when the moral subject considers the person of the other, the same feeling of respect awakens in it—since the other is also, by virtue of his or her reason, a possible source of moral law. The subject thus respects not the other's singular and irreplaceable personality but rather that which makes him or her similar to itself: the other's humanity, that is, according to Kant, his or her capacity to be the author of moral law. The sensible immediacy of the other's presence, beside or in front of oneself, produces various feelings, but they remain *pathological* and, as such, cannot enter the field of morality. Only the moral subject's inner certainty that, standing before the other, it is in the presence of another moral subject elicits respect in it. The "dignity"—for which there is no equal—of the reasonable being in the person of the other is not perceived in a sensible manner, it is deduced from the *fact* of the moral law in oneself. The subject, considering the other as the author of that law in the *same* capacity as itself, owes him or her respect. That is why one of the formulations of the categorical imperative requires that every person treat the humanity in his own person and in others *"always at the same time as an end, never simply as a means."*[13] Thus autonomy is the basis for the respect due the other: in human societies, even those receptive to the Enlightenment ideal Kant admires, humanity is, of course, not solely an end in itself, but it begins to be so when everyone respects the presence of the moral law in his own person and in that of the other. "At the *same* time," says Kant, everyone, naturally and inevitably, relates to the other in terms of his utility, if only to ask a service of him, but this fact only makes respect all the more indispensable. As a result, in addition to "the pure interest" in moral law stemming from its own rationality, there is an interest that is just as "pure"—that is, with no allegiance to any emotion or feeling and not beholden to the relations of utility that persist in spite of everything—in the person of the other, given that, through his reason, that person is the source of moral law in the *same* capacity as oneself.

Certain questions arise at this stage of the analysis: can the idea of a "pure" interest in moral law mark, without contradiction, the road of the moral subject's conduct? Does "respect" for the law, which bears witness to that interest, make it possible to deal *morally* and in every circumstance with the entreaties of those who live with you in society for a period of time? And finally, does it suffice to respect the other as the possible author—by virtue of his or her reason, that is, by virtue of an unrepresentable universal—of moral law, to understand both the other's dignity and his place within humanity?

From the perspective of that inquiry, Levinas wonders, first, whether, contrary to the exception granted by Kant, any interest, in spite of its liveliness, can ever be "pure," that is, free from any egoistic baggage and any calculation or ulterior motive. In fact, Levinas likes to emphasize the presence of *being* within interest—*inter-esse-ment*[14]—and links that presence to the inevitability of egoism. "The self-interestedness of being is dramatized in the all-out struggle of egos against one another." It threatens the peace that men try to establish among themselves, since that peace "does not resist self-interest."[15] Ethics completely reverses self-interest, suspends its inevitability. In shaking off the torpor of a subject that nothing can penetrate, in wounding it at the sensitive core of its perseverance in being, ethics awakens the subject to what it cannot give to *itself* as a gesture of proud autonomy: the appeal of the good. Yet that appeal does not come from self-interest of any sort. Ethics, according to Levinas, does not originate in self-interest, however pure—that is, relieved of the suspect baggage of some secret gratification—but rather in disinterestedness. It introduces a moment of pure gratuitousness into being, a dawning of pure goodness, because the appeal of the good never leaves the subject time to *self*-reflect, to consider it, and possibly to take an interest in it. Its urgent request defers self-reflection, does not leave the subject the luxury of measuring ethics by the yardstick of any self-interest, not even the "lively" and "pure" interest evoked by Kant. It obliges without becoming a matter of self-interest.

Levinas admires Kant because, he says, he forged the path toward the notion that sense is not necessarily an event of being. The *fact* of moral law in itself cannot be explained in terms of the phenomena of the sensible world or by means of theoretical and ontological reason. Nevertheless, this *fact* gives a positive and practical signification to certain ideas of pure reason, beyond the finitude of time and space. According to Levinas, there is "a mode of practical signification" in that philosophy, a mode "that remains, next to the theoretical access to being, an access to an unimpeachable sense," "as if, in reason, there was something for a being other than the fact of being."[16] That sense makes its appearance with the *fact* of moral law—not an empirical *fact (Tatsache)* but a *fact* of reason *(Faktum)*, since it is impossible to deduce it from a prior statement—as if ethics, and it alone, placed one on the path to a rationality that is not ontological.

But, in speaking of self-interest, Kant himself was not radical enough in pursuing that path. In insisting upon disinterestedness, Levinas intends to deliver the moral subject from the slightest traces of the receptivity of being. Is not self-interest yet another detour taken by the act of being? That implies, already at this point,[17] a return to ontology in Kantian thought, a return Levinas cannot abide, since, according to him, it implies inevitable violence: self-interest is never "pure" of all egoism, of all favor granted to oneself. The Kantian idea of a "moral interest" that is "purely practical and free," a self-interest befitting only a "finite being" and not God—only a finite being has "a need to be impelled to activity by something because an internal obstacle is opposed to it"[18]—therefore appears contradictory from Levinas's point of view. It does not compel sufficiently, it does not deliver the subject from ontological egoism, it even seems to condemn the subject to never move beyond it.

As a result, despite the clearly desirable respect it elicits among men, the duty to treat humanity as an end and never simply as a means, in one's own person and in that of the other, is open to dispute. For Kant, respect means that one is aware that the will is subordinated to a law it sets for itself. Like self-interest, respect makes sense only for a reasonable and finite being: an infinite being would not feel respect for moral law since it would not experience it as a demand contradicting its own propensities. The subject must respect the other because it recognizes him as a person, that is, as a finite and reasonable being, a potential author of moral law. That is why, Kant explains, only people—not things or animals—elicit respect. The animal will be loved or feared, but it will not be respected,[19] since its finitude is deprived of reason. Autonomy is thus the basis for the respect due to the person of the other.

Is it enough, however, to respect rationality in the other and to deliberate rationally on how to behave toward him or her? Does rationality

alone, a rationality I deduce in the other on the basis of my own, constitute the other's value? Of course, some will say, in a world in the grip of
violence and contempt for the other on a daily basis, that is already a great
deal. "Given the intermittence of feelings, I fall back upon the law. Unable to be faithful to the other, I attempt to remain consistent, to remain
in agreement with myself,"[20] that is, with what the reason within me demands of me, despite my possibly aggressive or even hostile feelings toward the other.

The subject's autonomy leaves no choice other than the intermittence
of feelings toward the other or the respect due him in his capacity as an autonomous person like myself. An autonomous subject *goes to* the other on
the basis of the moral law in him; it is not the alterity of the other that it
respects, but what he or she has in common with the subject, namely, reason. The subject thus sees the other as an alter ego, a finite and reasonable
being similar to itself. Yet that perception is obviously not immediate and
does not result from the encounter with the face of the other: it comes at
the end of a process of deduction carried out in complete solitude.

Levinas wonders whether the encounter with the other as alter ego suffices for morality. Is the quest for the other on the basis of the subject's autonomy the best path to take? In any case, it appears necessarily to lead to
an encounter with the other as alter ego—a reasonable being like myself—
and not as an alterity. That path is indispensable in the struggle against violence, which refuses to recognize the other as an alter ego, worthy of respect if not of love, and in the denunciation of a fanaticism blind to the
universality of the human. Levinas questions its sense, however: is that
sense good? He of course recognizes, with Kant, that in morality reason
acquires a "full vigilance" irreducible to any knowledge. The *Critique of
Pure Reason* sets limits on the claims of knowledge and calls for restraint
on the part of reason. But "from that adventure, essential to the human
within the Western tradition, reason (despite the passivity to which, in the
capacity of categorical imperative, it will not fail to bear witness) maintains its claim to activity, that is, to its primary or ultimate place within
the category of the Same."[21] Through a movement of self-reflection, the
Kantian subject identifies the other as an alter ego; as a result, according to
Levinas, that subject, despite its vigilance, misses alterity. That is why Kant
paves the way for a different philosophy, one whose sense would not move
from myself as a rational and moral subject toward the other but rather

from the other as a source of infinite uneasiness toward myself, a self that would thereby also lose his or her beautiful and proud autonomy. For, in tearing the self's finitude asunder, that face-to-face relationship with the other would awaken a *"de profundis* of the spirit,"* whose signification would remain unamenable to ontological rationality. That signification would call upon the moral subject to conceive of a transcendence within immanence or "a heteronomy of freedom that the Greeks did not teach us."[22]

The Evils of Heteronomy

Generally, philosophers emphasize the alienation inherent in all forms of heteronomy: there is supposedly no place for the idea of freedom within a context where heteronomy is present. Hence, before Kant, Rousseau's *Social Contract* argued for the freedom of peoples on the basis of a radical rejection of all heteronomy. However diverse its expressions, whether public or private, it is the equivalent of slavery. Nevertheless, people do not always realize this and it sometimes happens—this is the greatest danger, of course—that they consent to obey a master without looking for or wishing for a different life, since "slaves lose everything in their chains, even the desire to be free of them."[23] Does not "voluntary servitude" (La Boétie) lead a man to fight for submission to the master as if for his freedom? Against that perversion, which annihilates freedom de jure and de facto, Rousseau defends an idea of freedom based on autonomy, since only "obedience to the law one has set for oneself is freedom."[24] To be sure, everyone who joins the social pact gives up his own will, which is linked to his own interests and his particular desires, and obeys the general will of society; but, since everyone participates in that general will as a citizen, no one is alienated by that obedience. As a result, the civil liberty of every individual implies that he enter a space of political autonomy. Rousseau adds, however, that civil liberty is not sufficient; "moral liberty" must be added to it. Even in a political state devoid of all heteronomy, once one's existence is governed by the social contract, submission to individual impulses and appetites still represents a terrible slavery. Political autonomy thus calls for moral autonomy, which alone makes "man truly master of himself."[25]

Rousseau's analysis of autonomy had a profound effect on Kant, who also transforms it, however. As Hegel points out, did not the Reign of Terror, in its effort to eliminate all individual will, demonstrate the impossibility of reconciling the individual will with the universal will? Hegel notes, in fact, that "before the universal can perform a deed it must concentrate itself into the One of individuality and put at the head an individual self-consciousness; for the universal will is only an *actual* will in a self, which is a One." During the French Revolution, the Reign of Terror showed that "absolute freedom as *pure* self-identity of the universal will thus has within it *negation,*" the negation of any individual will.[26] It bears within it, as its obligatory and formidable corollary, the terror of death.

Kant nevertheless transforms the political schema of the *Social Contract,* since, in ethics, everything is played out within the subject. The individual and particular will—which the citizen, according to Rousseau, must renounce—corresponds to the will *pathologically* affected by the propensities of man's sensible nature, which is inclined to seek happiness. The universal will, on the contrary, is equivalent to the autonomous will, that which decides on its own to act in accordance with its notion of a priori principles. The battle between the universal and the particular thus moves inside each subject. Autonomy is to be defended within every person against his own inclinations and his own preferences, that is, against his sensible finitude. For all people, "moral necessity is *constraint (Nöthigung),* that is, *necessitation (Verbindlichkeit),*" it "commands" the propensities because the universality of its principles is incompatible with their particularity. Nevertheless, in order to succeed, it must also elicit in every man "the terrible respect" that reminds him of his "unworthiness" and humiliates his sensible nature. Then and only then, after that abasement, when the subject gives the feeling of respect "a practical influence" over its decisions, does it also tirelessly admire "the majesty of moral law."[27]

The citizens of Rousseau's *Social Contract* are not spontaneously in agreement with the general will. As individual people too attached to their own will and to their own self-interest, they often refuse to give them up on the pretext that they are citizens—to the point that the recalcitrants must sometimes be compelled to be free, that is, to obey that will.[28] In the same way, the Kantian moral subject is not immediately concerned with the universalization of the maxims behind its actions. If moral law—even though the subject is the author of it through reason—did not in itself produce the respect that humiliates the natural propensities in order to raise the subject toward the law, the subject would probably not obey it. In this case, the "terror" exerted within humanity by respect for the law comes to bear on the entire residuum of *pathological* attachment to his own interests. No one can avoid the ordeal of that "terror," since the voice of moral law "makes even the boldest evildoer tremble." Moreover, although every person is truly a law-making member "of a kingdom of morals" by virtue of his or her reason, he or she is never anything but its "subject" and not its "sovereign."[29] But—and here is the great difference between Kant and the revolutionary Reign of Terror—no one has any right to intimidate anyone else to make him or her moral. No one can lay claim to a higher degree of virtue than his or her neighbor in order to compel him or her to respect moral law. Such heteronomy would, in fact, destroy ethics. Some would obey no doubt, out of fear of reprisal, but that is the point: such a motivation would bankrupt ethics. Legality would be safe, since, in the end, people would submit to the yoke of the law rather than risk death, but ethics would disappear, since it rests solely on the purity of intention. According to Kant, then, it is truly within the soul of every person, and there alone, that the battle allowing the moral law to prevail over particularities unfolds. Yet, despite the progress every person can make, that internal battle lasts a lifetime, because, in this life, no one reaches the culmination of the violence of his or her inclinations and self-interest; no one possesses a "holy" will. That is why Kant says that, despite autonomy, moral law always presents itself to the individual as an "imperative." The paradox of that autonomy rests on the fact that "for the finite man, it is to be promoted within a context of constraint, obligation, and even debt, hence duty."[30]

Moral autonomy, then, does not tolerate any compromise with heteronomy. Kant turns his back on the heteronomy stemming from sensible nature in itself, that of individual self-interest and the quest for happiness, since these subordinate moral law to motivations external to its purity. But he also rejects with equal determination the heteronomy of the virtuous and "incorruptible" tyrant who would like to have men bow down, who would like to submit them by force to his will—supposedly that of the universal—even as he is prepared, to that end, to make them submit to terror and death. Kant also rejects the heteronomy, albeit less dramatic, of "so called *noble* (supermeritorious) actions," which are proposed as "examples" to children to predispose them in favor of such actions and elicit their enthusiasm.[31] Ethics is not based on imitation of the behavior of others and the eventual admiration that behavior produces. Even if, in certain people at least, such an attitude leads to apparently virtuous acts, it deprives people of their critical reflection and keeps them in the condition of minors. Admiration for others often blinds a person and turns him or her away from autonomy. History has shown what profound misery is inflicted on humanity by the fanatical passions that admiration sometimes elicits. In all these exemplary cases, the intrusion of alterity, in the form of the violence of sensible inclinations, or of the tyrant's will, or of admiration for other people's behavior, destroys the sole principle of morality, namely, autonomy.

In addition, even if a person, by virtue of his or her finitude and unlike God, does not possess a holy will but rather a will endlessly hindered by sensibility, ethics does not stem from the holy will of that God. Hence, Kant says, "the Christian principle of *morals* itself is not theological (and so heteronomy); it is instead autonomy of pure practical reason by itself."[32] It is never because God prescribes certain maxims that they become moral; on the contrary, it is because they are moral—stemming from the moral law within every reasonable being—that God prescribes them. Thus, the act of agreeing with what the God of the Bible commands by observing maxims does not imply that autonomy is called into question. The source of moral duties cannot lie in a will foreign to oneself, not even in God's will. In fact, even if it is wholly permissible to consider them divine commandments as well, it is never for that reason that the moral subject obeys them. In addition, if, as Kant admits, the individual ultimately recognizes that he needs God's participation to conceive of a realization of the highest good,[33] that recognition does not call the foundational autonomy of ethics into question. The differences between atheists and believers are irrelevant in the consideration of the fact of moral law in itself and in the respect it elicits.

Hence, Kant's indictment of heteronomy turns out to be final and definitive: heteronomy alienates the subject and destroys ethics. Will reading Levinas allow us to reopen the case? Levinas shares with Kant the idea that the prescriptive statements of ethics cannot be deduced from knowledge, and, like him, he thinks there is a mode of practical signification that does not depend on ontology. Nonetheless—and here we must carefully measure the distance between the two philosophers—that signification leads him precisely to reevaluate the idea of heteronomy.

Like Kant, Levinas has no particular taste for servitude and submission to the tyrannical will of the other. The heteronomy of the master-slave relation is clearly an evil from which one must liberate oneself, and God himself condemns it. The Bible says that the slave who, out of love for his master, rejects the good news of his liberation, will be marked by a sign of opprobrium. "His master shall bring him unto the judges; he shall also bring him to the door, or unto the door post; and his master shall bore his ear through with an aul; and he shall serve him for ever" (Exodus 21:6). Because he was deaf to the order announcing his liberation, he is branded in the ear, near a door or door post to signify his refusal to cross the threshold to freedom. The man who comes under a master's yoke cannot serve God, as the Talmud says (Berakhot 20a); he must be exempted from religious obligations. Finally, let us recall that the first law given to the Israelites when they were still in Egypt was to free the slaves. The Lord reminds them of this in Jeremiah (34:13–16) and reproaches the Israelites for disobeying: "Ye . . . polluted my name, and caused every man his servant, and every man his handmaid, whom he had set at liberty at their pleasure, to return, and brought them into subjection, to be unto you for servants and for handmaids" (Jeremiah 34:16).

No one owes obedience to a tyrant's law. Yet the risks of tyranny recur throughout history and in people's private lives, and the possibilities for it are vast. "It has infinite resources at its disposal, in love and money, torture and hunger, silence and rhetoric. It can exterminate in the tyrannized soul even the power to be offended, that is, even the power to obey on command. True heteronomy begins when obedience ceases to be an obedient conscience and becomes a propensity. The supreme violence lies in that supreme mildness."[34] The slave soul no longer experiences the order as such; love for the master blinds him to that distance. But, as a result, Levinas says, the tyrant no longer commands anyone, he simply makes use of matter offered up to his violence.

Levinas shows no indulgence for that formidable heteronomy or for the masochism that often accompanies it: that heteronomy is to be combated outside oneself and within oneself. The philosopher knows what a great risk to freedom it is to succumb to tyranny in the name of sublime causes but also in the name of love. Freedom must therefore anticipate its own shortcomings and arm itself in advance by setting up—outside the self—a reasonable, just, and humane order. It is therefore fitting that freedom should impose on itself a commandment exterior to itself, a commandment that will prevent it from regressing toward the archaism of tyranny. Yet, according to Levinas, that order cannot reside solely in the four cubits of rational law or in a "categorical imperative defenseless against tyranny."[35] It must find a written expression that will guarantee a person against his or her own temptation to return to Egypt and serve a master.

Nevertheless, the written law, the rational law of institutions—even if, as in Rousseau, it is an expression of the general will—is often a burden to people. In the impersonal reason of the law—whether moral or political—these people rarely recognize their own will, and they experience its weight as an alienating constraint. Levinas considers the possibility of a tyranny of the impersonal that, though founded on reason, nevertheless constitutes a tyranny. Can one force someone "to be free" by compelling him to obey the general will, as Rousseau prescribes? To respond to the moral imperative, is it enough, as Kant believes, to transpose that battle to the solitary interior of every soul struggling to obey the moral law in itself and ruthlessly expelling any temptation to succumb to heteronomy?

If tyranny, as Levinas says, is characterized by the impossibility of looking the other in the face, then the impersonal law of rationality, because it does not find the face of the other, does not suffice to abolish tyranny. That law still has a coefficient of violence since it knows nothing of people's faces: it approaches them "from an angle," on the basis of universal principles, ideas. The Kantian moral subject goes to the other on the basis of a form—the law—and does not let the faces of people trouble its autonomy. That is why concern for the law, despite its rational or reasonable foundation—which, according to Kant, guarantees the subject's autonomy and hence freedom—is not enough. A law that disregards faces remains violent. According to Levinas, the face intrudes on the subject's world as a weak and defenseless appeal that peacefully resists the tyranny "of brutality, but also of incantation, ecstasy, and love."[36] Yet it also reveals the violent, though often unrecognized, aspect of rational and impersonal autonomy: when confronted with the face, an imperative can be heard that is different from the categorical imperative proper to moral autonomy, and that imperative challenges the subject's proud autonomy.

Does not Levinas, then, argue for a new form of alienation? Is it possible to conceive of the heteronomic imperative, or the command of the face, without tyranny?

Human Election

Freedom allows for the human effort to rid itself of the grip of tyrannies, especially when they have long been accepted as the inevitable order of things. From that perspective, Kant describes enlightenment as "the human being's emergence from his self-incurred minority," when, for lack of education, as the result of intimidation, or for the sake of convenience, he is unable to use his own intellect.[37] The public and private use of reason by every individual thus constitutes the quintessential imperative of freedom. As a result, the criterion for the legitimacy of political law is expressed in terms of "whether a people could impose such a law upon itself."[38] As in ethics, that criterion does not distinguish between freedom and autonomy. In ethics, the autonomy of pure practical reason *is* freedom— "a free will and a will under moral laws are one and the same"[39]—and, in politics, autonomy and freedom are also declared indissociable. To escape the status of a minor and to gain access to freedom, one must have moral and political autonomy. Kant mounts a strong challenge to any resurgence of heteronomy, since it destroys the very principle of freedom.

Levinas's reflection is different, since he does not accept the notion that autonomy and freedom are identical concepts. He speaks of a heteronomy that, far from abolishing freedom, leads it to a path where it discovers the excellence of its moral "vocation." How are we to understand that reevaluation of the concept of heteronomy? For what idea of freedom does it serve as corollary? Can a subject that loses its autonomy truly hold on to the sense of freedom, and does the qualifier "moral" still apply to it?

Levinas also insists that freedom admits of violence. One must leave the status of a minor, or, as he reminds us, the condition of slavery, in pain and suffering. One must leave Egypt, flee it, in the throes of distress and confusion, since the sea and desert promise no reassuring sanctuary. In spite of Moses, then, there will always be a temptation to remain attached to Egypt and to submit once more, and for a long time, to Pharaoh's brutality or to the subtler but no less formidable violence that works its way into souls, in the name of "noble" causes that mask the tyranny of one person over another and make it acceptable. The temptation to turn back without crossing the Red Sea and the desert, or to leave Egypt without letting go of it internally, dwells within many minds. Seeing "the

Egyptian"—that is, the lie of a tyranny whose ambition is to efface God from the minds of people[40]—"dead upon the sea shore" (Exodus 14:30) does not always suffice to impel us to sing a song unto the Lord, as Moses and the children of Israel do (Exodus 15:1). Nor does it always suffice to make us go forward to the land of promise—a promise with an as-yet uncertain sense—without turning back.

Is there any hope that that uncertainty will be removed? According to Levinas, the purpose of that hasty and sometimes nostalgic departure or flight, far from the alienating heteronomy of Pharaoh and of all those who, even without apparent brutality, resemble him, is not, as it is for Kant, to make it finally possible to enter the beautiful promised land of autonomy. In the Bible, in any case, the Israelites leave Egypt in order to receive the Torah at Mount Sinai, not to bestow their own law on *themselves*. They exchange the tyrant's heteronomy for the Lord's, but they remain within heteronomy. Is there a difference between these two forms of submission to the law of another? According to an opinion recorded in the Talmud, the tablets given to Moses by God announce freedom: "And the tables were the work of God, and the writing was the writing of God, graven upon the tables" (Exodus 32:16). "Do not read *Harut* [graven] but *Herut* [freedom], since no one is truly free except he devote himself to the study of the law."[41] But clearly, that opinion is not self-evident and cannot be a philosophically acceptable argument. In addition, since all the commandments of that law are transmitted in the name of the Lord—"I am the Lord thy God, which have brought thee out of the land of Egypt, out of the house of bondage" (Exodus 20:2)—and in the imperative mode, which allows for no discussion, where is the space for freedom in the subject that hears them? The commandment "Thou shalt not kill" thus represents a categorical imperative of a very particular kind, since, contrary to Kantian imperatives, it does not emerge from the subject's will. It therefore appears that the reconciliation of that heteronomy with freedom constitutes an aporia. According to Kant, God's heteronomy, despite its content (concern for the life of creatures), which differentiates that law from that of a tyrant, still remains alien to freedom. Obedience to his precepts—however positive an effect they may have on human lives—keeps people within legality without allowing access to morality, which depends solely on respect for the subject's autonomy.

How, then, does Levinas reconcile heteronomy and freedom? On occasion, he quotes the verses that remind individuals of "the status—or lack of status—of strangers and slaves in the land of Egypt."[42] In fact, he says, although these verses can in no way "prove" the validity of a thesis—if they did, we would be outside the realm of philosophy—"they bear witness to a tradition and an experience" that merit considered reflection. Someone engaged in that reflection will not be concerned solely with the singularity of one tradition but, as a philosopher concerned with the universal, will ask whether these biblical texts—texts where the Hebrew letter has been covered over by the Greek letter[43]—bear a truth relevant to the human as such and, in this respect, whether they are worthy of the philosopher's attention.

Levinas notes that, in the Bible, the memory of the stranger's status is associated with the heteronomy of the commandment that prescribes respect for the stranger: "Thou shalt neither vex a stranger, nor oppress him: for ye were strangers in the land of Egypt" (Exodus 22:21). "This echoes a permanent *saying [dire]*[44] of the Bible: the status—or lack of status—of strangers and slaves in the land of Egypt brings man closer to his neighbor."[45] The person who has felt deep within his soul and in his flesh the suffering inherent in the status of the stranger and the slave bears within him a truth about the human that overwhelms and vexes him when he is confronted with his neighbor's weakness. The encounter with the defenseless nakedness of the face takes hold of him, shakes the pride and self-assurance he feels as a now-liberated man. That memory prevents him from settling definitively into being, from letting himself be seduced by tyranny, and from mimicking Pharaoh's behavior. That memory wounds his psyche and destines him to serve weakness without seeking to profit from it, dominate it, or simply disregard its appeal to him. But, Levinas insists, that attitude is not a matter of course, it is not natural, it must be commanded. The concern for one's own life and the self-interestedness of being—once we are out of Egypt—are not converted spontaneously or by an autonomous decision into a concern for the life of the other and a subordination of being to the imperatives of the good. The appeal of the good—in the form of the Lord's commandments in the Bible—solicits the subject; it is not the subject that decides, not it that posits the appeal.

What about freedom, then? Is it not paradoxical and philosophically unacceptable to conclude, as Levinas does, that the free person is pledged to his or her neighbor and that no one can save himself without others? And why does he refer to the particular history of the children of Israel coming out of Egypt in order to understand the human subject as such? Is it not a philosophical error, as Kant claims, to conceive of matters on the basis of texts external to mere reason?

Levinas distinguishes moral freedom from every philosophy of autonomy, which, according to him, is always under suspicion of being indifferent to the fate of the other. "Ethics begins when freedom, rather than finding its justification in itself, senses it is arbitrary and violent."[46] Yet the subject's awakening to the arbitrariness and violence of its freedom does not result from a self-reflexive movement or from the desire to universalize the maxims of its actions; it comes from an "investiture" by the other. "To philosophize is to return to the near side of freedom, to discover the investiture that liberates freedom from arbitrariness."[47] It is not autonomy but the welcome of the other that responds to that quest; the reawakening comes from the other. Confronted with the nakedness of the other's face, which is always threatened by violence and death, the man liberated from the tyrant's alienating heteronomy—like the Israelite coming out of Egypt—experiences his freedom with shame. "The presence of the Other—a privileged heteronomy—does not run counter to freedom but invests it."[48]

What does that investiture mean? What is the difference between the tyrant's alienating heteronomy and the privileged heteronomy of the other, if it turns out that the former is to be combated as what destroys freedom and the latter welcomed as what makes freedom moral? Submission to the tyrant abolishes freedom and has no value; it simply attests to the powerlessness, or even the masochism, of the slave. That submission is immoral since it prevents the slave from emerging into life as a subject; it wounds and bruises the subject without awakening it to the good. In the case of masochism—in a supreme perversion—it can even incite the subject to confuse the good with the intensity of the evil produced by submission. Conversely, the heteronomy of the face in its weakness awakens a person to life as a singular subject; it invests his or her freedom and makes an infinite request to it. The subject emerges in its irreplaceable uniqueness as a response to the appeal of the face that elects the subject. That election of one person and not another does not result from a partisan choice or a greater degree of attention from the elect: it is the response that determines election. The chosen subject is alone in hearing the appeal, not because others turn a deaf ear or are not called, but because it is in hearing, in letting the biblical "here I am" rise to the lips, that the subject becomes the elect, becomes itself.[49] Such is the liberating sense of the privileged heteronomy of the other: an election that brings the subject to its irreplaceable uniqueness. Unlike Kant, Levinas does not think that the subject is moral and free by reason of its autonomy but rather by reason of that election.

But, some will object, why does Levinas persist in using the vocabulary of wounds when he describes the encounter with the other as a trauma, or even as an obsession? Is that not a return in force of masochism, against which an ethics of autonomy would have to be defended? When he makes the moral subject a "hostage" to the other, does this not imply a tyrannical—that is, an immoral—heteronomy?

Levinas's vocabulary, marked by an intensity of undeniable suffering, signifies, first, that morality does not stem from one's finer feelings, nor does it emerge spontaneously. To obey the voice of the other's privileged heteronomy is painful because it reverses the natural impulses and the primacy of concern for oneself. Kant is in agreement with Levinas on this point: no doubt the Kantian "Thou shalt" comes from the voice of reason within oneself—and not from the other—but that voice also inflicts harm on spontaneity and egoism; it "strikes down" the impulses. In addition, despite their different sources, the prescriptive statements of both philosophers inflict harm in a second respect: they do not appeal to any prior knowledge that, in justifying them in terms of theoretical reason, would allow the subject to be in full intellectual agreement with what ethics requires. In fact, Kant does not deduce these statements from a prior knowledge any more than Levinas does; the moral "fact" imposes itself on a person and makes him cognizant of his freedom, but that does not broaden the field within which his speculations can legitimately exert themselves. His speculative intelligence is thus left in sufferance [en souffrance] as well.

To be sure, the suffering of the subject affected by the appeal of the face and the suffering of the subject that hears the voice of the categorical imperative do not have the same origin, but both carry a formidable weight as far as the advent of morality is concerned. Absent holiness, it seems impossible to do without that suffering. But must it be called masochistic, as it sometimes has been? Must one flee it at all costs as an accommodation with evil? Isn't that a misinterpretation? Such a characterization rests on a misunderstanding about what is at stake in that suffering, both for Kant and for

Levinas: freedom. To be sure, Levinas does not conceive of that freedom in the same terms as Kant, but, for Levinas as well, the suffering inflicted on ontological egoism is liberating. It frees up the breathing space indispensable for the emergence of the moral subject; it is a long way from the rigidity of an identity defined in terms of essence. It orients life toward an existence on the alert, a worried and responsible existence, which, because it delays self-reflection—"Self-reflection becomes an endless detour"[50]—severs one's bond to oneself and proscribes repose in being. Yet, strangely, that delay, far from destroying man, liberates him: it reveals his uniqueness to him, and therefore, his freedom. That uniqueness is to be conceived without reference to an identity or an essence; it is to be found beyond them. Or rather, it is a uniqueness to be found *again*, since, according to Levinas, the first fact of existence does not lie in the in-self or in the for-self but in the "for-the-other," or even in goodness. He adds that this means that every existence is a creature: the person called to being cannot escape by expecting volunteers to designate *themselves* in his place, he and no one else is solicited by an appeal that preexists him. Levinas describes that appeal as the goodness of the Good, of the Good that does not slumber or sleep. "A goodness always more ancient than choice: the Good has always already elected and solicited the unique, the only one *[l'unique]*."[51]

The anteriority of that election in relation to any choice assumed in the pride of an autonomy becomes apparent when the appeal of the face—or its heteronomy—wounds a person's self-importance and the firmness of his or her position in being. That is why, according to Levinas, "the specificity of the prescriptive statements is not and cannot be ensured sufficiently by the Kantian procedure," whereby only "the will that subscribes to clear ideas or that comes to a decision only out of respect for the universal" is considered good.[52] Such a will, in effect, obscures the first fact of election; it effaces it or claims to takes its place. There is no privileged heteronomy for Kant, since any heteronomy, including that of God or, quite simply, the heteronomy of any content of ethics, destroys the principle on which it rests because it exerts authority over it. By contrast, Levinas argues for a heteronomy of weakness. And, contrary to Kantian moral law, the law that emanates from that heteronomy is not expressed in a purely formal manner. It demands a precise behavior, whose sense lies in the commandment "Thou shalt not kill" (Exodus 20:13) or "Thou shalt love thy neighbor as thyself" (Leviticus 19:18).

The commandment of love—which is contradictory according to Kant, since the moral law must remain formal by necessity—has no pertinence unless it comes from love itself, from the goodness of the Good, which solicits a person at every instant of his or her encounter with the weakness of the other. This does not mean that that weakness is lovable or that it elicits a feeling of love but that, through it, the appeal of the Good makes itself heard to the elect. It is precisely in responding to that solicitation that a person becomes the unique or the elect. From that perspective, the "self" of the biblical commandment is not a premise but a result: that love is "thyself." The moral subject, in its unique and irreplaceable aspect, does not preexist that love but is the result of it.

The heteronomy of the law, signified in the Bible by the signature—"I *(anokhi)* am the Lord thy God"—addressed to the "thou" who is supposed to keep the commandments, does not signify an alienation or, as Kant would have it, a pure legalism that would never require the subject's interiority to adapt itself to moral imperatives. It constitutes the "living *presence* of love," its "harassment." Contrary to what Kant believes, Levinas writes, "love can be commanded, and it is even the very essence of love to command reciprocity. Only love can command love. Love commands love in the privileged *now* of its loving."[53] It commands us to love the men and women who, *at this moment*, are passing their lives on earth. Every instant of time is then renewed by that love, which does not signify a feeling or a passion for the other but a worry about his life and a concern to struggle against what threatens it. That uneasiness and concern are painful because they settle into oneself in spite of oneself, and, says Levinas, they even resemble a persecution.

Might individuals have the choice merely between two forms of persecution, that of tyranny and that of weakness? Or, in biblical terms, between that of Pharaoh and that of the stranger? For Levinas as for Kant, the need to do battle against the former is not simply deduced from the fact that it destroys the dignity of the humanity in man and makes the practical concern to universalize the maxims of his actions impossible for him. To struggle against the tyrant or to flee far from Egypt—even into oneself— is necessary if the irreplaceable singularity of the moral subject is to emerge. Tyranny, public or private, prevents the emergence of faces and names; it relies on confusion. The tyrant's persecution corresponds to the desire to keep everyone—a people or one's own kin—in the pain, sometimes unknown to oneself, of the indistinction between self and other. Under the tyrant's "law," no one exists face to face with the other, no one responds for the other. Every person's right to live is mortgaged by the tyrant, he determines it in accord with his own self-interest.

But must the outcome of the battle against the tyrant's persecution entail persecution by weakness? Although the sense of that form of persecution is clearly different, since it does not rest on any effective power to do harm, in spite of everything it does wound. Through it, the moral subject is prevented from resting, it discovers that it is accountable for the fate of the world. That persecution entails a responsibility beyond choice, a responsibility in the form of election that awakens the human in man—or in the moral subject—beyond identity, beyond essence. But that awakening, since it does not come spontaneously from the subject or from its decision to universalize the maxims of its actions, cannot fail to cause pain since that awakening reverses the spontaneous tendency to grant oneself priority and leaves no time for a self-reflection that would consider, in all serenity, the principle of the universality of one's maxims.

Is that reevaluation of heteronomy sufficient? Is there not also a "Kantian moment" in Levinas? In fact, the moral subject cannot respond solely to the individual face whose weakness or strangeness solicits it at this precise moment, and abandon the other faces to their fate, for the subject would thereby run the risk of being immoral, of confusing weakness and tyranny. Responsibility does not rest on a heart-felt and partial impulse or on intimidation in the face of distress; it remains inseparable from justice toward a third party. The moral subject must therefore know how to evaluate the situation between the other and the third party, or risk committing a travesty. The other is never the only one to suffer even if he believes he is, and nearby "all those other than the other obsess me, and already the obsession cries for justice, calls for moderation and knowledge, and is the conscience."[54] Yet, precisely, how are we to know—without self-reflection and without appealing to abstract principles for comparing the other and the third party—that the attention solicited by that individual face does not entail an injustice to another person, sometimes imprisoned within a mute and formidable distress? When the moral subject reflects upon the consequences, for the life of a third party, of the subject's response to an individual face, it is eventually led toward restraint or a moderation in the attention or goodness shown toward the other. That does not mean harshness or indifference but rather concern for justice; the subject thus takes universality into account.

Nevertheless, at this point, Levinas does not argue for a return to the cause of autonomy. In fact, unlike Kant, this moment, which solicits the conscience and self-reflection—the subject must compare incomparable entities, the other and the third party, and must possess the concepts necessary to decide a conflict without letting itself be moved by the weakness of one at the expense of the weakness of the other—is not the source of morality, which is still the appeal of weakness, but rather its maturity or its wisdom. That maturity or wisdom is always subordinated to the heteronomy of the appeal and cannot emancipate itself from it without veering toward the tyranny of the impersonal. At every instant, then, even when the subject compares the other and the third party or evaluates the evidence of a conflict on the basis of certain principles, the living source of ethics is still singularity. That memory must not be set aside—in the name of autonomy and its principles—otherwise, it may never be found again. Levinas insists that the unique and irreplaceable singularity of people has no opportunity to be taken into account—in ethics or in politics—if the subject does not begin with it and return to it. That does not mean that the subject falls short of the universality of the human but rather that the subject moves closer to it every day, out of concern for singularities. Levinas's reflection, unlike Kant's, is moored not in the concern to preserve an abstract and formal universality—the idea of humanity linked to moral autonomy—but rather in the concern to watch over concrete singularities. Levinas shows how, thanks to the heteronomy characteristic of the encounter with the foreign and vulnerable face, another idea of universality is brought to mind. That universality does not depend on principles professed in the name of the human—autonomous in relation to any singular allegiance—but rather on the response given here and now, before it is too late, to the uniqueness of faces. In fact, Levinas says, one must not turn one's back on singularity on the pretext of saving universality—otherwise, one will find nothing but the idea of it—but must respond to the singularity of the other in order to perceive the sense of universality implied by that response.

The significance of the references in Levinas's texts to the singularity of the Hebrew text and to the experience of Jewish persecution in history thus becomes clearer. That methodological approach, adapted to his reevaluation of heteronomy as the source of morality, does not entail negating the universality of philosophical concepts but is rather concerned with putting them to the test of a singular voice, a voice "whose dignity and sense have never been recorded by metaphysics and before which the philosophers veil their faces."[55] Levinas considers that voice, not to delight in its irreducibility, but to understand how it disorients and reorients philosophy. That voice, he claims, in questioning the primacy of the subject's autonomy and self-importance, leads us toward a philosophy of the human indissociable from the subject's election.

Conversely, just as Kant defends the absolute rights of autonomy and sees heteronomy as an inevitable corruption of the moral principle, he also expels from his notion of philosophy the intrusion of texts stemming from a particular tradition. Pure reason cannot act on the authority of texts alien to the universal concepts produced by the understanding—texts it would interpret hermeneutically—and thereby exceed its own limits. For its part, practical reason cannot consent to serve the singularity of persons without immediately introducing a coefficient of heteronomy that would destroy its principle and its universality.

Does not one of the major themes of that conflict between autonomy and heteronomy have to do with the status of sensibility relative to reason, for Kant and for Levinas?

f i v e   **Sensibility and Reason**

The Kantian subject, in wresting itself from the grip of natural facts and from its submission to cultural institutions, in emancipating itself from all Revelation, and in rejecting the authority, or even the exegesis, of books supposed to transmit Revelation, discovers the universality of the law as "a fact of reason." The subject's capacity to disregard sensible, cultural, and social data and to think and judge for itself, places it face to face with autonomy as the criterion par excellence of a human being's humanity. In retreating from the anteriority of modes of thinking and living, in refusing to define the human being in terms of its membership within a particular group, and within the customs and books of that group, Kant is able to put forward an idea of human universality irreducible to any traditional, concrete, and singular model of intellectual or practical behavior. "The idea of universal humanity assumes significance by virtue of a denaturalization of customs,"[1] a demonstration of their contingency, their conventional and particular character, which discredits them relative to reason. The universal principles that supposedly govern ethics cannot accommodate themselves to a contingent and singular source. As a result, moral obligation, supposedly valid for any person anywhere and at any time, imposes itself in its pure form only on the person who disregards the imperatives relating to a precise time and place, such as the appeal of a particular person on the day he is in distress. If one gave in to the urgency of that appeal, without self-reflection and without considering the principles that govern moral autonomy, one would reinforce pathology's hold over reason. The unfortunate person would promptly be aided, no doubt, and extricated from his difficulty, but there would be nothing moral in that act. The deed would thus fall short of the idea of humanity as the sole guarantor of the morality of maxims and acts.

Kant's confidence in reason cannot be breached by the limits of one's power to know, limits attributable to the absence of intellectual intuition. On the practical level, Kant shows how reason accounts for the "properly human" in a human being. That is the meaning of the idea of moral autonomy, an idea saved from any contamination by sensible heteronomy only by virtue of its formal universality. The recognition of the human in every subject—inasmuch as, by virtue of its reason, the subject is a possible author of moral law—and the feeling of respect toward the subject thus depend solely on that formal criterion. The humanity the moral subject intends to respect in itself and in the other is an idea that resists all concretization; that humanity is discovered when the subject turns its present attention away from particular human beings. The sensible eyes and ears of the Kantian subject are apparently not invited to participate in his entry into morality. Human finitude can be deduced from two factors. The first is that a human being is incapable of coinciding with the idea of humanity within himself because of the attraction that the pathological exerts over his will, despite his moral autonomy. The second—and this too is linked to the influence of the pathological—has to do with the concrete indeterminability of the idea of humanity.

In his quest for the human, Levinas does not seek to emancipate himself from any particular culture, but that does not mean that he submits to any one culture as to an intimidating authority. It is as a philosopher concerned with universality that he agrees to learn from a Book that, he says, bears witness to a particular tradition. He rejects the idea that fidelity to reason implies contempt for the heteronomous sources of thought. As a result, he does not see the subject as the power to disregard all particular determinations—as a pure autonomy—but as an unimpeachable relation with an alterity, the alterity of God, of men, and also of texts. The moral subject bears the trace of having been chosen by the alterity of a source— and not by a principle—that, from time immemorial, has exceeded the subject and dwelt within it. Conceived in that way, the subject does not preexist "that exteriority of the alliance";[2] it exists only through that exteriority and in it. The subject therefore cannot exempt itself from that exteriority in order to evaluate it critically and, if necessary, return to it in full autonomy. Levinas claims that when man seeks to grasp himself as a subject outside that exteriority, and wishes to place himself at the foundation of his own acts and thoughts, at that point precisely, he loses himself as a subject. The subject's interiority entails an exposure to the infinite prior to any conscious decision, "a demand on the Same made by the other within myself,"[3] or an insurmountable change that, in preventing autonomy and repose in an identity, makes the uniqueness of the subject—a uniqueness that cannot be refused—emerge. The simple words "here I am," spoken to a particular neighbor here and now, bear witness to that uniqueness, an act that does not depend on a voluntary decision.

As a result, the recognition of the human in every person is no longer beholden, as it was in Kant, to an idea of reason but rather to that "permanent *saying* of the Bible" relating to the obligation toward the stranger. For Levinas, the idea of humanity cannot be deduced from the formal effort of reason preoccupied with setting aside the heteronomy of the sensible world and the weight of particular traditions so as to prevent human universality from being compromised by their concreteness. On the contrary, as the biblical tradition had already said, it is the stranger who makes it possible to uncover the idea of humanity, in the mode of an obligation that is unimpeachable because not beholden to an autonomous choice. Levinas does not deduce from that fact that people are moral subjects, or even that they struggle to be so; but, despite his horror at the evil ceaselessly inflicted by people on other people, here and now, he concludes that the human is defined by the recognition of a moral vocation. Every man, he says, has the notion of that vocation even if he does not respond to it, even if he prefers the desolate paths of nihilism.

In view of that analysis, what is the status of sensibility for Kant and for Levinas? Is there not a difference between them regarding their assessment of classic oppositions—abstract/concrete, universal/particular, active/passive—and is not the status of reason in moral life also at stake?

Self-Love

Kant claims that "so distinctly and sharply drawn are the boundaries of morality and self-love that even the most common eye cannot fail to distinguish whether something belongs to one or the other." He adds: "The maxim of self-love (prudence) merely *advises;* the law of morality *commands.*"[4] The maxim of self-love has a precise aim: to maintain or increase the feeling of the pleasure of being. Yet I cannot desire, without contradiction, for it to become a universal law of nature—which is precisely what is at stake for moral law. Pleasure remains uncertain, dependent on circumstances, particular and ephemeral by definition. Therefore, it cannot serve as a universal criterion for morality. Hence the pleasure or satisfaction sometimes experienced after some deed that is termed "good" does not in any way constitute a criterion regarding the morality of that deed; in any case, such feelings commit you to nothing, determine no universal design. Internal experience and empirical and contingent feelings cannot influence the decisions of practical reason: "*to philosophize by feeling*" and to believe that you are making everyone a better person by appealing to his or her so-called finer feelings, leads people to their doom[5] because no morality can stand on such a fragile base. Kant challenges the existence of a "moral sense" that would supposedly determine moral law independent of the reason. Despite its subtlety, that "pretense," which holds that the "consciousness of virtue is immediately connected with satisfaction and pleasure, and consciousness of vice with mental unease and pain" is illusory.[6] The wicked person is often at peace with himself while the virtuous person worries that he has fallen short of his duty.

Nevertheless, Kant does not have absolute contempt for self-contentment. In fact, when that feeling, rather than constituting the foundation of moral obligation, is instead deduced from it, it becomes morally acceptable. Hence it sometimes happens, after a certain time, that observing moral law produces "a subjective feeling of satisfaction," which, says Kant, is legitimate and desirable. "To establish and to cultivate this feeling, which alone deserves to be called moral feeling strictly speaking, itself belongs to duty."[7] The concept of duty cannot be deduced from it; on the contrary, duty produces it. In that sense—and in that sense only—self-contentment has a moral value. It is the result of conforming one's acts to moral law: the subject feels satisfaction at having obeyed the law without giving in to the temptation of its own propensities.

But what, exactly, is the meaning of that satisfaction? Kant insists on the idea that the observation of moral law does harm to sensibility and any form of egoism *(Selbstsucht)*. Whether it manifests itself as excessive love of self *(Selbstliebe)*—as a *benevolence* toward the self indifferent to any other consideration—or as an arrogant self-*satisfaction*, egoism is always the enemy of morality. The term *self-love* characterizes the former expression of it, that of *self-conceit* the latter. Yet, Kant explains, if the moral law "strikes down self-conceit altogether" and leaves no room for pride, it "merely *infringes upon* self-love" without the aim of annihilating it, since it authorizes a *"reasonable self-love."*[8] Such a love is expressed in self-contentment, whose moral legitimacy is recognized by Kant.

Self-love, as long as it disregards any consideration other than itself, as long as pride casts a spell over it, feels humiliated by moral law. That law claims to dictate self-love's duty without paying it any heed and to impose strict limits on it. In Kant's philosophy, in fact, only reason knows how to set limits. According to him, that is its essential task in the theoretical and in the practical realm, to keep human beings from wandering out into boundlessness. An absence of limits is characteristic of madness, the madness of occultism, for example—denounced in "Dreams of a Spirit-Seer" as "the realm of shadows" and "the paradise of fantastical visionaries"[9]—but also the madness of reason's potential to wander into metaphysical speculations on God, the soul, and the cosmos, even though, in the absence of intellectual intuition, it does not have the means to make them objects of knowledge. Kant's critical point of view does not accommodate itself to enthusiasm of any kind; it tirelessly does battle against delirium and denounces *Schwärmerei* as a dangerous illusion, even and especially if it makes a strong impression on weak minds. Reason must be critical, which means that it must set limits on the claim to knowledge and denounce dogmatism as that which exceeds those limits and causes delusions. Yet, in ethics as well, enthusiasm, affects, and sensibility ensnare human beings, and reason must therefore—here again—check their momentum and submit them to its law. No spontaneous love—whether self-love or love of the other—has a moral value in itself, since its maxim remains un-amenable to universality. Nevertheless, Kant says, once love is humiliated and kept at a respectful distance by the law, it is not fated to disappear ab-solutely but rather to become reasonable. The moral law challenges all ex-pressions of pathological love on the grounds of their amorality but allows for a practical love.

What does that love mean when it is addressed to oneself? It seems par-adoxical at first since the moral law, in its impersonality, produces fear and respect in the human being but, precisely, never elicits love. "One can transgress the moral law, but one can never revolt against it," Kant re-marks. Only love can elicit love and revolt.[10] How, then, could the law on its own bring a *reasonable* or practical love into being? That love, indisso-ciable from respect—the only feeling both necessary and known a priori to the subject—is the result of observing one's own submission to the moral law in oneself. To be sure, at first respect deals a decisive blow to self-love, but it is precisely by virtue of the pain thus produced that it liberates one from a pathological attachment to oneself and makes one capable of prac-tical love. That love stems, therefore, from the positive outcome of the conflict between two sorts of principles: the right to satisfy one's own in-clinations and the duty to submit them to evaluation by a universal law. It thus entails for every person the recognition of his capacity to choose the law against his own impulses. Its target is not the unique and irreplaceable aspect of the person but rather what that human being shares with the uni-versality of men: his autonomy. Morally, the subject is entitled to experi-ence a certain satisfaction when, to the detriment of its immediate im-pulses and its emotional and sensible singularity, it has obeyed the voice of duty.

That voice constitutes an infallible guide valid for all human beings; it is that voice that authorizes a reasonable self-love, a love directed at the humanity in oneself and not at the ephemeral and fragile person of every individual. Rousseau describes that voice as a "divine instinct" that sup-posedly characterizes the excellence of human "nature,"[11] and he makes it an immediate given of empirical consciousness. But Kant associates that voice with reason and reason alone and therefore cannot promote any em-pirical self-love. On the contrary, one must disregard empirical self-love to become capable of hearing the voice of moral law.

How is that practical self-love expressed? Although it procures a certain satisfaction in carrying out the law, it manifests itself above all in its duties toward oneself or, more exactly, toward the humanity in oneself, since it is a duty to treat that humanity in one's own person as an end in itself. As a matter of fact, that is the only duty dictated to the self by practical love. That law, once delivered from its pathology—that is, from the sensible attachment to the irreplaceable and precarious uniqueness of persons, to the joy taken in their existence and the affliction caused by their abandonment, since none of that has any moral value—commands a practical concern for oneself that is expressed through duties. Hence the moral subject must not let itself be tempted by suicide or by false promises, when it feels overwhelmed by disgust or weakness. It must take care not to waste its talents,[12] even when it is seduced by laziness. It must not ask, in reference to every act, whether that act will bring it pleasure; it must consider the compatibility of the act with respect for the humanity in its own person. In addition, it seems valid to infer that the subject is entitled to require others to respect it in the same way, since reasonable self-love includes that reciprocity. The subject therefore should not accept being humiliated, deceived, or betrayed without demanding reparation for the humanity in itself that was thus offended and demeaned. In fact, if, to spare itself a conflict with its neighbor, the subject were to consent to being treated by him simply as a means—and not as an end—that would no doubt attest to the subject's fear of conflict but in no way to its morality. On the contrary, practical self-love demands that the subject know how to confront other people's violence against it and must refuse to be tolerant (due to moral weakness) of the contempt they have for the subject's humanity.

Therefore, practical self-love—like the love for others—is not the result of spontaneity of any kind. To achieve it, everyone must struggle against the influence of his sensible motives over his maxims and establish the primacy of the law, even while knowing that that struggle lasts an entire lifetime. In fact, no inclination is immediately moral; it would therefore be moral enthusiasm to claim "an inclination to duty" on the subject's part.[13] But the faculty of desire can submit itself to the legislation of reason and can find its a priori principles in that legislation. In that case, this faculty is called the will.[14] Practical self-love depends on the possibility of educating and submitting the faculty of desire to the principles of reason.

It is precisely respect for the majesty of the moral law in oneself that allows that submission. Conversely, a desire that is not submissive to the law—whatever its object and even if it gives rise to noble actions—has no moral value.

Levinas is not unaware of that distinction between pathological love and practical love, and he intentionally contrasts erotic love and "love without concupiscence." Nevertheless, especially in the latter case, the word "love" always has to do with the other and is not directed toward oneself. Does a reasonable self-love have no significance in his philosophy, then, in contrast to Kant's?

It is, in the first place, for a reason unrelated to Kantianism that Levinas calls erotic love "pathetic." That love leads you to discover a proximity to the other wherein the distance that separates you from him "is wholly maintained";[15] it makes you enter into a relation "with that which always slips away."[16] But Levinas does not regret that pathos, since, far from representing a failure in the relation between two people, it awakens you to the inaccessible character of the other. The dream of abolishing the pathetic from love, in a fusion or a communion, is not, according to him, a dream of love but of power, since it points to a dread of the alterity of the other and to the desire to efface it. The phenomenology of sensual pleasure proposed in *Totality and Infinity* confirms that view of erotic love but also announces its moral insignificance—or, at least, its ambiguity—because no responsibility can rest on the subject's erotic life without becoming precarious. The confusion between erotic desire and metaphysical desire, concupiscence and transcendence, is, in fact, the quintessence of ambiguity. Moreover, that love is lacking in disinterestedness: "To love is to love the love the Beloved bears for me, to love is also to love *oneself* in love."[17] And that self-reflection and self-satisfaction—the very happiness of feeling *oneself* loved—have no moral import.

Like Kant, Levinas then contrasts that pathetic love to another sort of love, a practical love, a love irreducible to a feeling of benevolence or pity and which thwarts even the will and natural propensities. He describes it as a "summons to a nonerotic proximity, to a desire for the undesirable, a desire for the stranger in one's neighbor—separate from concupiscence which, for its part, continues to be seductive through its resemblance to the Good."[18] Nevertheless, unlike Kant, Levinas does not think that love entails the submission of sensibility to reason. Practical love—love without concupiscence, therefore—still stems from sensibility, it comes into being as a result of the subject's vulnerability to the weakness of the other and of the stranger, the person who, in any case, elicits no impulse of love but rather a profound unease. Without requiring the slightest self-reflection, moral life begins the instant that weakness strips sensibility bare—"right to the skin, right to the nerves."[19] So begins a paradoxical love for the other, a love that, despite its obligation or because of it, corresponds to no spontaneous inclination or lust on the subject's part. It even reverses their direction, it imposes itself like the persecution of "a thorn pricking the flesh,"[20] and it strips the subject of its enjoyment of life, the certainty of its legitimate right to being and of its haughtiness. The encounter with the other affects the subject's sensibility and its flesh, it strips them bare and exposes them, it wounds them and fates them to be compassionate and to give the "gift that exacts a cost."[21]

Thus sensibility does not stand opposed to morality. On the contrary, sensibility is affected by alterity—altered without intentionality, passive therefore—and this constitutes "the ultimate secret of the subject's incarnation."[22] Nevertheless, the suffering of sensibility does not correspond to any deliberate search but occurs "in spite of oneself." Levinas does not favor either self-destruction or self-hatred, he does not ask that anyone mistreat *himself*—or let *himself* be mistreated—on the pretext that this brings one closer to those who suffer. Such a masochism presupposes the existence of a "self" that would exist prior to moral life—even in the mode of suffering—which is precisely what Levinas calls into question. And he does not perpetuate the illusion that asceticism is necessarily proof of the primacy of the concern for the other over concern for oneself. He is well aware that asceticism, even when it ravages one's own flesh, is liable to makes its peace with the gravest of the world's misfortunes. He simply says that, far from constituting an imprisonment or a shackling of one self to another, the vulnerable and mortal body, the flesh and sensibility, teach one the rightness of the ethical summons. It is by virtue of them that a person, without seeking the slightest humiliation, hence passively, is exposed or handed over, defenseless, to the other. That vulnerability exists prior to all love and all hatred, and it determines the moral response to the other. "Beginning with sensibility, the subject is *for the other*."[23] In a preoriginal manner, the subject is destined to respond for the other, without having wanted or chosen to do so.

How, then, could Levinas find a place for the Kantian idea of a reasonable self-love and for the claim that there are duties one owes oneself? Such a love makes no sense from his point of view since, according to him, the subject does not exist prior to its exposure to the other, does not exist safe within itself, but is the result of a movement toward the other. Yet that movement does not come about as the result of the ecstasy of an intentionality but from the subject's incapacity to lock itself in from the inside. The subject does not find "itself" by turning back on itself but, on the contrary, by letting go, by responding to the appeal of the other without having made the decision in full knowledge of the facts, by leaving its home. That response—or that practical love—and that leave-taking, never carried out once and for all, constitute the subject's election. They reveal the subject's uniqueness to itself.

Some will object that Levinas, in not requiring reciprocity in moral life as Kant does and in neglecting the idea of one's duties toward oneself, submits the subject to a great many risks. Do his rehabilitation of sensibility, his justification of passivity—indispensable for the emergence of a subject that does not return to itself—and his notion of its uniqueness, irreducible to an identity, suffice for morality?

At first glance, the moral subject seems pledged to the other in an exorbitant and dangerous manner, since the subject does not have the right to require the slightest compensation from the other. Whereas the face of the other—transcendent and poor at the same time—prohibits murder, calls for responsibility, and entails an obligation, Levinas says nothing about the face of the moral subject. It is clear, however, that that face also often risks affront, humiliation, and even death. No one is safe from violence, and even kindness can elicit hatred. Levinas is obviously aware of this, and, though he sometimes speaks of sacrifice, he does not defend martyrdom. Yet he does not believe in checking violence and hatred by imposing the limits of a reasonable self-love and requiring symmetry but rather by distinguishing between the tyranny of the other and his weakness and also by taking the third party into account.

How are we to understand that asymmetry? It means, first, that the subject cannot emancipate itself from moral obligation on the pretext that the other remains indifferent to the subject's fate. That asymmetry thus delivers the subject from the violence of mimicry and from a relation in which, on the pretext of an equality between the self and the other, "no one owes anything to anyone, no one can expect anything of anyone, except as the result of a contract."[24] Moral obligation does not depend on a contract whose clauses, freely determined and clearly stipulated, would keep everyone at a respectful distance. It does not rely on the memory of a commitment but on an unimpeachable appeal—or election—by the face, which, in its fragility, revives the Good's hold on the psyche. The subject, confronted with the face, in spite of itself awakes prisoner to an unconditional promise of responsibility toward the other, even if that other, for his part, perseveres in his being, completely deaf and indifferent to the subject. To expect him to treat me not only as a means but as an end before I ratify my election—to expect him to uncover himself "for me" in turn, in his confrontation with my face or, in Kantian language, to respect the humanity in me—entails a denial of my election.

Is not that formidable asymmetry in need of a lesson in wisdom? Or, quite simply, a lesson in "good sense"? Levinas says yes, since he corrects the asymmetry in two respects: first, responsibility for the other, even one who is violent and tyrannical, does not entail submission to his violence and tyranny; and second, that responsibility must always take into account the plurality of persons.

Submission to the tyrannical or violent other's hold over oneself, far from resembling the disinterested moral orientation described by Levinas, actually distorts the sense of that orientation. In that case, submission to the other rests on a concern for oneself, it points to no real concern for the other. What does it entail, in fact, if not fear or even terror—conscious or unconscious—about what will happen *to me* if I do not give in to the other? That is the exact opposite of the moral attitude described by Levinas, since, in such a case, submission to the other rests on the subject's uneasiness *about itself*. Its torment remains egoistic. Hence the subject has not left Egypt, and Egypt continues to insinuate itself into the secret recesses of the subject's psyche and to delay the moment when the subject acquires its freedom.

The Bible says: "And they shall know that I am the Lord their God, that brought them forth out of the land of Egypt, that I may dwell among them" (Exodus 29:46). Rashi comments on this verse: God brought them out of Egypt on the condition that he might dwell among them. But does not the distinction between submitting to tyranny and responding to weakness invite another reading? As long as the responsibility for the other is indistinguishable from obedience to the other's violence, however mild and friendly, the God who delivers the subject out of Egypt cannot come to mind. That God remains confused with a system of reward and punishment since the prisoner of Egypt—even if the prisoner does not know he is one—cannot think in any other way. His mind is clouded by the other's influence over *his* fate, and he often prefers to give in to the other and grant him priority; but that priority, and the peace it sometimes brings, have no moral value, they simply ratify the fear of the other. The tyrannical hold of the other over the self, a hold that often resurfaces again and again, must therefore be combated and its confusion with responsibility forcefully rejected. That battle and that rejection determine access to moral life, that is, precisely, to a life that ceases to be haunted by the concern for the self and its survival when confronted with the other.[25]

When ethics is at issue, the act of taking one's distance from the two figures of self-love evoked here—erotic love and the joy of feeling *oneself* loved, and submission to violence out of fear *for oneself*—governs Levinas's second correction to the radicality of asymmetry, namely, the act of taking the third party into account. "Earthly ethics invites us to the difficult detour leading to the third party who has remained outside love." Love is always tempted by the self-sufficiency of the twosome, the "I" satisfied with the "thou," as if the presence of the other exhausted the content of society.[26] The person obsessed with fear of the tyrant also does not perceive third parties, since he is too busy satisfying his master, persuaded as he is that such is the condition for his own perseverance in being. These third parties pass by as if they were nonexistent: he does not see them.

Therefore, the reflection implied by the presence of the third party—what is the other for the third party? Is the other persecuting him?—is an invitation to wisdom.[27] It presupposes, first, a liberation from self-love or concern for self. As long as self-love prevails, Levinas says, the third party quite simply does not exist. That also means that only the subject's awakening to practical love for the singularity of the other—or to responsibility—by means of the wound the other makes, and the subject's exceptional uniqueness, which that wound exposes, govern access to the third party as well. With the third party, then, rational reflection begins to consider the attitude to take toward both the other and the third party, but that reflection by itself does not allow the subject to perceive the singularity of the third party, a singularity that must therefore remain secondary. Rationality—a reflection on moral principles, for example—follows the ethical awakening: it does not produce it.

It is therefore on the basis of a different assessment of self-love that Levinas's view of sensibility can be distinguished from Kant's. In a sense, this is paradoxical: Kant grants a place for a reasonable self-love but gives no positive status to sensibility in ethics; Levinas rejects the idea of such a love—the ethical subject is the result of practical love for the other and does not exist prior to it—but he thinks that sensibility, in its vulnerability, is an unavoidable fact of ethics.

Do the concepts of the sublime for Kant and of disinterestedness for Levinas make it possible to better explain that difference?

The Sublime and Disinterestedness

The pure moral law, Kant says, "lets us discover the sublimity of our own supersensible existence." But since, at present, the human being continues to feel his dependence on sensible existence, the sublimity of that "higher vocation"[28] cannot be experienced directly. Nevertheless, it is anticipated in the feeling of respect, whose singularity—it is the only feeling produced by reason—does not simply attest to the effect of moral law on sensibility but also lifts the soul toward what lies beyond the sensible condition, toward the infinite. Respect, negatively defined in the *Critique of Judgment* as "the feeling of our incapacity to attain an idea *which is a law for us,*"[29] gives us a positive glimpse of the sublimity of our destiny. We have a notion of that destiny thanks to reason, but not an intuition of it, since its final goal exceeds our capacity to know.

The feeling of the sublime occurs in the presence of the boundless. In fact, no sensible, precise, and limited form "can contain the sublime properly so-called. This concerns only ideas of the reason."[30] And no sensible, adequate presentation of these ideas can be imagined by human beings. Nevertheless, when one experiences the sublime—when one awakens to the awareness of being superior to the nature in oneself—one gets a sense of what exceeds all possible knowledge. That experience, or that ordeal, which Kant assures us happens solely in the subject's mind, produces a disinterested satisfaction in the subject. For an instant at least, the subject transcends any pathological attachment to its sensible existence and any interestedness in being. It lets the free play of its imagination conform to the ideas of reason, which produces a disposition of the mind corresponding to the influence that practical ideas have over feeling.

Although Kant describes sublimity as a disposition of the mind—and not as an objective fact—he also reflects on the occasions that elicit it and describes man's encounter with "magnitude" or "the incommensurable" in all its forms as the most favorable circumstance for awakening that disposition. Everything that suggests the idea of what surpasses the subject's sensible interestedness in being—including the formidable forces of nature—produces the sublime in the subject. In fact, when confronted with the sometimes devastating force of nature—and provided that, in spite of everything, one is safe, that is, not fated to pass away immediately—one discovers in oneself a power to resist that gives one the courage to measure oneself against what, apparently, surpasses one. One is gripped by fear when confronted with danger, which makes one feel one's smallness, even one's dereliction, but that fear is soon transformed into a challenge. It is as if, in the face of the peril that might well destroy one's sensible body, one found within oneself an indestructible moral force against which nothing could prevail. That force would allow one to measure oneself against the apparent omnipotence of nature.

Hence, despite the ravages it produces, the irresistible and destructive violence of nature paradoxically elicits a feeling of independence in relation to that violence. In such a circumstance, one knows, without being able to prove it with a conceptual argument, that the humanity in one's own person will remain unvanquished, even if one's sensible individuality must truly succumb. The act of imagining the peril that hangs over life—and not that peril itself—seems propitious for fostering the disposition of the sublime mind. On that point, Kant does not hesitate to praise war "carried on with order and with a sacred respect for the rights of citizens," since, he says, war, by means of the incessant confrontation with death, produces the feeling of the sublime destiny of the person more than does a long peace, which, ordinarily, "debases the disposition of the people."[31] But, whether the danger comes from nature or from war, one must always be able to rise above fear if the sublime is to acquire meaning. The terrified person does not experience anything but his terror and remains indifferent to the question of his fate; he seeks only to save his sensible existence, even at the price of morality. That is why, Kant explains, a religion elicits the sublime only when it ceases to foster fear or servility and allows the faithful freely to recognize the conformity of their convictions to divine will.

The sublime leads the subject to experience a disposition of the mind "which is akin to the moral."[32] Just as moral law does violence to sensibility to better pave the way for respect for the humanity in one's own person and in that of the other, the sublime—through the play of the imagination—makes the human being feel the finitude of his sensible destiny to better awaken him to the magnitude of his supersensible destiny. Hence, on the aesthetic plane as well, the force of moral law manifests itself in the "sacrifice" of sensible finitude, a sacrifice indispensable to the revelation of the "unfathomable depth" of the "supersensible faculty, with consequences extending beyond our ken."[33] The effacement of the bounds of sensibility in the sublime turns out to be eminently positive: it allows the imagination to feel boundless, and "that very abstraction is a presentation of the Infinite, which can be nothing but a mere negative presentation, but which yet expands the soul." That is why Kant sees the commandment "Thou shalt not make unto thee any graven image, or any likeness of any thing that is in heaven above, or that is in the earth beneath, or that is in the water under the earth" (Exodus 20:4) as the most sublime passage in the Bible. That prohibition on representation, according to him, is quintessentially valid for "the representation of moral law and the disposition to morality in us."[34] It is precisely when morality finds itself stripped of all sensible representation—when the senses no longer perceive anything, when concepts remain devoid of intuition—that the moral idea imposes itself in all its excellence. Like the God of the Bible, *"the unfathomable character of the idea of freedom* quite cuts it off from any positive presentation."[35] Yet, that ontological impossibility, far from being regrettable, rather makes it possible to observe the force of moral law, the determination of which imposes itself on its own, without the slightest help from any sensible presentation and apart from any theoretical argument that would transform it into an object of speculative knowledge.

In nature, the sublime is linked to magnitude. Kant thus sees "the starry heaven" as its emblem par excellence. "Two things fill the mind with ever new and increasing admiration and reverence, the more often and more steadily one reflects on them: *the starry heaven above me and the moral law within me.*"[36] But what is the significance of that connection between the starry heaven and moral law?

The starry heaven elicits a sublime disposition of mind without, however, representing a threat to a man's life. To be sure, it reveals to him his own smallness when compared to its immensity but it does so in an admirable way, without disturbing him or exposing him to fear for his mortal fate. On the contrary, it reminds him of the significance of what, within him, exceeds that fate: moral law. That heaven, which seems indifferent to the individual's sensible fate—what is he in the face of its infinity? What does his present suffering matter to it?—nevertheless calms man. According to Kant, in contemplating it, everyone learns to liberate himself from concern for his individuality and his interest in persevering in his sensible being. That contemplative pedagogy reminds an individual of the only concern that counts: respect for the humanity in one's moral person and in that of the other. Nevertheless, that pedagogy is of a particular kind: its aim is to make one capable of a perception without imaginative or cognitive a prioris, since Kant asserts that, "to grasp the sublimity of the starry heaven," one must "contemplate it 'as one sees it,' and not as one imagines it or knows it to be."[37] The desire to escape the vertigo of one's own smallness when compared to the heaven, and to struggle against that shock by adopting an active attitude by means of the image or concept one forms of it, undermines at its very root the experience of the sublime, since its goal is to ignore the effect of the incommensurable on oneself. Therefore, one ought to learn to detach oneself from the influence of the image and the concept and to stand at the ready before the starry heaven but without cognitive activity. It is then that the human being discovers, as he does in ethics, the possibility of a sense beyond his capacity to know. The radical finitude of the theoretical access to the being of phenomena—produced by the absence of intellectual intuition—opens onto a sense that exceeds knowledge at the moment the reasonable subject *listens to* the voice of the moral law within him and *contemplates* the heaven "as he sees it." And it is precisely because, in both cases, the subject does not seek to acquire an imaginary or conceptual mastery of what it listens to or contemplates that it opens itself to a relation with a sense resistant to any gnosis. That is also why the contemplation of the sublimity characteristic of the starry heaven awakens one to an awareness of the sublimity of one's moral destiny, as if an invisible thread connected one to the other. The secret of that thread is found in man, since sublimity always entails a state of mind. It is as if the infinity of the starry heaven awakened him, beyond the adventure of being, to the idea of the moral obligation that has a hold over him without its requiring theoretical justifications.

Levinas subscribes to the need for eyes and ears relieved of all "transcendental imperialism" in order to give sense to ethics. But, in his philosophy, the eyes are solicited by a task more urgent than the contemplation of the starry heaven: they are appealed to by the face of one's neighbor and fated to respond to it. Therefore, Levinas does not give a privileged role to contemplation of the heaven; according to him, it does not have the significance of awakening man to an awareness of his supersensible destiny that Kant finds in it. It remains subordinated to the disinterested gaze cast on the face of the other, or, more exactly, solicited by it, imperatively, without the subject being able to escape or distract itself by trying to look at something else, at the starry heaven, for example. In Levinas's philosophy, the feeling of finding oneself before a magnitude irreducible to any concept or any image does not come from the contemplation of the heaven but from the loftiness of the face. "A presence dominating the one who welcomes him, coming from the lofty heights, unexpected and, as a result, teaching its very newness."[38] The face comes from elsewhere, from another shore, it calls upon the subject and the subject cannot erase the distance that separates them. It is the face that teaches, par excellence, transcendence, or "the very loftiness that is equal to its exteriority, namely, ethics." The prohibition on representation, which Kant describes as sublime, nevertheless remains in force, since Levinas says: "The other is not the incarnation of God, but precisely, by virtue of his face where he is disincarnated, the manifestation of the lofty heights where God reveals himself." God therefore remains invisible and unimaginable at the very moment that the idea of him comes to the mind of man, who knows he is solicited by the other man's face. Hence, for Levinas, "ethics is spiritual optics" par excellence, more so than the contemplation of the heaven.[39] To look at a face is to experience that which calls one's being and one's concern for oneself into question since, "through that commerce with the infinity of exteriority or of loftiness, the naivete of the direct impulse, the naivete of being that exerts itself as a commanding force, is ashamed of its naivete."[40] Shame surges up because the face's loftiness, inseparable from its poverty and nakedness, shakes the subject to the point of making it doubt its legitimate right to be before the face, confronting its misery. The awakening to disinterestedness is thus the corollary of an experience of loftiness or of infinity, which is more disturbing—because it is the source of an infinite uneasiness about the other—than the contemplation of the sublime loftiness of the heaven. Whereas the heaven speaks to the subject's *solitary* gaze about *its* supersensible destiny, the face destines the subject for concern for the other, a concern that defers concern for itself and even for its final destiny.

Levinas writes: "In metaphysics, the role Kant attributed to sensible experience in the realm of understanding falls to interhuman relationships."[41] This means that the moral encounter takes the place of intellectual intuition, which, for both philosophers, is absent from metaphysics. It orients metaphysics, gives it its sense, yet without allowing it to extend to a knowledge of God or of the soul's destiny. No knowledge of the supersensible results from the moral response to the weakness and the loftiness of the other. No theoretical knowledge of the being of phenomena emerges, then, but rather an inquiry that reverses the traditional privilege of the question of essence.

The loftiness of the heaven does not make the appeal of the Good audible, and it does not awaken the psyche to ethical disinterestedness. In itself, loftiness is inadequate; it must also announce alterity, that is, a spiritual resistance to the powers of the one looking at it. And only the face—and not a phenomenon, even a sublime one—teaches a person the meaning of that spiritual resistance, irreducible to the "hardness of the rock that shatters the hand's effort" or to "the distance of a star in the immensity of space."[42] The alterity of the face is not that of things; in its misery and its loftiness, it solicits the subject and is of concern to it, even though the subject can have no hold over it. The subject does not dominate the face as it dominates the alterity of things, which its science and technology defy. The face pits the infinity of its transcendence against the one who looks at it. Levinas explains that this does not mean a *very great* resistance—in that case, it would be the source of a sublime feeling. Rather, it is the ethical resistance of the *absolutely Other*, the defenseless resistance of weakness and nakedness, of exposure to the wound and to murder, the resistance without violence of what revives in a person, the trace of an idea unamenable to the memory of having been acquired or learned, the resistance of the "harsh seriousness of goodness,"[43] or of disinterestedness. It is as if that resistance—and not the resistance of an inaccessible firmament—awakened the psyche to the preoriginary alliance with goodness, whose antecedence in relation to evil Levinas has asserted. Despite the egoistic sedimentations of interestedness in being, prior to everything and to the other, which almost always keep us in a state of forgetfulness regarding that alliance, the face, in its powerlessness and in the threats hanging over it, would have the power to awaken the trace of the alliance.

The sublime does not suffice. It produces the idea of the subject's supersensible destiny but not that of the urgency of the task to be accomplished in this world, or, to be very precise, "under the sun." That is, on an earth where, so often, "everything is absorbed, sucked down, and walled up into the same,"[44] because, as Ecclesiastes laments, the sense of newness, of transcendence, and of alterity is disappearing. Yet, Levinas says, to find an exception to that immutable order, we should not lift our eyes to the heaven but rather open them to the faces of those who, in an ineluctably provisional manner, share with us an existence "under the sun." The shattering of immanence, however, does not presuppose an experience of the extraordinary or of the numinous; here and now, there are signs of it thanks to the "spiritual optics" of ethics, when the face calls upon the same—in the deepest part of itself—sobering it up and opening it to goodness or disinterestedness. That requires that we make a place for a mode of thinking governed by the irreducible alterity of the other in his concrete singularity. And that obviously presupposes subordinating the idea of what the other has in common with oneself—the abstract universality of the idea of humanity, for example—to that alterity. Were that not so, the other would return to the order of the world, thus justifying the disabused words of Ecclesiastes.

If, therefore, we are to examine more thoroughly the sense of the difference between the optics of sublimity and the optics of disinterestedness, we must reflect upon the different status that Kant and Levinas give to reason in moral life. Is Kant's distrust of what resists or stands against universality and abstraction the best safeguard as far as that status is concerned? Does Levinas's insistence on singularity, concreteness, and passivity anticipate an indictment of reason?

Activity and Passivity: Reason

The autonomy of the will and reason's capacity to determine *itself*, to be practical reason, argue for the morality of emancipating oneself from the yoke of the other as from any other form of alterity, such as the fear of a punishment or the promise of a reward. They also point to Kant's rejection—like that of Enlightenment philosophy in general—of the idea of the tragic consequences of original sin. "Augustinianism, which emphasizes the radical corruption of human nature and its incapacity to return on its own to the divine is thus attacked at its vital core."[45] For Kant, reason forever remains "the *highest good* possible in the world"; it has the privilege of being "the final touchstone of the reliability of judgment."[46] No sin has corrupted it and the human being, thanks to reason and all on his own, can therefore advance on the path toward his intellectual and moral perfection, without having to wait for help from somewhere else. According to the *Aufklärung*, such waiting only fosters the feeling of human powerlessness and superstition and corrupts the exercise of reason. No baptism to liberate the self from the grip of sin is necessary, or rather, that baptism is the result of one's own determination.

Kant denounces the dangerous illusion of those who, on the pretext of moving beyond the limits of theoretical reason, allow themselves to indulge in daydreams, in enthusiasm, or even in the anarchical use of reason. He also refuses to introduce a dimension of enthusiasm or anarchy into ethics: practical reason always remains on its guard. It is well known as well that he denounces submission to alterity as passivity on the part of reason and as a formidable figure of heteronomy.[47] Nothing is to be received from the other; reason must not give in to any seduction coming from outside itself. Does that insistence allow for no exception?

Kant admits that the emotions, despite their alterity in relation to reason, can contribute to moral education, at least momentarily. To be sure, "a mind that is subject to affects and passions is always *ill*, because both of them exclude the sovereignty of reason."[48] But emotion, in spite of its unhealthy character and unlike passion, has positive traits.

"For pure practical reason," says Kant, "the passions are cancerous sores; they are, for the most part, incurable because the patient does not want to be cured and shuns the rule of principles, which is the only thing that could heal him." Yet, although passion is always "a disease" that condemns the subject to "slavery" and is therefore "morally reprehensible,"[49] emotion can play the role of a provisional springboard for ethical motives. *Apathy* is a fundamental moral rule because emotion risks blinding us— hence compassion for a friend can become an injustice toward another person—but Kant does not rule out the possibility that emotion "could handle the reins *provisionally* until reason has achieved the necessary strength."[50] Despite the absence of wisdom it denotes, the pathological impulse to act morally can cause "the stirring of the soul . . . that has the good as its object." Kant does not hesitate to mention "an enthusiasm for a good purpose" in sermons and political discourses or even in the words we say to ourselves to encourage ourselves to act morally. Those who do not enjoy a "fortunate *phlegma*" of apathy and the strength of soul neces- sary for pure morality find a provisional stimulus in them. Kant gives var- ious examples, such as learning to face life's happy or unhappy circum- stances with a smile: "this illumination of the face gradually moulds [children] within as well and establishes a disposition to joy, friendliness and sociability which is an early preparation for this approximation to the virtue of benevolence."[51]

Kant's concession to the emotions on the anthropological and educa- tional levels does not impugn the philosophical principle of the autonomy of practical reason. It is the result of the obvious fact that human beings are made of flesh and blood and are not solely reasonable beings. Auton- omy is always played out in a sensible world, among sensible people who affect one another and whose self-interest rarely coincides with the pre- scriptions of moral law. How could such people despise their emotions or passions and, considering themselves solely the authors of moral law, act appropriately? Why should they, in fact, since to do so they would have to have already accepted the morality of that law?[52]

Kant is well aware that sensibility and affectivity do not easily allow themselves to be intimidated by the voice of morality. The passions make the subject completely deaf to what it prescribes and often the emotions are little better. Contrary to Stoic radicalism, however, Kant's philosophy seeks to attribute a subsidiary value to the emotions. Within the context of sensible finitude, they are to be purified but not made to disappear. They do not have the character of respect since, unlike it, they are not produced by reason, but, for a time, they can compensate for a person's moral short- comings. Kant is grateful for a certain "wisdom on the part of nature," which bestowed the emotions on human beings whose maxims here and now in the sensible world rarely have the value of universal law. Thanks to the emotions, human beings possess a provisional stimulus to moral action. To be sure, emotion, left to itself, lacks wisdom and runs the risk of inducing a person to behave in a manner inconsistent from the moral point of view. But, in spite of everything, reason can make use of emotion to encourage recalcitrants—those who, out of laziness or impatience, do not take the time to question themselves on the universalizable character of their maxims—in the service of the good. In that case, says Kant, emotion stems from the faculty of desire—that is, from the will, determined to act by the representation of a purpose—and not from sensibility.

Conversely, passion never stems from the will; it is alienating and constitutes a powerful enemy to morality. It deprives the subject of all freedom. Although Kant rules out the possibility of a corruption of reason, he admits that passion hinders, clouds, and reduces the exercise of reason. Despite the subtle reasoning the passionate man often displays, he has lost all aptitude for discernment and all concern for the universality of his maxims. He acts only in view of satisfying an inclination to which he has become a prisoner, and the reason in him is affected by a pathology that Kant believes is almost always a hopeless case.

Despite Kant's concession to the emotions, the categorical imperative is valid only within the framework of autonomy. It is valid only for a subject who is "unconstrained and free, that is, not limited by the other."[53] That is why passion—the act of being affected by an incommensurable alterity—represents the worst danger for reason. An action performed out of passion probably does not even deserve the name "action" and, as a result, practical reason must labor to expel far from itself any coefficient of passivity capable of obstructing its exercise. But, Levinas asks, is passivity truly only a hindrance and a misfortune? Can it not be championed and precisely in the field of ethics?

Levinas conceives of a new concept of passivity; he seeks "a passivity more radical than that of the effect of a causal series," and he associates it with "the *reverse side* of being," or with an anteriority "on the ontological level, where being posits itself as *nature*." He does not seek to grasp the birth of the moral subject in the idea of man-as-principle—an idea he declares inane—but, paradoxically, in that of a "radical passivity."[54]

That praise of passivity—a passivity that cannot be taken upon oneself and that is forever irreducible to a principle since its source lies in the unrepresentable—leads Levinas to conceive of the subject as already inhabited by alterity, as destined for it and exposed to it, without any voluntary choice on the subject's part. In this regard, he does not hesitate to speak of "a seed of madness in the depths of the psyche," of "psychosis," or of "delirium."[55] In fact, does not the summons that the moral subject receives to respond to the other—without that act stemming from a careful and deliberate decision, without the subject being aware of having done the other a particular wrong that it ought to repair—resemble madness? Nevertheless, Levinas sees that change in the psyche demanded by the Other, deep within itself, as "exactly the opposite of the [moral] meaninglessness" characteristic of a mental disturbance. He understands it as an election and not as an illness, as a blessing—Saying *[le Dire]*[56]—and not as a curse.

Some might object that it is difficult to distinguish the psyche solicited by the other in the mode of election—hence passively—from the psyche over which the other casts a spell in a maleficent manner. How are we to distinguish, in the other's hold on us, between the disaster of a curse and the timelessness of a blessing? Do not prudence and good psychic health require that we return to the Kantian certainty that autonomy constitutes the subject's sole safeguard? Do they not require us to concede nothing to Levinas in this area? Does not his rehabilitation of passivity, under cover of election, lead to the formidable danger of mental disturbance, a disturbance vehemently described and denounced by Kant in his use of the term "passion"?

Clearly, Levinas knows the formidable peril of mental illness. He is not unaware of the tragedy of those who, despite their moral good will, remain struck down by the intolerable suffering of finding themselves prisoners to deadly words. He does not praise mental disturbance but rather election; he admits of no complacency toward the fragility of psyches marked, to their misfortune, by the malevolent Said *[les Dits]* of the other; he seeks, beyond the Said, the trace of Saying that calls a person to life, to a responsible life, for that is election. The philosopher is well aware that the human Said *[Dits]* of the people nearest to oneself and of more distant people often destine the subject to mental disturbance and make it difficult to understand that Saying, but he continues to maintain that it is in responding to that Saying—and only in that way—that one is liberated from the gangues that hold one prisoner to the fallacious idea one has of oneself—identity—and that one achieves one's uniqueness as a subject. He does not pronounce in favor of submission, conscious or unconscious, to the imperatives, the violence, and the madness of the other but argues for an unimpeachable responsibility toward the other, for election, to be precise.

Yet that cause cannot be combined with the misfortune of a possession by a psyche other than one's own. Since the act of resigning oneself to that destiny makes the emergence of the moral subject impossible, one ought to combat its opprobrium. As Levinas insistently says, it is necessary to leave the servitude of Egypt and remember the harm it inflicts—especially on the psyche—in order to become capable of the moral encounter. The person who remains in Egypt in his heart, wherever that person may be in actuality, confuses election and alienation. Nevertheless, as the Bible teaches, no one leaves Egypt at one's whim and in a movement of proud solitude. No one leaves it without peril and, no doubt, no one leaves it once and for all. But it is because, from the "deep mire" (Psalm 69:2), despite the servitude in which that limbo keeps him, man can still hear the rustling of Saying, that he finds the strength to rise up and go. That Saying commands him to "leave" what he believes is fated, to leave behind what holds him captive. "Go toward thyself," *lekh lekha*, the Lord had already told Abraham (Genesis 12:1),[57] in a commandment that continues to resonate in the lives of individuals. Otherwise, why would that commandment matter?[58] Yet, as the Bible also shows, it is always a surprise to hear that voice. The sound of that voice does not depend on a voluntary decision, it seizes hold of the subject and liberates it, seizes hold of every person to liberate his uniqueness in relation to the other. It foils the deadly force's grip over the self—and, as a result, over the other. In order for the uniqueness of the subject to be born within an ego clutching to its identity—or for the soul to be born in man's closed-off self, in F. Rosenzweig's expression—that appeal must be heard. And that appeal—or that Saying—is more decisive than the torments inflicted by alienation on the other and by internal darkness, which are sometimes maintained with satisfaction. That appeal is liberating because it makes a person capable of perceiving—for the first time, perhaps—the face of the other, and because it introduces the sense of a responsibility toward the other whose source does not lie in reason but in Saying, hence in passivity. But that passivity is not the antithesis of activity; rather, it offers a glimpse of the sense of that "preoriginary sensitivity" to the Good, which keeps the human psyche from closing in on itself. It is this passivity that, despite the privilege of ontology, also introduces the idea of a rationality of transcendence.

"The attention Abraham paid to the voice that led him back to the ethical order by prohibiting human sacrifice is the loftiest moment of the drama," Levinas writes in an admirable passage on the "binding" of Isaac. From the sharp edge of that attention comes the renunciation of one's hold over the other—in this case, Isaac—even in the name of supreme causes, and the responsibility for his life. Faith, says Levinas, does not require us to disregard ethics, as Kierkegaard claims, it does not stem from adherence to irrational propositions. Rather, it liberates us from deadly mirages in the interest of ethics. Such is Saying: "An appeal to the uniqueness of the subject, a sense given to life in spite of death"[59] and in spite of the limits speculative reason imposes on itself in the metaphysical realm out of concern not to give in to its own paradoxes.

For Kant, despite the contradictions that affect the exercise of reason when it seeks to make metaphysics a science, reason must still always hold the reins. Ethics is no exception to that principle. Practical reason admits of no prior Saying, nothing beyond itself. To claim that reason is practical is, in effect, to assert that it sets rules for action but also to ensure that those rules have a force that sufficiently motivates the subject to act in conformity with what they prescribe[60] without needing the Saying of an alterity that commands the subject to do so. By contrast, Levinas invites us to conceive of an anteriority—Saying—that questions that supremacy of reason, even practical reason, since moral action begins only at the moment of that appeal.

What does that anteriority mean for freedom? What origin must we recover to achieve the difficult freedom of which Levinas speaks? Does the Kantian idea of a transcendent freedom make it possible to forge a path toward it, or rather, does it further accentuate the distance between the two thinkers?

s i x   **Intelligible Character and Anarchy**

All phenomena are subject to the determinations of time. They are governed, says Kant, by the law of causality as a *natural necessity*. The concept of freedom thus loses all pertinence with respect to phenomena since it follows from that law "that every event, and consequently every action that takes place at a point of time, is necessary under the condition of what was in the preceding time. Now, since time past is no longer within my control, every action that I perform must be necessary by determining grounds *that are not within my control*."[1] Time then appears as a figure of heteronomy more formidable than the hold the other's will has on oneself since, although one can do battle with the tyrant and struggle against enslavement for aims alien to those of the moral law in oneself, it appears impossible to rid oneself of that temporal causality, or of that causality as *natural necessity*. How could one interrupt the infinite chain or series of events that connect one to the past? How could one really *begin* something and be free if the act one performs today is entirely determined by what was? A philosophy that explains human behavior as exclusively the function of temporality—empiricism, for example—thus appears incapable of accounting for the human being's freedom and responsibility, since, if we were seriously to take temporal causality into account, the concepts of freedom and responsibility would implicitly be invalid and impossible.

Nevertheless, Kant does not intend, on the pretext of saving freedom, to deny that temporal determination and hand the human being over to blind chance. On the contrary, he continues firmly to embrace the idea that all phenomena are subject to the determinations of time. From that perspective, the human being is not an exception to the natural order; he is thus subject to its inevitable necessity. How, therefore, in spite of temporal determinism, would he be truly capable of beginning something, of performing a free action, that is, an action not dependent on what has preceded it? How can Kant conceive of such a possibility—a possibility reserved solely for the human being—if he needs *at the same time* to maintain—as Kant does—that the human being is part of the phenomenal world? Such is the aporia that the concept of transcendental freedom must resolve. In doing so, however, it also raises many difficulties in turn, in particular, the difficulty of conceiving of the connection between that freedom and an anteriority or an origin reaching back beyond human memory. Nevertheless, Kant assures us that only that concept of freedom "allows us to find the unconditioned and intelligible for the conditioned and sensible *without going outside ourselves*."[2]

Although Levinas, like Kant, confronts the complexity of the idea of beginning in time, he analyzes it differently. To be sure, he is no more willing to make the human person subject to the often formidable weight of temporal heteronomy and thus to inscribe human acts in a determinism that would make the emergence of the moral subject impossible. But his concept of freedom, unlike Kant's, implies precisely that we *go outside ourselves* to find the unconditioned and the intelligible. The origin exempt from memory, the immemorial, which makes freedom possible, makes the subject go outside itself, not to subordinate it to the regulation of its maxims by abstract and universal principles, and even less to yoke the subject to an alienating authority, but rather to give sense to its freedom, *anarchically*, prior to the subject's confrontation with the logos.

We must therefore follow the thread of that double inquiry relating to the idea of an anteriority that no human memory can grasp in full consciousness and that nevertheless gives sense to human freedom. Why do Kant and Levinas, despite their differences regarding its status, believe it is indispensable to understand the enigma of freedom in order to save it and, along with it, the moral subject as well?

Freedom and Temporality

The natural causality characteristic of the world of phenomena is thus the opposite of freedom. Yet, quite clearly, man, as a sensible and finite being, belongs to that world. He is born, grows up, and dies marked by the determinations of a biological, psychological, social, and historical time, which are not the result of any free choice. From that point of view, the acts he performs or the misdeeds he commits today are dependent on a past over which he has no control, and they therefore cannot be imputable to him as a free subject. Kant thinks that the causality that governs the phenomenal world cannot be breached. Far from accepting the idea of contingency, he describes that causality as a mechanism from which no one can escape. At every point in time, he says, the necessity of what has preceded—and which escapes everyone's power—weighs upon human acts. The human being is determined by "the series of events infinite a parte priori"; one merely extends them "in accordance with a predetermined order [that] would never begin of itself." That "natural chain"[3] thus seems to imprison him, to make freedom an illusion and, as a result, to destroy morality.

Nevertheless, Kant does not intend to exempt human beings from that chain in order to save ethics. The law of natural causality inevitably concerns the human being since his existence is determined in and by time. Hence, if he commits a theft, that crime is explained by the antecedents in his life, his bad upbringing or his unhappy childhood, for example. The causal series within which that theft is inserted allows for no exceptions, it makes it impossible that this deed "could have been left undone."[4] Because of the past's ascendancy over him, a past that hangs heavy with the implacable weight of its determinations on the present, the thief could have done nothing but steal.

Therefore, no external experience can demonstrate freedom or even lead one to conceive of the possibility of it. On the contrary, it seems to demonstrate the foolishness of the very idea. Internal experience is no more convincing, and, even if the thief wanted to do so, he could not legitimately claim to feel free to act as he does. In fact, according to Kant, all experience—even internal—is subject to the determinations of time. No psychological consciousness ever attests to freedom. By virtue of one's empirical character, one is determined to act in one manner or another, and even one's internal deliberations are marked by the seal of necessity. To be sure, one can claim that one feels free to act as one does and can embrace one's own act; one can certainly maintain that no authority has any influence over one when one deliberates—but all that is illusory. The data of consciousness can never serve as proof of freedom since they always depend on time. Moreover, to maintain that a being is free because the principle that animates it is purely internal—like a body that receives no external impulse in the course of its trajectory—is only a ridiculous artifice. A determination internal to the subject rules out freedom just as surely as an external determination, since it too depends on the past beyond one's power. And, for Kant, in order to be free it is not enough to make the effort to recognize necessity and to acquiesce to its hegemony.

Thus, natural necessity—the mechanism, as Kant says—indelibly marks the acts of every man. How, then, can we speak of freedom? How can we continue to defend autonomy, and, thereby, the very possibility of ethics?

Kant sets out a difficult and, at first sight in any case, a contradictory requirement: one must, he says, conceive of man as subject to the determinations of the past and, *at the same time*, as exempt from them. But "how can that man be called quite free at the same point of time and in regard to the same action and in regard to which he is nevertheless subject to an unavoidable natural necessity?"[5] To call him free, says Kant, one must recall that such a necessity is attached to a human being's act only to the extent that the act and its author are subject to temporality. Yet a human being is not simply one phenomenon among others; he has "consciousness of himself as a thing in itself," and, in this respect, he "also views his existence *insofar as it does not stand under conditions of time."*[6] He is conscious that he can be determined by the laws that he sets for himself through his reason—in an autonomous manner, therefore—or by a rational, that is, a free, causality. And, from that point of view, the series of acts that mark his life turn out to be entirely free, with each act resulting from a rational deliberation that, for its part, does not depend on any past whatsoever, not even on one's education. Moreover, Kant says, man's life is entirely imputable to him since it belongs, "with all the past which determines it," to the character he gives to *himself* and in accordance with which "he imputes to himself, as a cause independent of all sensibility, the causality of those appearances."[7] "Character," which in theology designates the ineffaceable imprint of a sacrament such as baptism, is thus defined by Kant as a law of causality, either empirical or intelligible. In fact, according to him, one ought to distinguish between man's empirical character, which is dependent on natural causality—that is, on the past—and his intelligible character, which is free from all influence by sensibility and exempt from any determination by time: man gives that character *to himself*. From that point of view, he truly begins a series of effects on his own, and, whatever his past, each of his acts is imputable to him. The acting subject "in its intelligible character, would not stand under any condition of time."[8] As a result, a theft committed today by any person, rich or poor, properly reared or mistreated by his family, that theft, inevitable in terms of his empirical character determined by the past, would, in terms of his intelligible character, turn out to be an expression of his complete freedom. From that point of view, poverty and mistreatment, for example, do not constitute extenuating circumstances, since that theft would be wholly the deed of the intelligible—hence free—character of that person. In addition, Kant says, the empirical character and the connected chain of acts to which it leads in the sensible world must also be considered an expression of the intelligible character. He maintains that the latter is "the transcendental cause" of the former, its "ground."[9] That is why feelings such as shame and repentance about a past act, even committed under tragic circumstances that ought to excuse it or attenuate the weight of its opprobrium on the conscience, continue to haunt the author of the act. One knows one is responsible for it because one was entirely free, by virtue of one's intelligible character, to commit it or to refrain from doing so. One's character is not received from nature or particular circumstances: it is chosen. Otherwise, the idea of human dignity would be impossible.

Elsewhere, Kant insists on the suddenness with which character is established, a "suddenness that is always epoch-making."[10] That moment, he says, resembles a "rebirth" *(Wiedergeburt)*; it has the "solemnity of an oath made to oneself." Freedom as autonomy is thus intact: one gives one's character *to oneself.* From that point of view, whatever the nature of the connection between a human being and those who precede him in time, he receives nothing from them; otherwise, they would corrupt his freedom. "That solitary baptism of autonomy transposes the traits of true baptism, which is always received from the other, to inside the boundaries of mere ethical reason."[11] But Kant obviously cannot accept that "true" baptism since he considers all figures of heteronomy to be a source of alienation—never of freedom—and, to save autonomy, he argues for a pure solitude. The moral imperative that imposes itself on us all is "not to go outside ourselves." Freedom and alterity are thus destined to remain two antagonistic concepts.

Since Kant conceives of time in terms of a strict mechanical causality, he is obliged to assert that the freedom proper to intelligible character—transcendental freedom—escapes time. No one can know and experience it without an obvious contradiction, since knowledge and experience imply the prism that regulates time and hence the mechanism. But, in the absence of all intellectual intuition, does the unique character—not subject to the conditions of time—that a person gives *himself* remain unknowable and secret to himself?

In spite of everything, the Kantian argument appeals to a certain moral *experience*—that of shame and repentance—to justify the idea of transcendental freedom. "A human being may use what art he will to paint some unlawful conduct he remembers . . . as something in which he was carried away by the stream of natural necessity—and to declare himself innocent of it; he nevertheless finds that the advocate who speaks in his favor can by no means reduce to silence the prosecutor within him, if only he is aware that at the time he did this wrong he was in his senses, that is, had the use of his freedom."[12] When the person's intelligible character is at issue, the circumstances of the act committed, which may be dependent on necessity—a person stole because he was compelled by hunger, for example—hardly matter. The reason within me, Kant says, simply wonders whether that act, even if it occurred long ago and is forgotten by everyone, "belongs to me as a deed," if it depends on my subjective spontaneity as a "thing in itself." A troubled childhood, bad habits, and deleterious influences play no role here: Kant assures us that even a child is responsible. Our series of actions has "as its basis a free causality, which from early youth expresses its character in its appearances (actions)."[13] A person's chain of actions does not inure him to the point of corrupting his will; rather, it is his will that, immutably, independent of time, chooses bad principles—or good principles—that extend their hold over the general tenor of his life by expressing themselves in individual behaviors and acts over time. But that tenor is not a destiny in any way; it remains at every instant, and from childhood on, an expression of freedom. Even though it is impossible to understand the causality of reason, Kant seems to admit that it makes its mark on empirical character. This raises the difficulty— from Kant's own critical point of view—that there might be an inference leading from the empirical to the intelligible. Does not critical philosophy bar it, in fact?[14]

But a formidable difficulty still threatens that freedom. Some will object that the cause of a person's actions, inasmuch as the person is a thing in itself, lies in God. Kant forcefully rejects such a proposition: a human being, he says, would then resemble "a marionette" or "an automaton, like Vaucanson's, built and wound up by the supreme artist."[15] Transcendental freedom would then become pure illusion; it would be subject to the determinations of time and space, and the human being, guided by "an alien hand," would lose all autonomy. God is not the cause of actions that occur in the sensible world, Kant assures us, even though he is the cause of the acting beings considered as noumena. According to him, the creation concerns only intelligible—not sensible—existence, and therefore escapes determinations of time and space. Since God ought to be conceived as independent of temporal and spatial ideality, it is altogether absurd to suggest that his actions are the cause of human behavior. To be sure, God's mode of acting on things in themselves escapes understanding, but, to save the idea of intelligible freedom, we need only know that it does not stem from natural causality.

Therefore, the quest for the unconditioned and for the origin must not, at any cost, lead one to go outside oneself; otherwise, ethics is destroyed. Therefore, even though the intelligible character's act of being born remains exempt from any effort of memory and imagination—since it is timeless—and, in that respect, remains unrepresentable, that act implies no recourse to an exteriority. Ethics is thus saved: freedom must always prevail, in fact, even over the idea of God, and each human being must therefore give his intelligible character *to himself*.

The immemorial anteriority of the choice of that character remains a foundational and a free anteriority. The difficulty of reconciling the idea of such a character with that of "good will"[16]—the concern to act solely out of respect for moral law—is coextensive with the impossibility of understanding freedom in terms of the laws of the mechanism at work in this world. How can I decide to act out of good will if the intelligible character I have given to myself resists, in its timelessness, any obedience to moral law? How can I even hope to improve myself? That objection would be valid only if Kant had assimilated the intelligible character to a "nature" that determines the subject once and for all, thus depriving it of its present freedom. But that is not the case: the intelligible character does not stem from a nature; it escapes the mechanical temporality of phenomena and thus does not hinder the exercise of good will. Nevertheless, to conceive of it without contradiction, one would have to be able to conceive of a "practical time"[17] distinct from phenomenal time, which Kant cannot do. According to him, in the absence of intellectual intuition, that concept remains inevitably captive to mechanical temporality. Because Kant is unable to conceive of that "practical time," intelligible character is called "timeless."

But that timelessness—or that inconceivable practical temporality—does not, in any event, refer to anything but itself. Moral law reveals to human beings the resources of their autonomy; they discover *on their own* that they are capable of transcending their sensible inclinations and of obeying that law. Clearly, the character a human being gives *to himself* does not depart from that rule. Its establishment has the "solemnity of an oath made to oneself";[18] it does not open on an alterity. In recognizing the immemorial nature of that oath made to oneself, the Kantian moral subject also encounters what it is destined to do: to obey the voice of practical reason in itself. And that reason receives nothing from the outside; it is, on its own, the source of the law. Nothing is to be sought for or hoped for beyond practical reason. The human quest ends with the principles of reason; it knows nothing of anarchy.

Does not Levinas, in arguing for an inspired reason and insisting, unlike Kant, on the enigma of anarchy, lead us to understand the immemorial in a different way?

The Exempted Origin

How does Levinas understand human interiority, in terms of this analysis of phenomenal time and of the timelessness of intelligible character? Although, like Kant, he does not separate it from a reflection on time and on the immemorial, that reflection leads him, unlike his predecessor, to set aside the preoccupation "not to go outside oneself." At the core of the psyche, he perceives the clarity, not of a principle that would make it possible to remain with oneself, but, on the contrary, of an anarchy that stands at the ready in the face of alterity. Levinas describes interiority as "the fact that, in being, the beginning is preceded, but what precedes does not present itself to a free gaze that could assume it."[19] How are we to understand these words?

In the twentieth century, the progress of physics no longer authorized the philosopher to cling to "the mechanism" as a way of conceiving of phenomenal time. The human sciences, for their part, insist on the fact that human interiority is marked—unbeknownst to the subject—by structures that precede its birth and hence escape its freedom, but which orient it, without, unfortunately, always allowing it to "choose life." Psychoanalysis describes the human psyche as structured by a transmission—spoken and, especially, unspoken—of desires, fantasies, and words that sometimes go back several generations. That transmission obliges the subject to locate itself in being while bearing the weight of an origin exempt from any effort of memory. "Through infantile amnesia, everyone constitutes himself on the basis of a lost letter, a concealed secret. When we take the first words of our history in hand, we are already inside. We are already on the road. Intrauterine life has marked us outside or on the near side of any mnestic grasp."[20] The beginning is therefore not accessible to rememoration; indecipherable and secret, in spite of any light cast upon it, with the help of psychoanalysis for example, it commands every person to emerge to his or her life as a subject against the background of its enigma. As a result, it cannot be the very principle of one's thoughts, one's decisions, or one's commitments by virtue of the act of reason itself, as Kant would like it to be. No one knows the exact meaning of the secret from which one emerges, unless, precisely, it is that one does not stem from the steadfastness and self-assurance provided by a principle.

Before the human sciences, the Bible—with its metaphorical language irreducible to the univocity of the concept and to the authority of a well-reasoned thesis, but which nevertheless "gives food for thought"—already evoked the secret of every origin, whether cosmic or psychic. Its first word—*Bereshit*—posits the inaccessible character of the beginning and invites us to separate the idea of origin from any assertion of principle. The word *Bereshit*, which, according to the Midrash in any case, could be translated as "for the first fruits *[reshit]*"—in view of a development, then—begins with the second letter of the alphabet, the letter of duality. From the outset, that word brings us face to face with an enigma that has remained unsolved: the absence of the first letter, *aleph*, the letter of unity.[21] The history of every creature stands in relation to that anteriority or that absence, it bears witness to them, in spite of itself and often unbeknownst to itself. Sometimes as well, the human psyche, haunted by that absence, believing it may have been betrayed by it, struggles to forget it by asserting a radical ontological solitude of everything that is and by positing principles that are supposed to arrest the growing chasm and make it possible to go through life in a free and sovereign manner, something often more similar to a project of mastery than to attention and responsibility toward the fragile alterity of creatures.

What, then, does Levinas's description of interiority mean? Although it does not simply ratify psychoanalysis's discoveries about psychic life and does not propose a new exegesis of the absent first letter of the account in Genesis, it shares the same point of view: the quest for a "preoriginary," immemorial, and unrepresentable moment, whose absence, paradoxically, hangs over the psyche. Levinas does not explain exactly what he means by the expression "what precedes," since no conceptual formulation can account for it fully. "What precedes" does not fit any representation—whether as image or as concept—and transcends any act of naming. Otherwise, that anteriority would veer toward an idea or a principle assumable by human thought and freedom and would no longer bring us face to face with the anarchical. Nevertheless, says Levinas, that impossible-to-identify origin, which slips free of concepts and escapes all intuition, leaves a *trace* in psychic life. "Something has already passed 'over the head' of the present . . . something that precedes the beginning and the principle," something that, properly speaking, has never been there and that "signifies apart from any intention to send a signal," something that "disturbs the order of the world."[22]

Levinas shows no particular love for the ineffable and the unsayable; he indulges in no *pathos* of the incommunicable. The unpronounceable and unthinkable name of that anarchy—its unknowable transcendence—does not exert an attraction, unlike the Prime Mover in Aristotle's philosophy. Movement toward that transcendence does not presuppose taking a mystical path, which, according to the philosopher, always raises the suspicion of self-satisfaction and egoism. No ecstasy of the subject, whether mystical or erotic, approaches it, no union constitutes its endpoint. Nevertheless, that transcendence, or that Absence, having withdrawn into the immemorial, does not abandon people to the pure dereliction of their ontological solitude. If that were the case, how could they even yearn for it after its withdrawal, and, sometimes at least, feel distress as a result? In spite of everything, does not the evocation of an absence suppose a perception or an impression—strange for the individual who has never encountered the Absent One—that one lacks something or someone? Levinas says that, although the Absent One does not point out the path toward itself and does not reveal itself in phenomena—especially not in those called sacred—it nevertheless leaves a trace, a trace that carries obligations regarding the undesirable alterity of one's neighbor. It has a significance, in fact, one that is irreducible to an explanation—in the encounter with a human face. "The face is in the trace of the absolutely bygone, the absolutely past Absent One . . . and which no introspection could discover in Oneself."[23] Contrary to what Kant taught, one must "go outside oneself" and give up the yearning for a return to self—on the pretext of freedom—for the immemorial to have significance. But, as a result, it signifies something entirely different from a promise given to oneself in the form of intelligible character.

The psyche that confronts the face does not thematize the trace but submits to it. The trace remains irremediably resistant to conceptualization, but, in an unlikely manner—since, as in Kant, it holds in check the metaphysical claims of speculative reason and does not correspond to any prior expectation—it awakens the subject to the idea of a third *person*. This person—and not an impersonal principle—Levinas designates by the pronoun "He." That "He," that "Someone," who has withdrawn "from all revelation and all dissimulation," escapes the determinations of ontological rationality. Nevertheless, Levinas does not hesitate to call him "God," even explaining from whence the idea of that God came to him, when he writes: "The revealed God of our Judeo-Christian spirituality preserves all the infiniteness of his absence, which is in the personal 'order' itself. He shows himself only through his trace, as in chapter 33 of Exodus. To go toward him is not to follow that trace, which is not a sign. It is to go toward the Others who stand in the trace of illeity."[24] It is to obey an immutable responsibility toward them and, as a result, to be unable to continue on one's own way along a path marked out by the determinations of a life as an autonomous subject, proud to owe loyalty to no cause except one's commitment made to oneself, without any relation to phenomenal temporality. It is to find oneself banished from the path where everyone comes to the other—if one comes to the other at all—only on the basis of one's own autonomy as a reasonable being.

Before analyzing that anarchical situation of responsibility and its consequences for freedom, let us pause to consider the sequence of terms chosen by Levinas: the Infinite, the Other, He, the Absent One, the God of Judeo-Christian spirituality, the God who shows himself through his trace in Exodus. In fact, if the significance of the trace comes about by following that sequence to the last term and, thus, by *remembering* that we read in the Book that Moses descended from Mount Sinai toward his people carrying the Tables of the Witness (*luhot haEdut*) rather than remain in a state of ecstasy before the Lord, what becomes of the idea of the immemorial? Does not Levinas, on the pretext of conceiving an anteriority—beyond any principle—that animates interiority and orients it, give a questionable credence—questionable for a philosopher, in any case—to the singularity of a tradition? Does not the analogy introduced—"*as* in chapter 33 of Exodus"—to understand the trace in which the face is located finally weaken the argument?

Interiority, says Levinas, requires that we conceive of an origin exempt from memory and from freedom. What connection does he establish, then, between that immemorial aspect and the exteriority of the Book, which, paradoxically, supposedly records the memory of it? One corresponds to the other, according to him: all internal life depends on books—"what is written in the soul is first written in books,"[25] he tells us—and, correlatively, books need that internal life since, without it, their Said no longer transmits any Saying. In order to be awakened, and to awaken others, the "wings of the spirit," at rest in the letter of books, await the breath of questions coming from a particular and living interiority that will question them. Because the vulnerable alterity of the letter troubles the subject, it imposes the responsibility to watch over its sense, that is, to offer the letter, without fail, the sanctuary of the subject's living questions. How can one sleep so long as sense is left in sufferance in the fragility of the letter? How can one sleep so long as the temptation to know so often and so violently replaces responsibility toward what exceeds theory and dogmas? Yet that state of wakefulness that takes hold of the subject shatters its interiority, reveals to it the unimpeachable orientation that dwells within it—from time immemorial—and gives sense to it: transcendence within immanence or the other within the same. "The other, rather than alienating the uniqueness of the Same, which it troubles and holds, calls upon it only in the deepest part of itself, in the part deeper than itself, where nothing and no one can replace it."[26] The immemorial, with no history proper to the constitution of the subject—the Other in the Same—so often covered over by the egoistic sedimentations inherent in any perseverance in being, trembles at the call from weakness, an appeal that, this time, is always linked to history. That does not mean that the immemorial is something virtual—it would then no longer be immemorial—but that it surges forth from an absolute past that, as in Plato's philosophy, begins with a dispossession, of oneself and of any idea one might have of oneself and of the other. That dispossession begins, and begins again, when one is confronted with the vulnerability of alterity, a vulnerability that is impossible to forget and that obliges one, contrary to what Kant taught, precisely to go outside oneself. To conceive of interiority— hence of the immemorial—in that way is not the obligatory endpoint of a rational and reasonable argument but rather a shattering produced by exteriority. That shattering, however, does not expose the subject to the obscure powers of the irrational and the emotional but lets it glimpse the sense of a rationality of transcendence.

That shattering, produced by exteriority, does not occur as a response to the dread produced by beauty, as in Plato's *Phaedrus*,[27] but as the result of the trauma produced by weakness—of the face but also of writing—whose appeal reverses the concern characteristic of transcendental subjectivity, which is to confine itself to the meanings it gives to phenomena. In this case, it is weakness—and only weakness—that saves the psyche's transcendence from the forgetfulness where it so often becomes mired.

But why evoke the God of Exodus as the secret source of the appeal addressed to the subject by the fragility of a face? Why does Levinas, rather than confining himself to the words "Infinite," "He," or "Absent One," go on to say that the Infinite shows itself through its trace "*as* in chapter 33 of Exodus"? Does that reference constitute an exclusive particularism by a philosopher concerned with the universality of his concepts?

The pertinence of that objection is valid only if we consider the word "as," which Levinas uses here, within the framework of a methodological and empirical prudence, concerned with the truth of the result proper to a comparison but unable to demonstrate it rationally. But, in this case, the philosopher does not use the word "as" from within that framework, which, according to him, is always prisoner to the theoretical ideal of the univocity of presence and being. His philosophy sharpens the desire to see that ideal come to an end. Nevertheless, says Levinas, the trace of the "He" rises to the surface in one's words when one does not take oneself for their origin, *as* in Exodus when Moses bears witness to the words of the Lord. The aim of that choice of simile is not to confer a theoretical privilege on the biblical text in order, subsequently, to be able to measure the philosophical propositions by its yardstick. Rather, that simile seeks to keep alive the sense of what surpasses ontological reason: "the ambiguity or enigma of the nonphenomenon, of the unrepresentable," "evidence from before the thematization attesting to a *'more' awakening a 'less' that it troubles-or-inspires.*"[28] That simile in no way supplements a weakness in the theoretical argument since, precisely, it waives any claim to knowledge. It attempts to say what lies outside theory and concepts without, nevertheless, veering into meaninglessness. It stands humbly in the trace of the immemorial from which the psyche takes its life.

In its timelessness, the unrepresentability of intelligible character corresponds to the Kantian imperative not to go outside oneself; Levinas, for his part, discovers, in the deepest part of oneself, a part deeper than oneself. The absolute past, "immemorial, unrepresentable, invisible,"[29] obligates me toward the other. But why does Levinas think that that obligation goes so far as to expiate the debt of being oneself? Does not the

Kantian determination to attend to *limits* in all things, particularly in ethics, represent wisdom in the face of such *excessiveness?*

The Unrepresentable, the Immemorial

The significance of anteriority exempt from memory differs in the two philosophies. Kant understands it in terms of a free establishment of character; Levinas understands it in terms of an anarchical election of the psyche by alterity, an election that assumes its meaning when one is confronted with the present vulnerability of one's neighbor. The Kantian moral subject gives its character *to itself;* its freedom is incompatible with susceptibility to the slightest trace of heteronomy, even if that heteronomy has the fragile and unconsoled features of a human face. In fact, in order to remain the sole principle of morality, the finite reason in a human being refuses to respond to the appeal of an alterity—to obey the voice of reason within oneself is still to obey oneself—and forcefully challenges the passivity of affect. Within the theoretical domain, reason itself sets the limits beyond which the transcendental illusion begins; in the practical domain, it determines those beyond or on this side of which amorality or immorality begins. In contrast to the limits in the power to know, there is, to be sure, the possibility of a practical signification that exceeds those limits—"the implications of moral action can be made explicit without becoming the object of any knowledge of being," Levinas remarks on this point[30]—but practical reason, in its turn, very precisely delimits the pertinence of the qualifier "moral" conferred on action. The subject's finitude implies consciousness of its limits; that finitude depends on an agreement to draw borderlines that also constitutes its greatness. In theory and in practice, this drawing of borderlines is neither subject to nor imposed by an authority external to oneself; it is always an act of the reason. It is reason that defends itself against the intrusion of the chimera of implausibility and the contradictions—insoluble on the theoretical plane—of metaphysical ideas; it is reason that denounces any effort to make ethics rest on a motivation apart from itself and that thus declares the affects or the authority of the other morally illegitimate. Moral action entails full independence in relation to the boundlessness of the passions and the imagination; it emancipates itself from all tutelage, even that of God's infiniteness. The human being is *internally* solicited by moral obligation, but that solicitation comes from him.

Levinas certainly shares Kant's idea of the limits proper to theoretical and ontological reason. What Kant calls "transcendental illusion" Levinas terms "idolatry," and, just like Kant, he denounces its dogmatism and its violent power over minds. Nevertheless, although he likes to emphasize his kinship with Kant in terms of his desire to conceive of a practical signification extending beyond the limits of theoretical reason, does he not make an extravagant compromise with excess in the practical domain? Although Kantianism broke with the dogmatic or so-called scientific wanderings of reason and "glimpsed, in the illusions of the transcendental dialectic, a first gleam of practical *truths*,"[31] the new-found sobriety it brought about remains indebted to a self-presence of the self that Levinas seeks to reawaken from its identity, or, as he explains, from its impenitence in being. But is not that idea an unjust accusation whose excessiveness, whose burden of uneasiness, and whose pain ought to be limited by a reasonable principle, a Kantian principle, for example?

Unlike Kant, Levinas does not seek merely to understand practically what exceeds the limits of being. "For Kant, the fact that reason can be naive and as yet inadequately reawakened, that it needs to beware of its self-assurance, is demonstrated in the theoretical adventure whereby reason, as always in the West, is vested with the mission of truth and tries its utmost to discover being."[32] Kantian vigilance is nevertheless interpreted as an *activity* and always refers to the unity and solidity of an "I think" or an "I want," which Levinas judges to be inadequately awakened. The limit of rationality—or of vigilance—is understood by Kant as a limit of activity. Ethics exceeds the limits of any possible theory, but, for its part, it constitutes a "full vigilance" and a "full rationality," that is, a full and free activity, "despite the passivity to which, as a categorical imperative, it will not fail to attest." That passivity does not call its activity into question; it comes from the insubordination of affect and of sensibility. In that philosophy, reason thus holds onto "its claim to activity, that is, its place, initial or ultimate, within the category of the Same." Levinas concludes that, although Kant limits the claims of reason to the theoretical field, in placing the emphasis on the free activity of reason in the practical field he does not break with the ideal of the Same. "Reason is identity that posits itself as Ego: identity that identifies itself—that returns to itself—through the power of its form. . . . That energy of identification's return to itself—that *vis formae*—is the activity of any act and, if it entails sobering up, it sobers up in the Same, as a coming-back-to-self."[33] This is confirmed by the fact that the immemorial aspect of intelligible character is a promise the self makes to itself. The immemorial keeps watch over that principle; Kant does not imagine going outside oneself since, according to him, that act would destroy freedom. As a result, the break with his philosophy becomes imperative for Levinas, even though he admires the fact that Kant found a sense for the human without assessing it in terms of ontology: "The fact that immortality and theology would be unable to determine the categorical imperative points out the novelty of the Copernican revolution: sense that is not measured in terms of being or not-being, with, on the contrary, being determining itself on the basis of sense."[34]

But the objection will be raised: why does Levinas make the Same, or the return to self, bear the weight of impenitence? Why does he judge the awakening of the reasonable subject insufficient so long as it does not go so far as to call its right to being into question? What, finally, does the debt to be oneself with which he burdens the moral subject mean?

In relation to these questions, Kantian critical philosophy obviously seems more moderate and more reasonable. Nevertheless, does not the categorical imperative already obligate a person to preserve his life out of duty, when the distaste for life and the temptation of suicide make their appearance? It is as if, for Kant as well, the worthy life stemmed from duty and from the debt. Kant says, in fact, that one must live in the name of the law, out of obedience to what it commands, even when one has no desire or joy: life is owed. The moral law requires everyone to choose life at the moment death tries to seduce him. Levinas takes this point a step further, since he does not hesitate to consider the question of the right to being as the primary question, "the question of sense par excellence," even if that question goes against nature. It is, he says, the question of the sense of being, or of its justice, a "pure question that asks *me* and where, against nature, thought awakens to its nontransferable responsibility."[35] Is Levinas's implausible act of taking things a step further in the order of moral questioning—implausible because it departs from the *criteria* of truth and falsity—thus to be made more reasonable?

The reflection on the trace teaches us that, far from constituting a promise the self makes to itself, the immemorial, which gives the subject its life, comes from an appeal from the Other, an appeal awakened by weakness and that extends to the question of the justice of being. Levinas describes that appeal as a breath of the spirit in the psyche or as propheticism—that is, the "very psyche of the soul"—and he asserts that "Kantianism does not replace it."[36] Kantianism does not replace the election of the same by the other because it refuses, precisely, to make a place for alterity in the psyche of a moral subject. But why would election raise the question within oneself of the right to being, "a question repressed most of the time and which reappears at the extremity of what is sometimes thoughtlessly called illness"?[37] Why would it accuse the self and make it bear the weight of an inexpiable debt, prior to any possible sins?

For Levinas, the debt certainly stems from the immemorial. As a result, no subject can claim to have acquitted itself of that debt; rather, it is driven to the wall by the debt. No one is ever out of debt where one's neighbor is concerned. Internal peace—if by that one understands an ideal of serenity—remains impossible and the yearning for repose condemned. The ego is burdened by a sin it did not commit: "there was time irreducible to presence, absolute past, unrepresentable. Did not the Good elect the subject with an election recognizable in the hostage's responsibility to which the subject is destined, a responsibility it would be unable to escape without contradicting itself and by virtue of which it is unique?"[38]

Yet, far from opening a rift of unhappiness or dereliction, the immemorial debt—or election—gives sense to the subject's life. Although the immemorial debt makes the accusation that there is no justification for being oneself, or even that one has usurped the place of another, that debt does not crush the subject. On the contrary, it justifies, for all eternity,[39] the subject's being in its place as a unique and irreplaceable entity. The debt does not result from duty—as Kant would have it—since, contrary to his view, it bars "getting a grasp on things." The subject never manages "to make ends meet" and to acquit itself; if it did, it would lose its moral significance. But that idea, which, at least in relation to the tradition of reflexive philosophy, seems an intolerable—and unlivable—exaggeration, for Levinas governs the meaning of the for-the-other. For Levinas, the desire to limit the debt—or to forget it, to efface all trace of it even—does not come from a commonsense reaction (I cannot pay for everything and everyone) but from a wish to be deaf to the immemorial appeal and from a conscience too hasty to acquit itself of evil on the pretext that it is not the cause of it. That wish is inherent in the self's installation in being and in a life for itself; that conscience is characteristic of the so-called common-sensical concern to limit responsibility by freedom. But that wish and that conscience are to be questioned—and accused—in order to awaken, against its wishes, the moral subject that slumbers within them. In that way, the *uniqueness* of the subject rises up—behind its identity as an ego inclined to defend *its* place in the sun, often at the cost of excluding the other—in response to the immemorial appeal, the appeal of the *goodness* of the good beyond being, of the good that neither slumbers nor sleeps[40] and that obliges us to take seriously a transcendence other than that of intentionality.

That obligation is experienced as a responsibility toward one's neighbor, a responsibility stemming from the immemorial appeal, and not from some contract, the stipulations of which would be limited by the will in its freedom. But the elected one finds the sense of his freedom in that obligation that takes hold of him, since no one can take his place and respond to the appeal. He then achieves his *uniqueness*, immutable and irreplaceable by anyone else. Such is freedom for Levinas: the awakening of the subject to its uniqueness, the uniqueness of election when confronted with the face of the other, whose weakness, in the trace of the immemorial, obligates it, beyond the effort to get hold of its identity as a transcendental subject and beyond the concern for itself. Such is also the dignity of that subject—"the dignity of the unique"[41] prior to that of the reasonable being prescribed by Kant—and, as a result, the awakening to a project more original than the categorical imperative: that of goodness as transcendence. That goodness is not appeased by "respect for the formal universality" of the law, and Kant is wrong to dismiss it too quickly as characteristic of the "passionate and sensible impulses."[42]

"Now I am pledged to the other with no possibility of abdicating,"[43] not even in death. Death does not put an end to the sense of the human, that is, the proximity to the Infinite. It interrupts the finitude of a destiny, but the human exceeds that finitude; it "signifies through transcendence and through the to-God *[à-Dieu]* in me, which is the calling into question of me."[44] The Infinite that shatters me and reawakens me to Saying prevents the grave from being a refuge.

Must one, then, conceive of the "otherwise than being" even unto death? Does not Levinas write that the subject's being "goes away for the other; its being dies in signification"?[45] Does not that philosophy, disregarding all limits and on the pretext of "the dignity of the unique" and of goodness, lead one constantly to run the risk of dying for the other, that is, the risk of sacrifice? Would not the wise Kantian determination to question oneself on the possible universality of the maxims of one's actions rightly denounce that risk as immoral? For how can I wish without contradiction for the maxim "Sacrifice yourself for the other" to become a universal law of nature? Can I want goodness to prevail over the rationality of the law?

Levinas does not ask the question in these terms, but he wonders whether that sacrifice is moral in relation to the *third party*. The sense of limits, he says, always stems from the question of the third party—though that question does not efface the immemorial and unrepresentable appeal—and the endless correction it introduces into ethical asymmetry. The law is not opposed to goodness but considers the implications of goodness in relation to everyone. It does not require that one forget the love without concupiscence for one's neighbor, which Levinas calls "responsibility"; it signifies the universality of that love. But the third party, that other neighbor and that neighbor of the other, is not there by accident; he is inevitably always there. Ethics is always lived in the plural: the slightest decision regarding this neighbor has repercussions on the third party. The third party thus obliges a person to ask questions about the justice of one in relation to the other and about his own justice toward one *and* the other. In what way would it be moral to sacrifice oneself for one and to forget the other? In what way would it be moral to hand the other over to the violence of the one to whom I sacrifice myself? That is a non-Kantian question, to be sure, but a question that, as in Kant, imposes the idea that ethics—at the risk of destroying itself—cannot despise a reflection on limits. "The third party introduces a contradiction in Saying, whose signification before the other went in only one sense until that time. That is, in itself, the *limit* of responsibility, the latent birth of the question: What am I to do justly? A question of conscience."[46] A question, then, of the subject's self-reflection *[retour sur soi]*, even though that reflection does not constitute a preliminary condition to hearing the immemorial appeal. No preliminary condition—that of self-consciousness or that of intelligible character, for example—can replace the immemorial.

The arrival of a third party imposes a pause and a "betrayal of my an-archical relation to *illeity* but also a new relation to it: it is *thanks* to God alone that I, a subject incomparable with the Other, am approached as an other like any other, that is, for me." It is *thanks* to God that the others, sometimes at least, show responsible behavior toward me and not because of my desire to base my responsibility toward them on their responsi-bility toward me. That would amount to making the conscience and self-reflection a preliminary condition. Levinas concludes: "The passing of God, of which I can speak only by referring to that aid or that grace, is pre-cisely the reversal of the incomparable subject into a member of society."[47]

Is the immemorial and unrepresentable debt reduced as a result of that "grace of God"? And why think it is a grace—rather than the formal uni-versality of the law—that makes a person a subject among other subjects, a subject worthy of respect, a subject that can hope that the other will be-have in a responsible manner toward it but one that does not base its own behavior on that hope?

For Levinas, the debt, or election, obviously remains: the immemorial never lets itself be forgotten and the unrepresentable does not fit the lim-its of any present situation. *Consciousness* that one's behavior toward that particular neighbor has implications for the universality of men expresses the living and responsible sense of that universality and not masochism or morbidity as some people claim.[48] As a result, the "grace" from which the subject benefits does not resemble the intervention of a mysterious "cause" that would alter ethical asymmetry and replace it with reciprocity. It means that the ethical connection to human plurality is also made in the trace of transcendence, or that it remains irreducible to a pact or contract because it comes from the alliance with the Good, whose preoriginary, immemo-rial, and unrepresentable character Levinas theorizes.[49]

The name of the immemorial thus differs in Kant and in Levinas. Their philosophies are profoundly *affected* by that difference. Transcendental freedom announces the promise of autonomy: in all circumstances, the Kantian subject will be marked by the concern "not to go outside itself." Therefore, neither transcendence nor alterity nor goodness nor the grace of God will alter the promised land of autonomy and the confidence in practical reason. In Levinas, the election of the unique—the unforgettable appeal of alterity or the alliance with the Good—obviously shifts the stakes of that reflection. In that case, the immemorial destines a man to alterity, it pleads the case of going outside himself and of not returning to himself, as if this were the subject's highest destiny or its vocation to holiness.

These ethical systems obviously require a great deal of a person, too much, some people say, even the impossible. Are virtue and holiness within human reach? Do not people simply wish to experience a little happiness on earth? Does the disinterestedness that virtue and holiness presuppose entail forgetting happiness?

seven   **The Question of Happiness**

Ever since Aristotle, the philosophical tradition has linked happiness to the contemplative life. Happiness differs from diversion since it is an eminently serious matter or, as Aristotle says, an activity that is valid in itself. Actions consistent with virtue belong to that category, since "to do noble and virtuous deeds is a thing desirable in itself."[1] As a result, the activity consistent with the highest virtue—the virtue of the mind, because of its contemplative character—will lead man to happiness and even to perfect happiness "provided [that activity] be granted a complete span of life."[2] Happiness thus stems from metaphysics—a knowledge of the most sublime beings and an understanding of first principles—and crowns the exercise of human virtue par excellence, that of the speculative intellect. It resides in the contemplative life, *Bios Theoretikos*, which does not mean a "life of study" or a life during which one gradually uncovers truth but the ideal—realized by Aristotle's God—of being able to devote all one's time to "contemplating . . . divine realities."[3]

Man thus achieves his perfection through the gaze cast on these realities and knows happiness as a result. Aristotelian contemplation *(theoria)* remains on the intellectual plane; its aim is to achieve the fulfillment of the intellect, without seeking to "surpass it to attain a transcendent object beyond it."[4] To grasp God or "the supreme intelligible," intelligence is sufficient; it is sufficient to lead man to bliss.

The certainty that there is a connection between happiness and knowledge permeates all of philosophy. For Spinoza, for example, supreme beatitude—virtue itself—still resides in the union of the thinking mind with God or Nature. The path of adequate ideas constitutes the unique, rare, and precious guide toward it. "The wise man . . . being conscious, by virtue of a certain eternal necessity, of himself, of God, and of things, never ceases to be, but always possesses true spiritual contentment."[5] In that philosophy, speculative reason remains the quintessential guarantor of human bliss, a bliss that frees the wise man from the painful chance events of temporality.

And yet, just as Kant shows that moral virtue does not reside in knowledge, he also breaks the connection between metaphysical knowledge and happiness. The *Critique of Pure Reason* shows the illusory character of such a knowledge: far from leading the human being to happiness, the speculative intelligence inflicts the torments of its paralogisms and antinomies on him. The absence of intellectual intuition makes it impossible to know things in themselves, and Kant points to "the *loss* of its hitherto imagined possessions that speculative reason must suffer." He adds that one must "deprive speculative reason of its pretension to extravagant insights"[6] and denounce the metaphysical dogmatism of those who—like Spinoza—ignore the limits inherent in the power to know and believe reason capable of an adequate knowledge of God.

From that point of view, to base human bliss on knowledge would be the equivalent of decreeing it henceforth impossible. Kant, and subsequently, Levinas, break the traditional connection between metaphysical knowledge and happiness. Nevertheless, their last word is not this disabused observation from Ecclesiastes 1:18: "he that increaseth knowledge increaseth sorrow." The pursuit of happiness, they say, cannot be the motive for moral behavior, since it stems from self-love, that is, from the subject's egoism. Nevertheless, the idea of happiness remains on the horizon of their philosophies. Kant evokes the moral subject's hope to become "worthy of being happy," and, in spite of everything, he remains faithful to the idea of a connection between virtue and happiness—the highest good—even if, to do so, he must resort to postulates relating to the immortality of the soul and the existence of God. As for Levinas, he speaks of a moral postponement of happiness although, unlike Kant, he does not conceive of a merit in being happy that would be proper to virtue. Nevertheless, the spiritual awakening, and even the very life of the human being, which he mentions as a corollary to the response to the appeal of the other, does not seem alien to a quivering hope for happiness.

The Desire for Happiness

Kant notes that all reasonable but finite beings—who are dependent on other people and on things to live and, especially, to live well—necessarily desire happiness. But do they know what that means? "Happiness" is a concept so undetermined that no one can form a precise idea of it, much less share it with others. The objects that are supposed to procure it, such as wealth, power, pleasures, or a long life, almost always produce worries, envy, bitterness, and suffering. To be sure, other philosophers before Kant had condemned these "false goods," the pursuit of which fosters the "sad passions" without procuring the slightest happiness, but they had contrasted them to the life of wisdom. Spinoza, for example, made knowledge by means of adequate ideas the sure and supreme guide toward the true good—the intellectual love of God—and, as a result, toward beatitude. But Kant breaks away from that perspective because he shows no mercy for knowledge and enlightenment: they do not guarantee happiness, he says, and instead they sharpen the perception of the inevitable ills that threaten everyone. Hence, even in the best of cases, the person seeking happiness has at his disposal only some empirical advice to be prudent but no determinate principle to achieve his end. Kant concludes: "Happiness is not an ideal of reason but of imagination, resting merely upon empirical grounds."[7] Thus, he seems to dismiss any possibility of finding happiness along the path of reason. Is there, then, no place for the concern to be happy when the question of ethics is raised?

In fact, the desire for happiness dwells in every human being: it is even "an unavoidable determining ground of his faculty of desire."[8] Therefore, Kant does not banish it with contempt; he simply says that no ethics that rests on it is valid. How could ethics be founded on something for which no law exists? If happiness were the object par excellence of ethics, the will could not conform to any universal practical law corresponding to it—since such a law does not exist—and would therefore never be good. "The principle of happiness can indeed furnish maxims, but never such as would be fit for laws of the will, even if *universal* happiness were made the object,"[9] which—in spite of the Enlightenment—still remains a very vague idea.

The concern for happiness thus remains alien to moral preoccupations. It in no way resembles the satisfaction a man may sometimes experience when, in spite of adversity, he has held fast and maintained his dignity without giving in to immoral temptations. "When an upright man is in the greatest distress, which he could have avoided if he could only have disregarded duty, is he not sustained by the consciousness that he has maintained humanity in its proper dignity in his own person and honored it" under circumstances where, for example, a lie might have gotten him out of a difficulty? But, Kant insists, "this consolation is not happiness, not even the smallest part of it."[10] He claims that, in spite of the world's contempt or derision, that man, in his own eyes in any case, has not diminished in personal value, even if he has lost social status, the recognition of others, and even the taste for life.

It is therefore essential to distinguish between the doctrine of happiness, which is founded on empirical principles, and moral doctrine, which relies exclusively on a formal universal law. But Kant is adamant that "this *distinction* of the principle of happiness from that of morality is not, for this reason, at once an *opposition.*" In addition, "pure practical reason does not require that one should *renounce* claims to happiness, but only that, as soon as duty is in question one should *take no account* of them."[11] To work toward satisfying conditions that customarily seem to allow one to characterize a life as happy—such as skill, health, or wealth—is even a part of duty since, by virtue of them, one will have a better chance of accomplishing one's moral task without risking the temptations of covetousness, theft, lying, and even murder. Misfortune, Kant insists, often makes it possible for perversity to make its way into a soul to the point of persuading it of the permissibility of a wicked act that would supposedly put an end to one's own unhappiness or to that of one's fellow man.[12]

The moral subject must therefore not look down on happiness—its own or that of others—but the moral subject cannot without contradiction want the maxim of happiness to become universal law. Happiness always depends on an uncertain *content*, particular to every person, and often even indebted to suffering inflicted on others, whereas ethics stems from the pure *form* of law. The desire for happiness attests to the hold self-love, egoism, and self-interest have over people, but it imposes itself on them, since it comes from the finitude proper to everyone. No one is entirely self-sufficient; everyone depends on many things to live, or simply to survive, and, when these things are lacking, suffering increases. Hence the constant anxiety to procure the necessary things for oneself and to not lose them. But, since that dependence also constitutes a threat, some philosophers, the Stoics, for example, wanted to challenge it. They thus confused self-sufficiency and happiness, assimilating the latter to independence in relation to every *thing* that does not depend on oneself and, ultimately, to ataraxy. For Kant, however, their severity, despite its heroism, is a *moral fanaticism,*[13] since it incites a person to transgress the limits of pure practical reason. Does not the renunciation it leads to resemble arrogance and the error of a chimerical moral perfection? Instead of wanting to surpass human limits, is it not better to attend to an ethics compatible with "the limitations of finite beings"?[14] And, for that reason as well, must one not divorce the principle of morality from the desire for happiness? That does not mean promoting austerity, asceticism, or ill will toward oneself: like any reasonable and finite being, the moral subject maintains the concern for its happiness, but that concern remains constantly subordinated to the obedience of moral law. Kantian ethics differs from an ethics of renunciation; it simply presupposes that, when considering the potential morality of the maxim that presides over an act, the desire to be happy does not enter in. To "make *eudemonism,* if not into the entire principle of morality then at least into a part of this principle . . . is precisely the way to be without any principles." An action taken with happiness as the motive may well resemble in every respect an action stemming from a pure moral principle; at the same time, however, it corrupts and weakens the moral disposition, whose "value and rank . . . consist in demonstrating, without concern for these motivating forces and indeed by overcoming all their commendations, strict obedience to nothing but the law."[15]

By virtue of his finite condition, no human being escapes the desire—and even the need—for happiness. They are the expression of self-love or egoism, which, before being a moral defect, constitutes the very ontology of the subject. Levinas says, "For Kant, the ego rediscovers itself in that need for love,"[16] and agrees with him in linking happiness and egoism. But Levinas, again like Kant, does not condemn the desire for happiness and is mistrustful of Stoic intransigence. He says that the fulfillment permitted by happiness "is worth *more* than ataraxy."[17] Nevertheless, his critique of Stoicism is based on a non-Kantian argument: Stoicism is not in error because it surpasses the limits of pure practical reason but because, despite its rigor and its constant imperatives, the self-sufficiency—in renunciation—that it promotes has no affinity with concern for the other. In fact, despite its magnitude, the inner freedom of the Stoic does not suffice; it is at the mercy of the suffering of torments and does not respond in any way to the pain of the innocent.

But does the desire for happiness participate in such a concern? Does it not constitute an egoistic installation in being, indifferent to the weakness of one's neighbor? Must not the ontology of the subject, precisely, be thwarted so that a little good may come into the world?

After the very somber tone of the pages on the *there is [il y a]*, or the anonymity of being that surrounds man and suffocates him, Levinas's description of happiness constitutes the first bright spot. Following the horror, the weariness, and the tragedy of depersonalization endured by the man handed over, defenseless and unforgiven, to naked and threatening being, to night and the profound misfortune of being chained to oneself, comes a first breath, a first forgiveness, or even a "first ethics," an ethics inseparable from happiness, "the ethics of the fruits of the earth."[18]

Like Kant, Levinas thinks that the desire for happiness dwells within every person, and, also like Kant, he links it to dependence on goods which, beyond their immediate necessity—the bread one needs to feed oneself—and their usefulness, also make possible the enjoyment of life. "The relation of life to its own dependence regarding things is enjoyment, which, like happiness, is independence." "To think, to eat, to sleep, to read, to work, to warm oneself in the sun"—these are not pointless activities or accidents of being, in contrast with which asceticism would be better. Rather, they "make life worthwhile."[19] To live *on* something is not simply the regrettable price of human finitude; it signals the first emergence of the ego outside the grip of the *there is*, or the neutrality of being. Hence, by feeding oneself, everyone enters into a relationship with the *alterity* of things, one transforms it within oneself and acquires one's independence. In fact, when hunger and thirst, for example, become needs requiring satisfaction, they wrest man "from the anonymous threats" of the *there is* and make him "a being independent of the world, the true *subject* that has become capable of procuring the satisfaction of its own needs."[20] A man's needs differ from that of a beast, and their satisfaction depends on labor, which puts him in a relationship with the alterity of things, which he transforms and enjoys. These needs extend to the desire to possess shelter and goods by getting a foothold in being, and, it would seem, a firm foothold. According to Levinas, that is the ideal of happiness for the European man: to feel his existence confirmed by his appetite for life, to identify freedom and satisfaction and to possess money as the measure that he belongs to the world and that the world belongs to him.[21] That would also be his revenge—a lasting revenge, he believes—on the agonizing neutrality of being.

Unlike Kant, Levinas adds knowledge to what is, all things considered, a classic list of what many consider a good. The ego concerned with its own happiness—or its salvation away from the formidable grip of *there is*—seeks to understand the world, to appropriate it conceptually. Enjoyment then becomes knowledge, insight, and understanding. The ethics of "the fruits of the earth" ends with the equating of thought with its object, as if psychic life culminated in the excellence of realizing the possibilities proper to ontological reason. Yet, here again, as in any relation requiring satisfaction, the alterity of things and persons is condemned: the concept takes the place of the enigma, and intellectual and technical mastery breaches their exteriority. Philosophical happiness would be bound up with that profound allergy to alterity: in substituting ideas for people and themes for interlocutors, the philosopher would like to be deaf to the alterity of every human individual. In refusing to question the ancient and violent complicity between being and concept, thought and knowledge, the philosopher would gain the advantage of remaining within the immanence of familiar sites, intellectual ones in this case.

Levinas then establishes a series of equivalencies: "To be myself, atheistic, at home, separated, happy, and created—these are all synonyms."[22] Enjoyment liberates the ego from being overwhelmed by the *there is*, it suspends the horror of depersonalization and installs every person in a world that has become *his* world. That happiness is atheistic since it is self-sufficient, does not yearn for God, and is visited by no desire for the Wholly Other. But, according to Levinas, that does not entail vanity or pride; on the contrary, he says, "it is a great glory for God to have created a being capable of seeking him or hearing him from afar, on the basis of separation, on the basis of atheism."[23] It is also a risk, however, that of forgetting God in the enjoyment of things and in the intoxication of a rationality and a knowledge that disregard or scorn any question relating to their limits.

On this last point, Levinas clearly shares Kant's wisdom about the limits imparted to ontological reason. Like Kant, he is mistrustful of the enthusiasm—the inebriation, as he prefers to call it—characteristic of the person devoted to his or her chimera who has forgotten the limits assigned by reason to the possibility of knowing. Like Kant as well, Levinas believes that these limits do not so much constitute a failure as pave the way for a moral philosophy not dependent on ontology. In addition, he explicitly recognizes that he feels "particularly close" to "Kant's practical philosophy."[24] Nevertheless, in the case of happiness, although both Kant and Levinas link it to the subject's egoism and refuse to put it at the center of moral preoccupations, though without condemning it, they do not evaluate its persistence in the same way. Hence, Kant's reflection on the worthiness to be happy by means of morality justifies the concern for happiness to the point of making it an ultimate hope, whereas Levinas announces its postponement as a result of the ethical uneasiness caused by the weakness of the other but without postulating such a hope.

No happy installation in being can be guaranteed to last. The presentiment of the fragility of being and the observation of the tragedies that undermine and destroy it trouble one's self-assurance and good conscience. That is why, according to Kant, one must stand firm, whatever the empirical conditions of life, and not base ethics on the desire to be happy. That does not mean giving up happiness but rather introducing a new parameter into self-reflection: that of *worthiness*. The moral subject becomes worthy of happiness, even if the circumstances of its life belie that hope. But, Levinas objects, must not the quest for that worthiness be subordinated to the uneasiness that gets hold of a person, without remission, it seems, when confronted with the vulnerability of that person's neighbor?

Worthiness and Ethical Uneasiness

Virtue, says Kant, makes one *worthy* of being happy. It is therefore "the *supreme condition* of whatever can even seem to us desirable and hence of all our pursuit of happiness."[25] Yet worthiness is valid only for reasonable beings who obey the moral laws that they set for themselves, since it entails the impossibility of measuring and establishing an equivalence or a price. The things that satisfy one's needs and inclinations have a *market price;* those corresponding to taste, a *fancy price,* "but that which constitutes the condition under which alone something can be an end in itself has not merely a relative worth, that is, a price, but an inner worth, that is, *dignity.*"[26]

A human being's qualities—his working abilities, his humor, his imagination, even his speculative intelligence—have a price, but they do not constitute his dignity (or worthiness) since they are relative to an end that remains external to them. Conversely, "fidelity in promises and benevolence from basic principles (not from instinct) have an inner worth":[27] the dignity of a human being depends on it. Nothing replaces these qualities, whose value does not come from the result—to keep one's promise can lead to unhappiness—but from the intention, that is, from the maxim of the will in accord with moral law, regardless of one's feelings—one may have no confidence in the person toward whom one keeps one's promise—and regardless of one's interests.

What, then, does "becoming worthy of being happy" through virtue really mean? It appears that, at first, Kant seeks to eliminate all justification of happiness on the basis of the qualities distributed unequally to human beings and the various accomplishment these qualities allow. The high intelligence of one person and the abilities of another may lead them to the conditions for a happy life, but that does not mean they are worthy of happiness. The potential public usefulness of their qualities may, to be sure, elicit admiration and recognition, even approval, but that does not make them any more worthy of happiness. Kant rejects the idea that the end pursued in the exercise of certain qualities—even consequences favorable for an entire society, or for humanity as a whole—can ever determine one's worthiness to be happy. "Dignity" or "worthiness" designates the capacity for each person to be the author of moral law, and the "worthiness to be happy" designates the use of that capacity—and only it.

Therefore, the results obtained by virtue of other capacities, for the good of society, for example, are lacking the sole claim necessary to make the person *worthy* of being happy. Nevertheless, when one practices virtue, one is not seeking happiness; otherwise, one would lose, precisely, that worthiness to be happy. One would behave "morally" with an aim external to duty, and, as a result, one would not behave morally and would lose that worthiness. Behavior that imitates moral conduct for motives external to morality—that is, legality—does not make one worthy of happiness, even if that behavior benefits others, even if it apparently makes others happy. And the quest for happiness for its own sake makes a person lose that worthiness to an even greater extent: "The more a cultivated reason purposely occupies itself with the enjoyment of life and with happiness, so much the further does one get away from true satisfaction."[28] That is why Kant asserts that "mere worthiness to be happy, even without the motive of participating in this happiness, can interest us in itself."[29] For the virtuous man, the obligation of the law suffices; he does not need an external motivation and he does not say to himself, "I am going to become worthy of happiness by obeying the law." If he did so, he would immediately lose that worthiness. The worthiness to be happy does not imply a happy life. The virtuous man can—and often must—do without the recognition of others, and he may even be despised or mistreated. In addition, that worthiness, in order to maintain its purity, also seems to require that it remain unknown to oneself.

Kant nevertheless links it to the idea of a kingdom of ends, the realization of which is dependent on obedience to moral law by all reasonable beings. That kingdom—or that systematic connection "of rational beings . . . through the giving of their own laws"—constitutes itself on the basis of everyone's obedience to the moral law, without exception. But since the fact that one follows that maxim in no way means that the other does the same, that kingdom is endlessly postponed, and the moral subject cannot hope that it will come about, finally favoring "his expectation of happiness."[30] That really means that such an expectation does not disappear in the virtuous man, even though his conduct is not dependent on it. To be sure, he may regret that his respect for moral maxims does not lead others to respect them as well, but he cannot subordinate his own morality to that of others toward him; if he does, he will be immoral. Kant—and Levinas after him—thus does not require any reciprocity when virtue is at stake: it is always up to oneself to begin. That is the only hope if the very idea of a kingdom of ends is not to disappear from people's minds, in spite of its being constantly contradicted; or, more modestly, in Levinas's words, if a little good is to come about in the world.

The worthiness to be happy and the expectation of happiness do not correspond. The coincidence of virtue and happiness remain in suspense, despite the denials of ethical systems—Stoicism or Epicureanism—that seek to conceive of an identity or an analytical connection between the two. Kant does not share their opinion: despite their insight, he says, these philosophies did not see that "happiness and morality are two specifically quite *different elements* of the highest good and that, accordingly, their combination cannot be cognized *analytically*."[31] That is why, in the absence of the highest good, that is, during this life, the virtuous man has little chance of being happy—contrary to the allegations of the Stoics or Epicureans—and that contradiction remains a torment to the mind but also, as Kant teaches, an opening toward a move beyond ontological reason.[32]

Although Levinas also thinks that, during this life, the virtuous man's happiness is not the order of the day, his argument differs from Kant's propositions. He says that there is no analytical connection between virtue and happiness, not because the maxims of ethics and those of personal happiness differ in principle, but because an inextinguishable uneasiness inhabits the moral subject.

Uneasiness often catches one off guard, but it sometimes takes the form of a keen consciousness of the fragility of happiness. Levinas remarks that those who experienced the concentration camps and Jewish clandestinity during World War II were forced to admit the relativity—not the derisiveness—of everything that appeared indispensable: "One can do without meals and rest, smiles and personal effects, decency and the right to lock one's bedroom door, paintings and friends."[33] But it is not a question of giving these things up for lost as if they were goods without importance. On the contrary, especially during the darkest, most uncivilized hours, the moral subject must feel responsible for the peacetime values now being held in scorn. Yet that does not suffice: even in the absence of any threat hanging over the subject and its family, that subject cannot enjoy its happiness in peace. In fact, the encounter with the extreme fragility of the other's face constantly suspends its enjoyment of life and, against its will, calls into question its egoism and atheism.

Before the face, the very idea of a connection between virtue and happiness veers toward impropriety. Unless one refuses to hear the appeal when confronted with its weakness, no one can be content to let his herds graze like Abraham, to dig his wells like Isaac, to build his house like Jacob, or to cultivate his garden like Epicurus.[34] The simple, happy life is destroyed by the heteronomy of the face: it is that face—and not the concern for the moral law proper to an autonomous subject—that accuses the subject, in its egoism and atheism, of confusing the installation in being with the good.

Does that mean, as Blanchot suggests, that the encounter with the face substitutes anxiety about the happiness of the other for concern about one's own happiness, in such a way that no moral subject can ever wish to be happy? According to Blanchot, Levinas's philosophy is the equivalent of saying: "Let happiness come to everyone, provided that, through that wish, I be excluded from it."[35] Worrying about the other would not only require that the subject renounce its own happiness in order to help the other and work toward *the other's* happiness; it would also imply that the subject wishes to be excluded from any eventual happiness. That interpretation is questionable, however. In its radicality and its justification of one's own suffering, it goes even further than these words by Dostoevsky: "Let my life go, if only my dear ones may be happy."[36] It seems to misunderstand the meaning of the relinquishment produced by the encounter with the face.

In fact, the heteronomy of the face does not in itself nullify the desire for happiness but rather awakens the subject to a different perspective on the happy life. The subject is reminded, through that heteronomy, of what one is almost always unaware of when one is enjoying life: the fact that the cost of happiness is the other's unhappiness. To enjoy life entails exploiting the other and silently consenting to the injustice he suffers, or, even more decisively, usurping the other's place. According to Levinas, a happiness that is blind and deaf to the suffering of the world is punishable not because it contradicts moral law, but because it rejects the immemorial debt of election, even in the case of a simple and wise happiness that, apparently, does no harm to anyone. Does not that debt go well beyond the sins actually committed? "Saints, monks, and intellectuals in their ivory towers are punishable just men,"[37] Levinas observes. Do not personal perfection and the happiness of acquiring knowledge—bliss itself according to an entire philosophical tradition—stem, despite their nobility, from a quest for personal salvation and, as a result, from a form of egoism? Obviously, to make such a claim would be to introduce a ferment of noncontingent worry in the so-called happy life, a ferment that seems therefore to bar it forever, if, in the Kantian manner, one defines happiness as "a rational being's consciousness of the agreeableness of life uninterruptedly accompanying his whole existence."[38] But does that really entail a decision to exclude oneself from any happy life on the pretext of morality, or does it entail awakening to a different idea of happiness? In fact, if, according to Levinas, even the serenity of meditation or retreat cannot make one's own rights take precedence—if that serenity still has an immoral aspect—in the face of the suffering of the other, it is not because of masochistic self-satisfaction but out of concern to awaken the subject to certain imperatives, which he calls "happy commitment" or "austere happiness without self-satisfaction." That happiness constitutes all the nobility of the human subject solicited by the suffering of its neighbor, all the nobility of its election.[39]

The face-to-face encounter contests the ego's happy appropriation of the world and opens an irreducible breach in its present. Diachrony intrudes in the existence of the subject exposed to the order of the face; it postpones the subject's tranquility and obliges it to experience a temporality shaken by the intrusion of the immemorial. The subject no longer considers remaining within itself, even though no memory of having made a commitment of responsibility comes to it. Like Abraham, the ego is obliged to get out of its country and away from its kindred (Genesis 12:1), without knowing or foreseeing the hazards along the path to which its response fates it. It is solicited by "the goodness of the diachronic"[40] and has no time to critically examine its commitment. Confronted with the face, it loses its innocence of being and its right to enjoy in all serenity the shade of its vineyard and fig tree. Is not that humble place also a "usurpation of the places that belong to the other man already oppressed and starved by me"?[41]

Does not Levinas issue a verdict against happiness with no possibility of appeal? Does he not add that the face, in the trace of the Absent One who beseeches me, troubling my separate and atheistic happiness, directs me toward an endless responsibility? "There is no end, no final term. The Desire of the absolutely Other will not be satisfied like a need and vanish into happiness."[42] The God evoked in this passage—the God of Exodus 33—the God Moses cannot see but who transmits the Tables of the Witness *(luhot haEdut)* to him, creates the hole of Desire without filling it and without ensuring any happy outcome. But why does not this God "transcendent even unto Absence" provide happiness? Because, Levinas says, he obliges everyone to be good. And that obligation is "better than the goods to be received,"[43] since, thanks to it, man awakens to an idea of happiness different from that of a full satisfaction of his desires.

To conceive the possibility of a moral act or of human responsibility toward the face, Kant and Levinas argue for a postponement of happiness. Nevertheless, in maintaining that the subject can make itself worthy of being happy—though it rarely is so in its lifetime—does Kant not offer a glimpse of hope for the human being? In spite of the constant and cruel disappointments of history—and also because of them—must not the moral subject postulate that virtue and happiness—the highest good—will one day be brought together? Does Levinas not share that hope? Like Kant, he describes the moral life without letting the subject catch a glimpse of the slightest hope of reward for its time. On the contrary, he insists on the necessity of responding to the appeal of the face—in the trace of the hidden God—without expecting consolation or remission for one's trouble. But does the absence of postulates on practical reason in Levinas mean that he is definitively abandoning the notion of a union of virtue and happiness?

Postponement and Hope

Virtue, inasmuch as it makes us worthy of being happy, is the *supreme good.* Nevertheless, without happiness, is it the complete and ultimate object of hope? Kant does not think so: "Even in the judgment of an impartial reason, which regards a person in the world generally as an end in itself,"[44] happiness, he says, must necessarily accompany virtue. Such is precisely the highest good. For how could a reasonable being in his perfection, endowed with omnipotence—to posit the thinking of that being as a hypothetical—wish for a person to be truly worthy of happiness and yet not participate in it? Would it not be contradictory if that being's power did not obey his holy will?

The highest good thus entails two determinations—virtue *and* happiness—which do not logically imply each other, contrary to the assertions of the ancient Greek schools such as Stoicism or Epicurianism. As a result, although the connection between these two determinations must be firmly maintained, that connection, in spite of everything, is not an immanent relationship of cause and effect. The virtuous man suffers, the wicked man is spared, and, to claim happiness, it is not enough to experience an inner contentment due to consciousness of one's virtue in the face of private or collective misfortunes—while often refusing to call them such—to consider oneself happy. All serenity is fragile because it is never truly free of sensibility, and the unvarying intellectual contentment procured by the awareness that moral law is independent of one's propensities is only an approximation of happiness. Kant concludes that a human being cannot obtain the highest good on his own, even though it is required by practical reason. He can and must simply work to become worthy of being happy.

The expectation of "happiness in precise proportion to virtue"[45] is justified as far as reason is concerned, even though a person cannot observe the realization of that happiness. "The whole object of practical reason," namely, the highest good, does not constitute an object of knowledge—the limits of pure theoretical reason remain in force—but the imperative for its realization lies within practical reason. It is truly practical reason that asks "to add to the aim of its goal so that it may be complete what it excluded from its principle so that it might be pure."[46] And what it excluded was happiness. Kant then concludes that the connection between virtue and happiness is transcendent in nature and, from that point of view, he deduces two indispensable postulates. These do not entail a return in force of "speculative excess": they do not produce knowledge and are even alien to any gnosis—but they give hope. Their sobriety, so unamenable to dreams of paradise or hell, even though they invite us to conceive of something beyond time, avoids divagations and enthusiasm. These postulates emanate from reason—from pure practical reason—and not from the imagination. They do not entail extending one's knowledge into the realm of the supersensible—the critique of the transcendental illusion remains unassailable—but they provide a practical viewpoint on or significance to that realm.

Levinas considers at length that feature of Kantianism in particular: "There is a *hope*," he remarks, "a world accessible to a hope. In existence determined by death, in that epic story of being, there are things that are not included in that epic, significations that cannot be reduced to being. That hope can have no theoretical response, but it is a motivation in itself. That hope occurs in time and, in time, goes beyond time."[47] The Kantian subject, despite its finitude, would thus conceive of the imperative for a signification other than the theoretical access to the being of phenomena, of a signification surpassing the limits imposed on its finitude, namely, time and space.

To respond to the rational imperative of the highest good—or to that a priori hope inherent in finite reason—Kant introduces two postulates: the immortality of the soul and the existence of God. These prove nothing regarding the soul's ultimate fate or the existence of God, but they provide a glimpse of a relation with the infinite that is irreducible to any knowledge. "The sense of that hope in despair does not undo the nothingness of death; it allots to death a signification other than that which it draws from the nothingness of being. That hope does not respond to a need to survive."[48] What is at issue, then?

The moral subject's will, dependent on its sensibility, never achieves holiness but can only move toward it. Human finitude excludes the possibility that the human being's will could conform perfectly to the law, even though that conformity is the determining condition for the highest good. To resolve that contradiction, Kant introduces the idea of an *infinite progress* toward holiness, which ultimately supposes the immortality of the soul. A human being's consciousness of his moral progress in life allows him "hope for a further uninterrupted continuance of this progress, however long his existence may last, even beyond this life . . . in the endlessness of his duration."[49] The postulate of the soul's immortality does not presuppose any particular thesis on the nature of the soul, but simply expresses a free subject's hope that it will participate, beyond time, in the highest good, even if the kingdom of ends for which it worked during its life has not yet come into being. Levinas comments that it is as if, "in the human, and behind the *Sein zum Tode*, the story of a hope of immortality were reaching its climax, a hope not measured by length of time, by perpetuity, and which, as a result, has in this 'forever' a temporality *other* than that of being-unto-death."[50]

Since the connection between virtue and happiness is transcendent, Kant must nevertheless postulate an adequate cause that reconciles, in a proportionate manner, the worthiness of the person and happiness. The existence of God is thus necessarily linked to the possibility of the highest good. "It is morally necessary to assume the existence of God."[51] God is the origin of the synthesis—which is beyond human powers—between virtue and happiness. God, who had no role to play in Kantian ethics—otherwise, there would have been an infringement on the principle of autonomy—imposes himself with the moral act, when a human being wishes, and legitimately so according to Kant, his virtue to be in harmony with happiness. The moral law leads to God; it does not depend on him. It supposes a God who satisfies the demands of practical reason, a God who, in his timeless intuition and supreme intelligence, observes the progress of a person in this life and beyond death and considers it equivalent to perfection. That God, in his omnipotence, thus allows for a proper proportion between well-being and virtue to be finally established beyond time. That God's holy will, then, is in harmony with his omnipotence, since these are the two attributes Kant uses to evoke him. That "God looks, and gives nothing. Even his gaze does not constitute a gift, since it resides solely in his eternal nature and not in his love."[52] But, despite that silence regarding love and grace, Kant links the kingdom of God to Christianity. He maintains that Christian doctrine provides a concept of the highest good "which *alone* satisfies the strictest demand of practical reason."[53]

Ethics is the rational condition for happiness; religion adds the hope of obtaining it but, Kant insists, moral conduct cannot be subordinated to that hope without destroying itself. It is not in vain that a human being becomes worthy of being happy; nevertheless, morality would remain intact even without that outcome. A human being has the freedom to become independent from sensibility and to act in accordance with maxims that conform to moral law but, in order for his will to be entirely in tune with that freedom, he needs time and even something beyond time. He must—and can—progress indefinitely. That is why that freedom, to complete its work—to make a human being worthy of happiness through virtue—opens on the hope of the immortality of the soul and the existence of God.

In this analysis, Levinas points out, in particular, how practical reason puts an end to the contradictions of speculative reason. Does Kant not acknowledge that his postulates make it possible to resolve concepts that speculative reason left in suspense? Practical reason confers existence on "ideas that were only regulating principles for speculative reason"; it posits "freedom, God, and immortality beyond experience."[54] In metaphysics, then, the task of supplementing the lack of intellectual intuition in man falls to practical reason but with one limitation: the moral subject knows of the existence of God, of the soul, and of freedom only *"from the practical point of view."* It does not know them as they are in themselves. The field of speculative knowledge remains welded to the limitations of sensible intuition. Ethics opens on an order of signification independent of ontological rationality and makes it possible to imagine a rationality of transcendence. It does not extend the domain of knowledge but teaches that there are significations that exceed it.

Nevertheless, despite that proximity to Kantian philosophy, does Levinas not seem to disregard the hope that, under God's eyes, moral progress—and the worthiness to be happy—will finally be recognized? If the Desire for God (or of God) is not extinguished in happiness, as he says, what does it mean that the psyche opens onto the infinite?

Levinas describes it this way: an "opening of dis-inter-estedness, of sacrifice without reward, of discourse without response or echo, which 'trust in God' and prayer must have the strength to achieve. An opening of the self to the infinite, which no corroboration can match, which proves itself only by its own excessiveness."[55] That opening—or that awakening of the psyche—is not subordinate to anything other than itself. It expects no reward; it does not hope that a God will grant it—proportionate to its progress—the happiness of which it has made a person worthy. Or, more exactly, it is in itself that reward or that "austere happiness" characteristic of the psyche's election by the infinite.

Is not the Kantian idea of a synthetic connection between virtue and happiness thereby called into question? Does Levinas not argue for an analytical connection that nevertheless in no way resembles the "inner fortress" of Stoicism and in no way guarantees man against suffering or persecution? That connection implies that happiness should be dissociated from the egoistic enjoyment of life by a separate and atheistic self that is at home in the world and inclined to relate everything to itself. The happiness of election is more than an installation; it resembles a constant advance toward the most Desirable. That is, in fact, the meaning of the word "happiness" in Hebrew: *Ashrei* denotes the leg of a journey (*asher* means "to walk"). *Ashrei*, happy, is he who meditates on the law of the Lord

(Psalm 1:2) and who is undefiled in the way (Psalm 119:1), even if an outward look at his life perceives only its pain.

For the Jewish tradition, happiness is experienced as a "walk" toward God; the study of his Word and obedience to what it prescribes constitute its highest point. The Zohar (243a) teaches: "Happy the portion of he who devotes himself to the Torah as he ought, happy is he in this world and in the world to come." To study "as one ought" does not mean to bow to the norms of truth but to struggle to find new sense in the words (*hidush*) so that they might live and allow others to live. To study is happiness because it is a walk that transfigures one's days and because it does not merely hearken back to the same thing. In its vivid language, the Zohar (243a) assures us that such happiness is transmitted to God, who goes to the Garden of Eden to meet with the upright. He then produces the written and spoken words of his Torah, whose sense has grown thanks to every person's study and life. He looks at these people and takes delight. That look and that happiness of God represent the highest reward for a human life.

Levinas meditates on the worth of that reflection on happiness, often mocked by those who want to consider themselves liberated from the sense of the "to-God" [*à-Dieu*] for which diachronic time is the only path. These people even condemned the "to-God" for its incapacity to commit everyone to fight for actual happiness on earth and for a real share of it. The attention to the weakness of the face resembles the attention to the fragility of the verse. Are not both the face and the verse located in the trace of the Absent One, and do they not await, from the very core of their powerlessness, a subject that will rise up and respond, that is, one that will walk toward the Absent One? The ethical impossibility of persevering in the enjoyment of life when confronted with the face and the impossibility of haughtily closing one's mind and fixing on dogmas when confronted with the Book awaken the mind and prevent slumber. That awakening—or that happiness—postpones all egoism; it troubles the subject and keeps it on the alert, and the subject thereby discovers the diachrony of sense at the very instant that it suspends the subject's reassuring attachment to an essence, a possession, or an enjoyment.

Some raise an objection to Levinas: is that really happiness, after all? And in any case, what is the value of that awakening in the face of the dereliction and barbarism of the twentieth century, and why call that great austerity happy? Is it not a mockery and an indecency to conceive of happiness in that way, given the countless personal and collective tragedies that continue to aggrieve people's hearts? In addition, does not this happiness, on the pretext of ethical awakening, run the risk of sanctioning the inability to struggle effectively—by means of adequate political institutions, for example—against man's hatred of and terrifying violence against other men?

Such an indictment misunderstands the sense of "austere happiness" glimpsed by Levinas. He does not seek to counsel patience to the persecuted or to console the afflicted with the idea of a promise whose fulfillment is still to come, in this world or in the next, and even less does he seek to deny the need for just political institutions. The God who comes to mind at the instant a man, overwhelmed by the weakness of the face, sees his enjoyment-in-being called into question does not console him of his unhappiness since it requires him to respond to it, by political means if need be. These means become necessary with the appearance of the third party, but—to remain just—they must never imply that the happiness of a single face should be sacrificed for the sake of an abstract cause, since even "the happiness of humanity does not justify the unhappiness of the individual."[56] That hidden God, whose meaning awakens in the psyche of the responsible subject, does not give any transcendent justification to suffering that would lighten the subject's task. He does not promise compensation or reward by virtue of the imminent or distant advent of his Kingdom. He prefers to elect the subject so that it will respond—in its uniqueness as a person—to the weakness of creatures. God, says Levinas, assumes meaning beyond theological systems "without promising anything,"[57] He inspires an uneasiness in the subject that paralyzes its *conatus essendi* and makes its unimpeachable responsibility toward the other emerge. Yet, paradoxically in terms of an egoistic conception of happiness—as the fulfillment of my desires and aspirations—it is precisely at the instant of that awakening, always on the brink of a new awakening, that another way of envisioning happiness comes into being. Election makes the subject patiently breathe in harmony with the source of all life. The subject's response to the appeal, lurking in the most secret part of the face's weakness, through its own existence as a unique and irreplaceable subject, awakens it to the sense of that "austere happiness." That response allows the subject to approach the Infinite to which the face bears witness, even though no theoretical knowledge is ever commensurate with its witness. And that proximity to the Infinite is the loftiest hope.

In the tradition of Kant, then, Levinas dissociates happiness and knowledge but without conceding the Kantian idea of a moral possibility of "making oneself worthy of happiness." Since, according to him, the loftiest idea—that of God—always risks being retracted, the desire for God is not consumed or fulfilled in the happiness of a knowledge or a contemplation, and, of course, even less in a possession or a coincidence. It is experienced as an obligation to serve, in proximity to the Infinite, in a disinterested manner without intentionality, where the sense of distance increases as one draws closer. In ethics, that experience is expressed in the idea that the subject, open and vulnerable to the other, is never discharged of its debt, since its response increases its sense of responsibility. Yet it is precisely in that way that a person, unhappy to be driven back into himself, finds he is "sobered up from his inebriation in being" and obtains salvation. The absence of the "He" who solicits a person through the face—or through the verse—is revealed to be the mode of His most precious proximity. In responding to the weakness of the face, the subject is liberated from self-imprisonment; it discovers that the Infinite dwells within it. But the happiness of that discovery is not added synthetically, as it is in Kant, to the virtue of a reasonable and finite subject. In this life, that happiness, despite the barbarous and desperate hours of the twentieth century, is inseparable from the very practice of responsibility.

As we reach the end of this philosophical reflection, let us consider the meaning of the relationship Kant and Levinas establish between ethics and religion.

e i g h t   **Ethics and Religion**

V ery early on, Kant understood virtue as obedience to the law, rejecting the idea that it depends on any fear of punishment in the
next world. "Is it not rather the case that actions will one day be
rewarded because they are good and virtuous in themselves?" In fact, experience shows that many people, in spite of their religious convictions,
give themselves over to vice without any great anxiety, simply working
craftily to shelter themselves from the consequences of their acts. A "nobly
constituted" soul, for its part, has difficulty tolerating the idea that everything is over upon death and hopes for a future life. Kant concludes that
it is upon the feelings of such a soul that we, justifiably, ground "the expectation of a future world" rather than claim to incite moral behavior by
maintaining hope in another world. "Such is also the character of the *moral
faith:* its simplicity is able to dispense with many of the subtleties of
sophistry; it alone and uniquely is fitting to man in whatever situation he
finds himself, for it leads him directly to his true purposes."[1]

Kant remained loyal to that *moral faith*. He asked educators "not to present the moral catechism mixed with the religious one (to combine them into one) or, what is worse yet, to have it follow upon the religious catechism," but always to set it out first. Otherwise, "the religion that [the child] afterwards professes will be nothing but hypocrisy; he will acknowledge duties out of fear and feign an interest in them that is not in his heart."[2] In no case can moral behavior be dependent on a belief in God, since that would be the equivalent of founding it on heteronomy, which, de facto and de jure, would bankrupt it. The idea of God as a supreme moral being is not at the foundation of ethics, but is rather deduced from it, as the rational hope linked to the imperative of the highest good.[3]

Nevertheless, Kant's texts make frequent allusions to Christianity, and he does not hesitate to give a privileged status to that religion and to speak of Christ as a model for pure moral intention. We ought therefore to consider the meaning and import of these references in terms of what he calls "moral faith." That faith, to be sure, does not presuppose any adherence to a credo, since Kant rejects the dogma and authority of so-called holy history, but one must wonder, in spite of everything, why he judges the use of that expression legitimate. Why is practical reason the bearer of a faith?

Although Levinas also thinks that God is not at the foundation of ethics, he maintains that the idea of God comes to the subject's mind at the instant it responds to the weakness of its neighbor. The two philosophers nevertheless describe the moral act without appealing to the presence—and even less to the power—of God. On the contrary, it is against the background of his absence that ethics comes about. But what does that absence mean? Can it have the same meaning for a philosopher like Kant, so concerned with autonomy that he decrees any trace of heteronomy in human conduct immoral, and for Levinas, who, by contrast, intends to rehabilitate a certain idea of heteronomy, and precisely on the ethical plane?

As a result, do Levinas's references to Judaism have a role similar to those Kant makes to Christianity? To what order do they belong if it is true that Levinas does not wish to found his ethics on them and intends to present an argument whose scope concerns the humanity—and not the Jewishness—of a man?

Although both philosophers, inspired by their reading of the Scriptures, make a place for the idea of holiness in their ethics, does that entail, finally, and for both of them, an imperative that makes ethics and religion ultimately, but not foundationally, interdependent?

The Absence of God

Kant says that the source of the concept of the good cannot lie in the will of God without bringing about the ruin of autonomy and, thereby, of ethics. Nevertheless, in the few pages in which he reflects on man's practical fate in relation to his theoretical faculties, he radicalizes that view, since he asserts that God must not be present to the world, in order that the subject may have the capacity to behave morally. It is satisfying, he says, that nature, which some have seen as a *cruel stepmother*, does not allow them to perceive God. It is good that human finitude bars access to the knowledge of God and to proofs of his existence. In fact, says Kant, the opposite *hypothesis* would lead to disastrous consequences for man, and would even destroy the value of the world in God's eyes.

Suppose, therefore, that nature had presented man with the enlightenment he lacks and that he possessed a metaphysical knowledge: *"God and eternity with their awful majesty* would stand unceasingly *before our eyes. . . .* Transgression of the law would, no doubt, be avoided, what is commanded would be done; but . . . most actions conforming to the law would be done from fear, only a few from hope, and none at all from duty." Man would lose all freedom: his behavior would be "changed into mere mechanism in which, as in a puppet show, everything would *gesticulate* well but there would be *no life* in the figures." In losing his moral value, the person—and the world itself as a result—would also lose any value "in the eyes of supreme wisdom."[4]

Clearly, the idea of God implicit in these lines turns out to be very disputable. It is "the terrifying eternity of Haller" and "the terrifying God of Jakob Böhme in all his formidable majesty that appear, and, as a result, men are no longer anything but Vaucanson's marionettes." There is no trace of mercy in God, and no hint of his love emerges from these lines. But must one conclude that this passage is "horrid" and enigmatic and go on to suggest that Kant has *"perhaps* gone too far in his suppositions"?[5]

Since freedom constitutes the cornerstone of his ethics, Kant of course intends to avoid determinism and fatalism. But he also rejects the idea that

God should be present in the world—in nature or in history—in such a way that a human being would act out of fear of that presence, or in the expectation of some reward, rather than out of respect for moral law, in such a way, that is, that he would lose all his freedom. According to Kant, if one knew and perceived the power of God, one could no longer act out of good will but would be in the grip of fear. As a result, it is a positive thing that God should show himself "neither in the nature of the physicists nor in history."[6] To be sure, God's greatness is manifest in the starry heaven, but nature—which supposedly responds only to the questions a presiding judge asks it[7]—remains silent on the subject. In fact, according to Kant, no correct philosophical argument makes it possible to say that God intervenes in history to punish or to correct the course of things. The disaster of Lisbonne in 1755 was not, as was sometimes maintained at the time, a punishment or a warning. "There is not sufficient material there to construct an antinomy of pure reason."[8] Man can no more prove the existence of God by referring to the course of historical events than he can by observing nature. Kant always keeps human finitude present in his mind, but that also allows him, from his perspective, to save freedom and ethics.

Ethics depends solely on reason. And reason does not need God or the support of an institution such as the Church to make its voice heard. In not recognizing as legitimate any authority external to itself, it also rejects the idea that norms of behavior—moral, social, or religious—should be dictated to it in the name of Scripture. Reason can, to be sure, make use of a biblical passage and seek to give a meaning to it that will improve human beings, but the verse in itself does not have any authority. Apart from that use, in fact, the Bible holds little interest for Kant, who assimilates the study of its narrative passages to "a barren addition to our historical cognition."[9]

In ethics, Kant turns to the logic of a simple principle: "Each must, on the contrary, so conduct himself as if everything depended on him. Only on this condition may he hope that a higher wisdom will provide the fulfillment of his well-intentioned effort."[10] But that hope can never become a motivation without leading to the destruction of ethics: one must not turn to God when acting out of good will but, on the contrary, one must behave as if he did not exist, as if he had abandoned human beings, and consult only the voice of reason in oneself. "In allowing us to conceive of (but to suspend theoretically) the existence of God, freedom, or the immortality of the soul, the union of virtue and happiness, the concept of a 'postulate' of practical reason ensures that radical dissociation and, in sum, assumes the rational and philosophical responsibility, the consequence *here below, in experience*, of that abandonment."[11] Yet if that is the only truly moral behavior for a Christian, this also means that "Christianity cannot respond to its moral vocation, or ethics to its Christian vocation, except by enduring the death of God here below, in phenomenal history, and well beyond the figures of the Passion." Would Christianity then be "the death of God, which Kant thus announces and recalls to Enlightenment modernity"?[12]

Every trace of exteriority and alterity—God, the Book, nature—is banished from the mind of the Kantian subject considering its duty. The time of moral action requires the solitude of good will, since the principle of universality that founds it is not transmitted through worship, study, or contemplation shared with others. Atheists and believers are equally invited, by the reason within them, to do their duty in a solitary manner. They could hardly encourage one another to come to morality, since they would thereby run the risk of exerting an influence over one another, raising the danger of heteronomy. In addition, the believer faces the great difficulty of having to chase from his mind any fear of God and any hope in him in order to act in total purity, that is, morally.

All the same, can an equivalence between that absent God of ethics and the death of God be legitimately established? Kant's description of autonomy does not entail an emancipation from all antecedence; it is equivalent, de facto and de jure, to the unconditional obedience by a *finite* and *receptive* subject to moral law as a *fact* of reason within itself. Ethics shows that the intelligence "is absolutely master of itself within its limits," and that "reason does not invent its objective principles but appropriates them in obedience." But does not that description of the moral conscience fundamentally resemble that of "self-consciousness *before God*"?[13] Whether the moral subject calls itself a Christian or an atheist—at the instant of its living obedience to the law—in spite of its solitude it experiences no abandonment or dereliction. It *knows* that it *itself* is entirely solicited by the "voice" of reason within it, wholly called upon to make its good will a holy will. Yet that "knowledge" is not a theoretical knowledge—the limits on speculation remain in force—and Kant does not hesitate to call it "belief" or even "moral faith."

Practical knowledge is equivalent to the imperative and disinterested petition of an inner duty that does not depend on the empirical state of the world and of the person. The desolation of one and the bliss of the other, war and peace, are not taken into account as a justification or as an excuse when ethics is at issue. What one must do is dictated to one unconditionally; one can do nothing but comply since, in such circumstances, the introduction of external and contingent variables that supposedly dispute the validity of one's duty destroy ethics. But why does Kant call that duty "moral faith"?

Such a "faith" implies no adherence to irrational, indemonstrable, but appealing propositions; it pushes aside the imagination and does not yield to any temptation to attract God's benefits to oneself by virtue of obedience to his Word. In ethics, Kant repudiates any "word" whose source does not lie in reason. Nevertheless, the term "faith" remains pertinent, since no theoretical knowledge grounds moral obligation; the latter is imposed, and speculation has no right to examine its protocols and expectations. That obligation thus implies a move toward something "otherwise than knowledge." "The loss of its hitherto imagined possession that speculative reason must suffer"—the demonstration of the existence of God, for example—also entails the impossibility of deriving ethics from a theology or an ontology. Because of human finitude, the absence of transcendent intuition deprives man of any possibility of proving God—via ontological, cosmological, or transcendental means—and leads Kant to denounce the imposture of metaphysical dogmatism and to "make a place for *faith*."[14] And that place is very precisely the place of ethics. It seems that if, as Derrida maintains, Kant announces and recalls the "death of God" to modernity, that death is only speculative in nature. Does it not pave the way, this time in a positive manner, for an absolute moral imperative pure of any compromise with the ideas people form of God? Does not that imperative, because it resists the indictment of theoretical reason, exceed the limits of speculation and reveal—on the practical plane—the excess, indemonstrable as such, on which man *lives*? It is an excess, or a sense beyond being, or even a philosophy of the infinite despite finitude, that, remarkably according to Levinas, constitutes the "corollary of an ethics."

In any case, it is within that interpretive tradition that Levinas reflects on Kantian ethics and considers the enigma of a transcendence that to many appears to be absent or to have vanished. In this world, God does not reward virtue. He does not punish vice, as the human hope for consolation or justice would like, and the all-too-tragic spectacle of history lends credence to "strange rumors about the death of God or the emptiness of heaven."[15]

If, contrary to Kantian teaching, the moral imperative imposes itself on the subject in a heteronomous manner when it is confronted with the vulnerability of an always unique and irreplaceable face that awakens it to its preoriginary and unimpeachable responsibility, does that mean that, for Levinas, ethics is backed by a theology? According to Levinas, encountering the face is the equivalent of hearing the biblical imperative "Thou shalt not kill," and we have to wonder if that encounter is imaginable as such outside the framework of a philosophy stemming from the Bible.

Levinas's *philosophical* approach presupposes no proof of the existence of God and implies no elaboration of any theology, positive or negative. The traditional attributes of power and justice, which Kant retains in his postulate regarding the existence of God, do not appear in Levinas's work. He does not develop any discourse *on* God and does not speak *of* him; nevertheless he evokes the *to-God* as an indispensable and unimpeachable corollary of a reflection on meaning. "We do not think that the meaningful can do without God, nor that the idea of being or of the being of beings *[l'être de l'étant]* can take its place, to lead significations toward the unity of sense, without which there is no sense." But he also maintains that "it is the analysis of sense that must deliver the notion of God that that sense conceals"[16] and not the reverse.

Men, in their weakness and their pride, habitually form an idea or an image of a God who supposedly responds to their needs or their distress, who is ready to intervene in nature and history to save the best men and to punish the wicked. By virtue of that idea or that image—which places God within "a system of reciprocities and exchanges" wherein the man preoccupied with himself constitutes the center—men also denounce his absence, since life almost always disappoints such an expectation from God. That, according to Levinas, is the origin of the "famous paradox, which has become commonplace, regarding the death of God."[17] But, he asks immediately, is not the status of that vanished God problematic? Is not that God dependent on a religion that the person demands "for himself"? And, as a result, does the disappearance of that religion and of that God, in view of human dereliction, leave only the alternative between doing without religion and God altogether or claiming to still believe in him in order, no doubt, not to have to give up the hope of consolation? Levinas does not think so but seeks another path. Claiming that that religion and that God "do not exhaust the message of Scripture,"[18] he paves the way for a more demanding and more living notion of God. And although that God does not found ethics for Levinas any more than for Kant, the thought of God comes to mind thanks to ethics.

It is therefore the analysis of sense—of orientation[19]—which must lead toward that God. Contrary to the great tradition of reflexive philosophy, Levinas believes that the subject does not find its orientation by returning to itself or by consulting its own roster of principles, even one with a universal scope such as Kant's. The orientation comes from the Other, not from oneself: unless one wants to neutralize sense, heteronomy and the freedom required by it cannot veer into autonomy. The movement of the self toward the other, a movement awakened by the other, does not return to the self; otherwise, it risks a loss of sense, risks falling back into economic calculation. Levinas calls this movement "Works" *(Oeuvre)*, and even "liturgy" or "*to-God.*" He concludes: "Works, conceived in their most extreme form, require a radical generosity of the movement that, within the Same, goes toward the Other. As a result, they require an *ingratitude* on the other's part. Gratitude would be precisely the movement's return to its origin."[20]

The Kantian postulate of a God who, beyond the subject's death, would make it possible for the subject's happiness to be finally proportionate to its virtue, cannot be taken into account here. According to Levinas, that God remains too dependent on a hope *for oneself*, marked by economics and calculation. The absolute orientation toward the Other—sense—does not allow it. But does that mean that the God who comes to the moral subject's mind must remain *ungrateful?* It is not enough that the man who acts morally—placing the response owed to the other and to the third party as the judge of his own interests—does so without expecting a reward or a salary, from a God or from men, *as if* that God were ungrateful or absent. We need to understand the necessity of ingratitude—or the absence of reciprocity—as a safeguard to ethics and religion. Levinas says that we ought to act without expecting to enter the Promised Land, working for *a time without me* and for an eschatology without hope for oneself.

Was God ungrateful when he did not permit his faithful servant Moses to enter the Promised Land? The God who comes to the moral subject's mind, who fills no need and meets no expectation, even as the subject observes the ingratitude of people and looks with bitterness or acquiescence at the land that will soon hold its body—is that God a living God or, as for Kant, a postulate of reason? Is it a postulate, different from Kant's to be sure, since it relies on no hope for oneself, but still a postulate in spite of everything?

The *to-God* assumes its sense in the simple and fragile words with which a subject indicates its brotherhood with the other, apart from any expectation of reciprocity or gratitude. It therefore does not correspond to any particular postulate of reason—to any theoretical belief regarding the existence of God, even if that belief, as in Kant, depends on practical reason. It does not call for a theological construction regarding divine predicates and does not commit anyone to proclaim faith and devotion. It humbly bears witness, unbeknownst even to reflective consciousness, to the infinite responsibility that precedes the commitments made and assumed in complete freedom, bears witness to the responsibility Levinas calls election. It is by virtue of the human words "Here I am," which respond to the weakness of one's neighbor, that the *to-God* trembles on one's lips. Man lets an idea of God come and grow in these words, in them and through them, an idea that he often does not know dwells within him.

But why posit that correlation? If, as Levinas maintains, the sense of the word "God" emerges under the circumstance of the "Here I am," does that sense come to the mind of the person who pronounces the "Here I am" or to the one who hears it addressed to him or her, or to both? Why, in spite of his warning against all dogmatic—positive or negative—theology, and his refusal to found ethics on faith, does Levinas speak of a *to-God*?

According to Levinas, the man awakened to his uniqueness as an irreplaceable subject when confronted with the face of the other that beseeches *him*, and hence subject to the new-found sobriety of election or of the *for-the-other*, makes meaningful a *uniqueness different* from his own: that of the transcendence of the *to-God*, to be precise. That transcendence emerges from the most secret part of his words, it breaks into them—without having to be taken for a "new proof of the existence of God"—at the moment of the never-completed awakening of a subject to its uniqueness or election. It is as if the absent or hidden God, lamented, invoked, or condemned in distress or powerlessness, trembled in the words of the man awakened to his uniqueness before the other, as if that absent God, that God whose transcendence is irreducible to any concept, was revealing himself in that propheticism of the soul. "That Revelation is love for the other man, that the transcendence of the to-God, separated by a separation behind which no genus common to the separated entities can be recovered . . . that the relation to the Absolute or to the Infinite has an ethical significance— . . . this describes only the circumstances under which the very sense of the word 'God' comes to mind, and more imperiously than a presence."[21] In this case, the word "Revelation" does not mean the unveiling of an essence. Rather, as in the biblical context, it describes an act of descending: the descent of the word "God" onto human lips. The book of Exodus (19:20) says: "And the Lord came down [vaiered haShem] upon mount Sinai," giving the ten commandments, in particular, "Thou shalt not kill," the imperative for which Levinas hears in the other's face. Therefore, in its language stubbornly resistant to conceptual abstraction and ontology, the Bible describes how the word (davar) of God comes down to men.[22] But does the to-God differ from that act of descending? Does Levinas not seek to understand, through that reflection, how transcendence descends into the finitude of human words? And does he not show thereby, contrary to proud Kantian autonomy, how the subject's finitude is permeated by the infinite, how it is inhabited by a transcendence outside all theoretical and ontological knowledge?

It is, in the first place, to the mind of the responsible subject that the idea of God comes (down), at the very instant of the subject's obligation, at the instant of its uniqueness before its neighbor, or in the instant of its election. But does the other perceive that to-God? Levinas does not say so explicitly. His analyses adopt the point of view of the moral subject, not that of a person who might be the object of its solicitude. All the same, in speaking of "bearing witness"—"the way for the commandment to reverberate in the mouth of the very one who obeys, to 'reveal' itself before any act of appearing"[23]—does Levinas not suggest that the other is called upon to hear the to-God when the moral subject responds to him? Is not the act of bearing witness addressed to the other? Is not the other the target of the act of bearing witness as Levinas understands it, the way the infinite passes the finite into the moral subject? Thus the other as well will— perhaps—hear the "glory" of God in the moral subject's response to him.

That glory is commensurate with the powerlessness of that God to take the subject's place. It differs, says Levinas, from any ontological majesty in that it resembles the "peace announced to the other,"[24] the subject's responsibility for the other even to the point of substituting itself for him.

The subject's awakening to its uniqueness as a way of the *to-God*, the idea that the *mind* exceeds the capacities of reason, and the propheticism of the psyche show that Levinas conducts the exercise of practical reason in an excessive manner and, in any case, a manner irreducible to that of Kant. The moral word or command does not come from oneself but comes down into oneself to reveal a subject to itself, its uniqueness wrested from its identity where that uniqueness still slumbers. And yet, although this analysis certainly differs from that of the Kantian subject, paradoxically, it answers Kant's question: does God allow virtue and happiness to be in harmony? It answers that question without requiring, as Kant did, that one await God's judgment of the virtuous man's soul after his death.

Does the absence of God—of the God who meets one's demands for oneself—signify his indifference to human effort? Does it imply a definitive dereliction and resignation to ontological solitude? Although there is no doubting it in terms of an economic conception of the divine, for Levinas, that *ingratitude* of God opens on an awakening of the subject, which constitutes the true response of that God. That is also why the *to-God* is not a postulate but rather the very life of the moral subject. Such is the response or the *grace* of God: it is not measured in terms of power or social success but solely in terms of the proximity of the word that makes it possible to live by inducing the awakening, in giving birth, perhaps, to a quivering happiness commensurate with the fragility of the infinite within oneself. And that awakening—always to be exempted from relapses into the perseverance in being—finally opens on a hope that is not alien to that which Kant describes by the name "highest good," since death does not necessarily constitute the endpoint of the awakening. But, as in Kant, "it is not to a need to survive that that hope responds" but rather to "a temporality *different* from that of being-unto-death."[25]

Transcendence cannot be appropriated by any religion, by any institution, or by any body of doctrine. Kant nevertheless speaks of Christianity, and Levinas of Judaism. We ought therefore to consider the significance of these references.

Christianity and Judaism

The defense of moral autonomy turns out to be incompatible with the slightest concession to religion and to the idea of Revelation: "Morality in no way needs religion . . . but is rather self-sufficient by virtue of pure practical reason."[26] As a result, although Kant speaks explicitly of the "Son of God," whom he considers "the prototype of moral disposition in its entire purity," he immediately adds that he does not see him as a supernatural being, a suffering servant, or a Messiah, even less as a worker of miracles or a messenger of grace, but as "our master of moral truth," the man who realized "the ideal of a humanity pleasing to God,"[27] that is, the moral Ideal conceived by reason. "The Christian principle of *morals* itself is not theological (and so heteronomy); it is instead autonomy of pure practical reason by itself, since it does not make cognition of God and his will the basis of these laws but only of the attainment of the highest good subject to the condition of observing these laws."[28] The "Son of God" teaches the philosopher nothing he or she does not already understand; he brings no "good news." His death and resurrection do not so much intrigue the reason as bring attention to the dignity of its good and pure moral intention. And Kant explains that he "seeks in the Gospel not the foundation of his faith but its confirmation."[29] That nevertheless leaves open the question of the meaning and nature of that confirmation. Why would pure practical reason need to be "confirmed" by the exteriority of a text or a supposedly inspired word? Why, in its universality and timelessness, should it seek the support of *that* particular and historical text, namely, the Gospel?

The expression "Son of God" does not signify that Kant accepts the mystery of the Incarnation: for him, Christ is not God become man but the Ideal of practical reason. He understands him within the limits of mere reason. According to him, the only thing about a religion that deserves to be retained stems from its moral content, from the internal moral intention that animates those who embrace it. Kant pays no attention to the historical narratives in the Bible, and he considers the rites and laws of religion—particularly those of Judaism—as a pure external constraint without value. He seeks no historical confirmation in the Gospel for the teachings proper to reason, but he thinks that if Christ, as a man, realized the moral Ideal expected of every person, then he showed that the human

path has its endpoint in the excellence of that Ideal, whatever the historical, social, and cultural conditions of life. That is why Kant completely
separates the person of Christ from history, from the way of life and religion of the Jewish people, presenting his birth and the course of his existence as an enigma: "there *suddenly* appeared . . . a person whose wisdom,
even purer than that of the previous philosophers, was as though descended from heaven."[30] According to Kant, Christ therefore has nothing
to do with the Jewish tradition, of which he is nevertheless the son by ge-
nealogy and upbringing according to the Gospel itself, and Kant draws a
stark contrast between Christianity and Judaism, and, in fact, all religions
other than Christianity. "He believes that, in doing so, he is purifying
Christianity and referring it to the absolute ethical norm, instead of
seeking, like Lessing and a good part of the *Aufklärung* stemming from
Leibniz, a conciliatory eudaemonism."[31]

But is that all he believes? He asserts that the origin of Christianity resides in a "total abandonment of the Judaism in which it originated,
grounded on an entirely new principle." Yet, in order to support that con-
viction that Christ's pure moral intention is truly without precedent, he
does not hesitate to deny Judaism the slightest moral content and to define its faith as a purely statutory faith, that is, as *slavish* and *mercenary*.
"For whatever moral additions were *appended* to it, whether originally [in
Christ's time] or only later, do not in any way belong to Judaism as such."[32]
Kant thus radicalizes Spinoza's thesis—well-known in his time—which,
despite its severity toward Jewish Scripture, conceded that the latter Scripture taught justice and charity to the ignorant. Kant sees Judaism only as
a political association without the slightest moral content. The ten commandments, he says, had the aim of maintaining the political state; they
were constraining laws given "with no claim at all on the *moral disposition*
in following them."[33] Given Kant's criterion of the autonomy proper to
good will, this means they had no moral value and no religious value, in
fact, since to obey precepts out of fear is, according to Kant, equivalent to
serving an idol. In the end, Jewish Scripture holds no interest apart from
the historical. But, since the Hebrew language—whose fate appears very
precarious to Kant (astonishingly, he claims that we "have only one single
book"[34] written in that language)—allows for no extensive study, even that
historical interest, that is, the reality of the events and the sense to give
them, remains problematic.

Christianity, a Christianity delivered of all mysticism and alien to the infamous "scandal" of the cross, thus remains the single and unprecedented cornerstone of Kantian moral faith. Sanctification by faith requires that the human being never subordinate virtue to worship. As it happens, the concept of virtue is drawn from the human soul: no fear of god can impose it, only love from "*free choice* and from pleasure in the law."[35] Neither Judaism nor any other religion—to the extent that Judaism even deserves that name—meets that criterion, according to Kant. Consciousness—pure interiority without external expression, not even the humble and solitary *utterance* of a prayer—remains the only guarantor of faith.

The feeling that faith concerns only interiority and the mistrust, or even contempt, for the liturgy, rites, gestures, and acts that inscribe faith within an exteriority correspond on the religious plane to the ideas that ethics rests exclusively on good will, and that acts, in spite of their potential benevolence, never prove the subject's morality. Kant says: "I seek to extract the moral teaching (of Christ) by isolating it from all the New Testament precepts. It is certainly the fundamental teaching of the Gospel; the rest can only be an auxiliary lesson" designed to come to the aid of human *fragility*. For Kant, the only thing that counts is "the pure [moral] doctrine" at the foundation of the Gospel "amid the mélange of events and revealed mysteries."[36] It is through that doctrine in its supreme simplicity, independent of any theological doctrine, that religion can unite with the purest practical reason, in order, in particular, to resolve the moral conflict between the good and evil principle within man.[37] Christ, who appeared *suddenly* in a world of darkness, asks nothing other than what practical reason requires: goodness and purity of heart, that is, good will.

Like Kant, Levinas is wary of the irrationality characteristic of myths, and he condemns mystical emotion and pathos. To him, the precept "Let them not enter the sanctuary in a drunken state"[38] seems to be a major religious requirement. And such rigor is also indispensable if one is to respect the moral content of religion. The path leading to God necessarily includes concern for one's neighbor, and, to Levinas, a preoccupation with one's own salvation is unseemly in a world beset by evil acts of violence at every moment. Unlike Kant, Levinas does not defend a pure, internal moral faith, and he gives a positive meaning to the rites, gestures, and acts that inscribe faith in *exteriority*. He does not find the often-harsh ritual discipline required by Judaism alien to faith and ethics. Although he does not give it a sacramental value, he sees it as a rule indispensable for elevation and awakening. "The law is effort. Daily fidelity to the ritual gesture requires a courage calmer, nobler, and greater than that of the warrior."[39] The act of sobering up—or of awakening—is not the result of autonomy or the effort to act out of good will; it entails obedience to precepts that reverse a person's immediate tendency to grant himself priority and preference in all things. It is honed at every moment by these precepts, which tell the faithful of the immemorial, provided they consent to hear these precepts as addressed to them.

Levinas invokes the need for a pause—marked by memory of the Law—between the self and nature, "in the smallest practical actions," even, for example, as an act of gratitude for the gifts of daily life. Through the mitzvah—religious obligation—man also performs gestures and acts of humanity the urgency of which cannot depend on his good will. And, whereas Kant claims that such behaviors—in spite of the benefits they bring—do not stem from ethics but solely from legality, Levinas believes they educate one's moral disposition. Judaism, he says, introduces "a border of roses" between the spontaneous egoism of the living and the human vocation; in its heteronomy, the law compels the act of decentering required by an attention to alterity. Levinas thus forcefully challenges the notion of a pure internalization of the Law. For him, it is neither a religious ideal nor a moral ideal. In a formulation unamenable to the Kantian thesis of pure moral autonomy and, above all, to the words of Christ in the Gospel of Matthew (5:17), he asserts without ambiguity: "The pure and simple internalization of the Law is only its abolition."[40] Yet no one is required to choose between the Law and love, as a certain Christian teaching adopted by Kant would have it, since the Law "is not a moral formalism, but the living *presence* of love," its "harassment even."[41] Without it, the humble and fragile exteriority of the living finds itself defenseless in the face of the dangers of egoism.

That analysis of Judaism, of the Law, and of the rite is clearly demarcated from that proposed by Kant. The misinterpretation of the meaning of the rite (the "living *presence* of love") as the notorious "Jewish legalism" may be "the trait most characteristic of Christian thought."[42] Is Kant's interpretation any different? But that misunderstanding and the forgetfulness it carries with it regarding the attention to exteriority—since only internal faith would count—are also dangerous for ethics. Is it enough that, out of good will, one works toward one's inner purification and struggles to obey the moral law within oneself, if one does not discover the need to inscribe one's intention in an exteriority? To be sure, it sometimes happens in Judaism that obedience to precepts becomes overly scrupulous, obsessive even, but that justifies not contempt and mockery but rather further education, unless the meaning of that obedience is misinterpreted. And, for Judaism, pure interiority does not suffice for the sanctification of daily life. Nor does it suffice for ethics, since one's neighbor cannot stand to wait until love coincides with what the hour requires, or, in Kantian terms, until the will, absent holiness, becomes pure good will. Ethics was not "appended" to Judaism, as Kant claims; it constitutes its first impulse, since man's duty is to remain his "brother's keeper" come what may (Genesis 4:9). As the biblical story of Abel's murder teaches, God does not protect weakness; it is up to man to watch over it. That moral obligation, which is not a matter of choice and is too often subordinated to the love of God—as if it constituted only a secondary article of faith—nevertheless gives spirituality its full significance, a spirituality that does not separate the desire for transcendence from the sanctification of life.

Is there, as a result, as H. Cohen has claimed, "an extremely profound concordance between the provisions of the Kantian system and the prophetic orientation located at the foundation of Judaism"?[43] Kant did not think so in any case, since he saw Judaism only as a set of statutory laws and its "ethics" as pure legalism. Besides, in founding ethics on an "act of reason," does not Kant challenge propheticism? With Cohen, ought we, in order to rescue that concordance, to consider propheticism—the descent of the spirit into man—as a metaphor for Kantian autonomy? In any case, that is not Levinas's conclusion. He willingly recognizes his proximity to Kant in that, in the Kantian examination of the reasonable subject, "the implications of moral action allow themselves to be made explicit without becoming the object of any knowledge of being."[44] But he does not think that propheticism and heteronomy can be reduced to the act of reason and autonomy. Reason, he says, is capable of "keeping watch without intentionality," which leads it to become part of an order, or a disorder, where it is no longer "either knowledge or action, but where, unseated from its status by the other . . . it is in an ethical relation with the other, in proximity to one's neighbor."[45] Nevertheless, the claim that that exteriority—that of the other in this case—could "unseat" reason, inspire it, and awaken it to responsibility does not stem from Kantianism, but it does remain faithful to propheticism.

Despite their different assessments of Christianity and Judaism, do not Kant and Levinas both consider holiness as an ultimate obligation? How are we to understand holiness in relation to the idea of humanity that emerges in their philosophies?

Holiness and Humanity

Kant says: "The moral law is holy (inflexible) and demands holiness of morals, although all the moral perfection that a human being can attain is still only virtue, that is, a disposition conformed with law *from respect* for the law."[46] The virtuous man is not holy; he is aware that human finitude goes hand in hand with a "continuous propensity to transgression." No human being is endowed with a holy will, a will that conforms perfectly with the law. The virtuous man is thus not unaware that he sometimes obeys moral law for impure motives, out of physical inclination or fear, for example. In addition, given that "the depths of the heart are unfathomable," no one knows himself adequately to assert without hesitation, "when he feels the incentive to fulfill his duty," whether "it proceeds entirely from the representation of the law or whether there are not many other sensible impulses contributing to it."[47] A saint would obey without having to struggle against such motives, and he would be spared that doubt. But no person achieves that ideal; one can only hope to progress indefinitely toward it. As for the wicked man, he is not inevitably destined for evil since the evil in him, despite its radicality, does not constitute an absolute or a fate. Far from being diabolical, he can also straighten himself out and convert, and Christ, "the prototype of moral disposition in its entire purity,"[48] can serve as an example to him. Nevertheless, because of the *bent* of his nature, no human being is capable of an absolutely upright resolution regarding his duty; he prefers to stoop to lying and making peace with his egoism, to loving his sin. Therefore, no human being accedes to the holiness that is nevertheless required of him. As a result, that bent elicits "a profound anxiety, because it has no conceivable human solution and, as a rationalist, Kant seems to have very little belief in a higher Grace, though it be necessary."[49]

Holiness—purity in the will's disposition toward the Law—is thus the moral ideal par excellence. But, since it remains forever unattainable because of the finitude and the bent of human nature, the virtuous man can only move toward it, hoping for an immortality that will allow him to continue to pursue his efforts after his death. Kant says that, in God's view, all these efforts are equivalent to holiness: "The *eternal being*, to whom the temporal condition is nothing, sees in what is to us an endless series the whole of conformity with the moral law, and the holiness . . . is to be found whole in a single intellectual intuition of the existence of rational beings."[50] Therefore, hope postulates that the firm resolution to act constantly out of respect for moral law—the purity of intention—will be considered by God's intellectual intuition as an equivalent of holiness, despite the inevitable shortcomings of the virtuous man, whose nature, finite and bent like that of any man, can never be in a state of pure and definitive harmony with the voice of reason within him.

But does an intention of holiness suffice? Must not the subject's acts corroborate it? Kant himself raises the question—"How can this disposition count for the deed itself, when this deed is *every time* (not generally, but at each instant) defective?"—and he suggests we resolve that objection by distinguishing the deed, as a phenomenon linked to time, from the intention as a supersensible reality. The deed, he says, "according to our mode of estimation . . . always remains defective," and that estimation also stems from sensible nature, subject to time and space. But reason postulates that the supersensible intentions from which the deed results and which often remain unknown to oneself, will be judged "by him who scrutinizes the heart (through his pure intellectual intuition) to be a perfected whole."[51] Hence, once more, despite the positive character—of doing justice, feeding the hungry, or clothing the naked—that acts can effectively take on in the eyes of the other and in one's own eyes, Kant maintains that a person's acts would never allow one to draw the slightest conclusion regarding a person's virtue and a fortiori his holiness. In ethics, only their author's internal intention, secret and invisible to human eyes, counts. It is truly that intention—and it alone—that the one who scrutinizes hearts, independent of the temporality inherent to life, lays bare and judges. It is on that intention that the hope for the highest good rests.

Despite the insurmountable distance that separates a person from holiness, the obligation to it is an integral part of ethics and particularly of one's duties toward oneself. According to Kant, the biblical precept "Be ye holy" (Leviticus 20:7) means that human beings must do their duty with an upright and pure intention. But, he acknowledges, "objectively, seen in relation to the moral aim as a whole"—the intention *and* the acts—the precept "Be ye therefore perfect" (Matthew 5:48) is more fitting.[52] How are we to understand this? What distinction does Kant make between holiness and perfection? It seems that the imperative for perfection does not require that the human being abstain at every moment from lying, stealing, and so on, out of respect for the law. It rather enjoins him to constantly endeavor "to perfect all of the particular virtues associated with the various duties of virtue."[53] Holiness is "the supposed *possession* of a complete *purity* of dispositions of the will," but that ideal remains inaccessible to all *finite* reasonable beings because of the incoercible share of their sensibility. By contrast, virtue denotes "the moral disposition in *conflict*"[54] against every form of heteronomy, particularly that of the natural propensities. Yet only that conflict—or that virtue—remains within human reach. Despite the claims of moral fanaticism to the contrary, no human being achieves holiness. That is why, if the moral law is *holy*, it always presents itself to the subject as a law of *duty*, whose voice, demanding and harsh, is without mercy, without indulgence, and without forgiveness for human weaknesses. According to the Kantian criteria, no man is holy, therefore, but that voice, rather than consoling him for his inevitable failure or announcing Grace, firmly reminds everyone, up to the last moment, that the "*humanity*" in his person and in that of the other "must be holy to him."[55] The virtuous man is the one who, through a struggle lasting his entire lifetime, responds positively to that duty.

Nevertheless, since the virtuous man's respect for the holiness of the humanity in himself and in the other is not directed at the singular and fragile concreteness of the person, but only at the universal moral Law of which he is the author, the term *holiness* is fundamentally linked to the abstraction of a principle or an idea—the *idea* of humanity—rather than to the concrete reality of the uniqueness of every vulnerable and carnal human face.

On this point, Levinas objects: Is it certain that expelling sensibility from the register of ethics constitutes one of the parameters required to respond to a holy vocation, as Kant teaches? Is respect for the formal universality of the law sufficient for the person interested in holiness? Has not Kant linked sensibility to the egoism of passion in a way that is too harsh or too hasty? Levinas rejects the idea that the "*holy* imprudence" of sensibility, also called "goodness" or "love," stems from "pathology, as denounced by Kant" or from "the abyss of the arbitrary,"[56] where the sense of the universal is lost and from which one must deliver oneself to progress toward holiness. On the contrary, he thinks that no one can despise that "*holy* imprudence" without running the risk of confusing holiness with an ideal of personal perfection that is anxious about its own salvation, hence egoistic. For Levinas, then, that "holy imprudence"—that goodness or love—must be reevaluated, since it alone offers a glimpse of the sense, irreducible to an idea of reason or to a principle of the holiness, not of humanity, but of every human person's uniqueness.

How are we to understand this? The words "goodness" and "love," often hypocritically bandied about, certainly contradict the universality of the moral Law and distance one from the ideal of holiness when they express only the fragility and partiality of a heart-felt impulse. But Levinas refuses to abandon these words to some sentimental meaning: according to him, the true sense of goodness and love is revealed in the responsibility toward the other, irreducible, of course, to the intimidation and weakness one feels when confronted with the other's demands or to the passion the other inspires. From that perspective, Levinas links goodness and love to a reflection on holiness, which he defines as "the most profound upheaval of being and thought by means of the advent of man." The human—as an *advent* rather than an *idea*—gradually makes its way into being when the transcendence of the sensible face of the particular neighbor, in the trace of the immemorial, close by and different—that is, holy[57]—inspires nonerotic love in the subject, that is, responsibility toward the other. That love can lead to sacrifice, to an anxiety about the death of the other more prevalent than anxiety about one's own death. That is holiness, or "the rationality of the Good more lofty than any essence. The intelligibility of goodness. That possibility, in the sacrifice, of attributing a sense to the other and to the world which, without me, counts for me, and for which I am answerable . . . is an ecstasy toward a future that *counts* for the ego and for which it has to answer: but a future without-*me*, meaningful and future, which is no longer the to-come [*à-venir*] of a protained present."[58]

The hour of holiness[59] is indissociable from the hour of justice, when the third party intervenes, imposes a reflection on the neighbor's attitude toward him, and asks for a response by the subject that takes them *both* into account; and that hour of holiness is without reciprocity. Otherwise, its gratuitousness or disinterestedness would be compromised. The hour of holiness is thus the time of the subject's election or its accession to its own uniqueness, expressed by the simplicity of the words "Here I am."

The distinction Levinas draws between holiness and perfection does not coincide with Kant's. Holiness does not lie in a constant effort toward personal perfection but in the willingness to conceive of and to welcome the vulnerability of the other as an imperative for oneself, an imperative through which the self accedes to its irreplaceable uniqueness. Levinas does not naively claim that people are holy, but he maintains that the human psyche can conceive of holiness and that its humanity resides in that very capacity. The psyche understands the sense of the imperative for holiness— "Be holy" (Leviticus 20:7)—when it feels itself called into question in and through the love of its neighbor and of the stranger. It is, in fact, truly to the "holy imprudence"—imprudence at least in the eyes of those who advocate concern for oneself in all things—of that anxious love that, according to Levinas, the Bible invites us. And he even says that Kant, in the midst of the Enlightenment, called the Bible "that old holy book." The conceptual plenitude of that holiness would clarify the ultimate sense of the creature and the role falling to the humanity of man, the core of that condition, of that adventure or intrigue.[60] But that holiness exceeds the limits of simple ontological reason, since it does not stem from one's own decision or plan but from an inspiration by the humble and fragile proximity of alterity. In making this claim, Levinas does not undertake a plea in favor of the irrational, but he describes the opening of the psyche to what he calls a rationality of goodness or transcendence beyond ontological rationality. For him, that opening appears close "to the practical interest of pure reason." Did not Kant say that speculative reason ought to accept practical propositions "as a foreign good handed over to it" and "transcendent" in relation to its own realm? Setting limits on "speculative excess"[61] does not contradict reason—for Kant, it is still an activity of reason—but opens on the good. To conceive, with Levinas, of a rationality of goodness does not mean one gives in to irrationalism but rather that one conceives of what surpasses ontological rationality and gives it an ethical meaning.

Holiness differs from the sacred and lies in the effort to live tuned in to the immemorial appeal. The latter, however, differs from the voice of practical reason within oneself; it does not embrace any abstract and universal principle but allows one to hear the voice of the "living God."[62] That voice does not invoke respect for the *idea* of humanity but teaches responsibility toward every sensible and threatened face and only then toward humanity. Consciousness of the universal—the universality of the human in this case—does not begin, according to Levinas, with an agreement about a theoretical or practical *idea* but with the "holy imprudence" of the response here and now to the holiness of a singular and irreplaceable face.

Primo Levi writes: "That look was not one between two men; and if I had known how completely to explain the nature of that look, which came as if across the glass window of an aquarium between two beings who live in different worlds, I would also have explained the essence of the great insanity of the third Germany."[63] In the twentieth century, the idea of humanity, assaulted by so many tragedies, was destroyed, and it continues to be destroyed with the humiliation and murder of each face. Principles and ideas, tested by history, thus seem futile or terrible. When they teach respect for man, they remain cruelly powerless on their own to calm, or even to moderate, madness and the destructive passions. And it is sometimes in the name of principles—the superiority of a race or the universality of a class—that murders and atrocities occur and are given justification.

No philosophy can change that tragic course of history. Clearly, neither Kant nor Levinas can liberate man from his share of darkness, destruction, and disaster. Kant never forgets the finitude of men. "Humanity is not God," and holiness remains forever beyond reach. "All the same, inasmuch as humanity is a transcendental Idea of reality, it defines an ultimate end that can be approached in an asymptotic manner. As a *reality*, humanity is an asymptote in relation to the *Idea* of humanity, which itself is subject to God and to the profundity of his plan."[64] That hope for an asymptotic approach toward the idea of humanity *as end in itself*, despite the cruel disappointments of history, "the folly and caprice,"[65] is in harmony with the Enlightenment. Kant had no illusions about the possibility of improving the course of history, but he thought that a rational preparation would contribute toward—slight—progress along the path of that asymptote.

The twentieth century destroyed that hope. Even today, humanity, murdered in the person of millions of human beings, remains at the mercy of the most deadly passions. Is history only an illusion, then? V. Grossman writes: "The human being . . . is as stationary as a granite cliff. His goodness, his mind, are immovable. The human and humane element does not increase within the human being. What kind of history can human beings have if their goodness is static?"[66] Is history, as Grossman believes, only the struggle of evil against the spark of goodness that remains, invincible because powerless? Is it only "a battle fought by a great evil struggling to crush a small kernel of human kindness"?[67]

In close proximity to that thought, Levinas sees the sign of an extraordinary God, who, without promising anything, takes on meaning "beyond a past shaken to the point of atheism,"[68] the sign of a God who arrives and becomes thanks to the response of those he elects for an unremitting service. Such is the call to holiness or responsibility. It does not depend on an *idea* of humanity but on the attention paid to every singularity, since it is through that singularity—and through it alone—that the *idea* of humanity acquires a universal sense.

Even though history remains threatening and catastrophic at every moment, in the grip of the passion to exert power over the other and the temptation of death, is it absurd to conceive of the moral subject? Kant and Levinas do not accept that idea, and their philosophies do not seek to console the weak. They simply say, in a manner both timely and untimely, that attending to ethics remains the human task par excellence. The reflection on the *moral subject* in a world marked by objectivism, scientific speculations, and by the negation in some quarters of any specificity to man, also constitutes a point of resistance. But, in its fragility, and in the face of the constant perils, is that point invincible?

The task of the *moral subject* is to allow that question to receive a positive response.

n o t e s

Introduction

1. R. Descartes, *Méditations métaphysiques* (1640), trans. G. Rodis-Lewis (Paris: Vrin, 1963), Second Meditation, 24.
2. See F. Lurcat, *L'autorité de la science* (Paris: Cerf, 1995), part 1, chap. 2: "De l'homme neuronal aux neurosciences," 105–24.
3. E. Levinas, *Entre nous* (Paris: Grasset, 1991), 36–37.
4. E. Levinas, *Humanisme de l'autre homme* (Montpellier: Fata Morgana, 1972), 87.
5. See L. Lazare, *Le livre des Justes* (Paris: Lattès, 1993), 130–31, 75–76.
6. *Groundwork of the Metaphysics of Morals* (1785), in I. Kant, *Practical Philosophy*, trans. and ed. M. J. Gregor (Cambridge: Cambridge University Press, 1996), 59.
7. E. Levinas, *Dieu, la mort, le temps*, ed. J. Rolland (Paris: Grasset), 75.

Chapter 1: The Critique of Intellectualism

1. G. Steiner, *In Bluebeard's Castle: Some Notes towards the Redefinition of Culture* (New Haven: Yale University Press, 1971), 30.

2. Special issue of *Connaissance des Arts* devoted to Zoran Music, 34.

3. See Plato, *Apology of Socrates* 29e.

4. I. Kant, "Idea for a Universal History from a Cosmopolitan Point of View" (1784), trans. L. W. Beck, in I. Kant, *On History* (Indianapolis: Bobbs-Merrill, 1963), 21.

5. Ibid., 12, 20, 22, 25.

6. Steiner, *In Bluebeard's Castle*, 63.

7. T. Todorov, *Face à l'extrême* (Paris: Seuil, 1991), 155.

8. I. Scholl, *The White Rose: Munich 1942–1943*, trans. A. R. Schultz (Middletown: Wesleyan University Press, 1983), 78.

9. See K. Löwith, *My Life in Germany before and after 1933: A Report*, trans. E. King (London: Athlone, 1994).

10. E. Levinas, *Totalité et infini* (The Hague: M. Nijhoff, 1961), 60.

11. Remarks by I. Kant regarding his *Observations on the Feeling of the Beautiful and Sublime* (1764), quoted in L. W. Beck, *Studies in the Philosophy of Kant* (Indianapolis: Bobbs-Merrill, 1965), 9.

12. E. Levinas, *Noms propres* (Montpellier: Fata Morgana, 1976), 180–81.

13. D. Hume, *An Inquiry Concerning the Principles of Morals*, ed. C. W. Hendel (Indianapolis: Liberal Arts, 1957), 4.

14. Ibid., 5.

15. D. Hume, *A Treatise of Human Nature*, ed. L. A. Selby-Bigge, 2d ed. (Oxford: Clarendon, 1978), 458.

16. Hume, *Inquiry Concerning the Principles of Morals*, 6, 94.

17. I. Kant, *Observations on the Feeling of the Beautiful and Sublime* (1764), trans. J. T. Goldthwait (Berkeley: University of California Press, 1960), 60. Among the English empiricists, let us also mention Shaftesbury, Hutcheson, and Burke.

18. See I. Kant, *Critique of Practical Reason* (1788), in I. Kant, *Practical Philosophy*, trans. and ed. M. J. Gregor (Cambridge: Cambridge University Press, 1996), 171: "More refined, though equally untrue, is the pretense of those who assume a certain special moral sense." See chap. 5 below.

19. I. Kant, remarks relating to *Observations on the Feeling of the Beautiful and Sublime*, in the French translation of this text, *Observations sur le sentiment du beau et du sublime*, trans. V. Delbos (Paris: Vrin, 1969), 66.

20. Kant, *Observations on the Feeling of the Beautiful and Sublime*, 60.

21. Ibid., 60–61.

22. Ibid., 63.

23. Kant, *Groundwork of the Metaphysics of Morals* (1785), in *Practical Philosophy*, 84.

24. See Z. Klein, *La notion de dignité humaine dans la pensée de Pascal et de Kant* (Paris: Vrin, 1968), 60.

25. See chap. 2.

26. [Throughout this book, the term "sensible" will be used in its sense of "capable of being perceived by the senses" or "of or relating to the senses" (*Webster's Third International Dictionary*)—trans.]

27. E. Levinas, *Autrement qu'être ou au-delà de l'essence* (The Hague: M. Nijhoff, 1974), 5.

28. E. Levinas, *Humanisme de l'autre homme* (Montpellier: Fata Morgana, 1972), 71,75.

29. Ibid., 82.

30. R. Hilberg, *Perpetrators, Victims, Bystanders: The Jewish Catastrophe, 1933–1945* (New York: HarperCollins, 1992), 214.

31. E. Levinas, *Quatre lectures talmudiques* (Paris: Minuit, 1968), 75.

32. E. Levinas, "Philosophie et transcendance" (1989), in E. Levinas, *Altérité et transcendance* (Montpellier: Fata Morgana, 1995), 54.

33. See chap. 2.

34. Levinas, "Philosophie et transcendance," 56.

35. See Rashi's gloss on Leviticus 10:2: "Let them not enter the sanctuary in a drunken state," which appears as the epigraph to the chapter "Au-delà du pathétique" in E. Levinas, *Difficile liberté*, 2d ed. (Paris: Albin Michel, 1976), 13.

36. "What Does It Mean to Orient Oneself in Thinking?" (1786), in I. Kant, *Religion and Rational Theology*, trans. and ed. A. W. Wood and G. Di Giovanni (Cambridge: Cambridge University Press, 1996), 17 [translation modified. The Cambridge edition says "unbelief of reason"]. See also the translator's introduction to the French edition of this text: *L'oeuvre de Kant*, trans. A. Philonenko, 2 vols. (Paris: Vrin, 1993), 38.

37. R. Descartes, *Méditations métaphysiques* (1640), trans. G. Rodis-Lewis (Paris: Vrin, 1963), 46.

38. Levinas, *Totalité et infini*, 20; Plato, *Phaedrus* 249a, 265a.

39. Kant, "What Does It Mean to Orient Oneself in Thinking?" 16.

40. Ibid. [translation modified].

41. Levinas, *Altérité et transcendance*, 54.

42. [The King James Version says: "All that the Lord hath said will we do, and be obedient"—trans.]

43. Levinas, *Quatre lectures talmudiques*, 91.

44. I. Kant, "On a Newly Arisen Superior Tone in Philosophy" (1796), in *Raising the Tone of Philosophy: Late Essays by Emmanuel Kant, Transformative Critique by Jacques Derrida*, ed. P. Fenves (Baltimore: Johns Hopkins University Press, 1993), 52.

45. Levinas, *Quatre lectures talmudiques*, 95.

46. Kant, "On a Newly Arisen Superior Tone," 68.

47. Ibid.

48. Ibid., 71.

Chapter 2: Good Will and the Face

1. E. Levinas, *Autrement qu'être ou au-delà de l'essence* (The Hague: M. Nijhoff, 1974), 126.

2. I. Kant, *Groundwork of the Metaphysics of Morals* (1785), in I. Kant, *Practical Philosophy*, trans. and ed. M. J. Gregor (Cambridge: Cambridge University Press, 1996), 49.

3. Ibid., 50.

4. Ibid., 52.

5. Ibid., 58.

6. Ibid.

7. I. Kant, "On a Supposed Right to Lie from Philanthropy" (1797), in *Practical Philosophy*.

8. Kant, *Groundwork of the Metaphysics of Morals*, 80.

9. Kant, "On a Supposed Right to Lie," 65 (the case in which the subject is harboring a fugitive).

10. I. Kant, *Lettres sur la morale et la religion*, trans. J. L. Bruch (Paris: Aubier-Montaigne, 1969), 143.

11. V. Jankélévitch, *Traité des vertus*, vol. 2: *Les vertus de l'amour* (Paris: Bordas, 1970), 523, 522.

12. Ibid., 543.

13. H. Jonas, *Le droit de mourir*, trans. P. Ivernal (Paris: Rivages, 1996), 40.

14. Ibid., 51.

15. Kant, *Groundwork of the Metaphysics of Morals*, 80.

16. G. Krüger, *Critique et morale chez Kant*, trans. M. Régnier (Paris: Bibliothèque des archives de philosophie, Beauchesne, 1960), 89.

17. Kant, *Groundwork of the Metaphysics of Morals*, 86, my emphasis.

18. Krüger, *Critique et morale*, 148.

19. Ibid., 115.

20. E. Levinas, *Noms propres* (Montpellier: Fata Morgana, 1976), 167, 169.

21. Kant, *Groundwork of the Metaphysics of Morals*, 53.

22. E. Levinas, *Entre nous: Essais sur le penser-à-l'autre* (Paris: Grasset, 1991), 259.

23. E. Levinas, *Totalité et infini* (The Hague: M. Nijhoff, 1961), 277.

24. Kant, *Groundwork of the Metaphysics of Morals*, 88.

25. Levinas, *Entre nous*, 121.

26. Ibid.

27. Levinas, *Totalité et infini*, 188.

28. E. Levinas, *Autrement que savoir* (Paris: Osiris, 1988), 61.

29. E. Levinas, "Transcendance et hauteur," in *Cahiers de l'Herne/E. Levinas* (Paris: L'Herne, 1991), 63.

30. I. Kant, *Religion within the Boundaries of Mere Reason* (1793), in I. Kant, *Religion and Rational Theology*, trans. and ed. A. W. Wood and G. Di Giovanni (Cambridge: Cambridge University Press, 1996), 155–56.

31. See chaps. 3 and 8.

32. Kant, *Religion within the Boundaries*, 156.

33. Ibid., 154.

34. I. Kant, "The Conflict of Faculties" (1798), in *Religion and Rational Theology*, 276.

35. Levinas, *Totalité et infini*, xv; and, for the quotation, 56 ("La merveille de l'idée de l'infini").

36. Ibid., 154.

37. Ibid., 170. On incompletion, see chap. 8 below.

38. E. Levinas, *Humanisme de l'autre homme*, 45.

39. Ibid., 49.

40. Kant, *Groundwork of the Metaphysics of Morals*, 75.

41. Levinas, *Humanisme de l'autre homme*, 46.

42. Ibid., 50.

43. Ibid., 51.

44. Levinas, *Totalité et infini*, 173.

45. Ibid., 175.

Chapter 3: Good Precedes Evil

1. I. Kant, *Groundwork of the Metaphysics of Morals* (1785), in I. Kant, *Practical Philosophy*, trans. and ed. M. J. Gregor (Cambridge: Cambridge University Press, 1996), 61.

2. I. Kant, "On the Miscarriage of All Philosophical Trials in Theodicy" (1791), in I. Kant, *Religion and Rational Theology*, trans. and ed. A. W. Wood and G. Di Giovanni (Cambridge: Cambridge University Press, 1996), 28.

3. I. Kant, *The Metaphysics of Morals*, part 2 (1797), in *Practical Philosophy*, 560.

4. E. Levinas, *Noms propres* (Montpellier: Fata Morgana, 1976), 182.

5. Ibid., 181.

6. I. Kant, *Religion within the Boundaries of Mere Reason* (1793), in *Religion and Rational Theology*, 90: "How it is possible that a naturally evil human being should make himself into a good human being surpasses every concept of ours. For how can an evil tree bear good fruit?" See also 89.

7. Ibid., 93.

8. I. Kant, *Critique of Practical Reason* (1788), in *Practical Philosophy*, 164.

9. I. Kant, "On the Common Saying: That May Be Correct in Theory, but It Is of No Use in Practice" (1793), in *Practical Philosophy*, 288. For the example of the child, see 287–88.

10. Kant, *Religion within the Boundaries*, 122.

11. G. Krüger, *Critique et morale chez Kant*, trans. M. Régnier (Paris: Bibliothèque des archives de philosophie, Beauchesne, 1960), 25.

12. See Kant, *Religion within the Boundaries*, 142n.

13. Kant, *Critique of Practical Reason*, 163–64.

14. V. Grossman, *Forever Flowing*, trans. T. P. Whitney (New York: Harper & Row, 1970), 67.

15. On respect, see chap. 5.

16. See Kant, *Critique of Practical Reason*, 199.

17. Kant, *Religion within the Boundaries*, 117: "It cannot corrupt his reason" [translation modified. The Cambridge edition says "He {the human being} cannot bribe his reason"].

18. Ibid., 122.

19. Ibid., 90.

20. Ibid., 112.

21. Ibid., 117n.

22. Ibid., 80.

23. Ibid., 118.

24. J. L. Bruch, *La philosophie religieuse de Kant* (Paris: Aubier-Montaigne, 1968), 72.

25. A. Philonenko, note 2, regarding p. 74 of I. Kant, *La religion dans les limites de la raison pratique*, in *L'oeuvre de Kant*, trans. A. Philonenko, 2 vols. (Paris: Vrin, 1993), 1340.

26. See P. Ricoeur, *Le conflit des interprétations* (Paris: Seuil, 1969), 304. See also chap. 7 below.

27. Kant, *Religion within the Boundaries*, 109.

28. Levinas, *Humanisme de l'autre homme* (Montpellier: Fata Morgana, 1972), 80.

29. Ibid., 81.

30. Ibid.

31. E. Levinas, *De l'existence à l'existant* (Paris: Fontaine, 1947), 161.

32. Levinas, *Humanisme de l'autre homme*, 80.

33. Ibid., 81.

34. Ibid.

35. E. Levinas, *De Dieu qui vient à l'idée* (Paris: Vrin, 1982), 257.

36. J. L. Chrétien, *L'effroi du beau* (Paris: Cerf, 1987), 36.

37. Levinas, *Humanisme de l'autre homme*, 80.

38. Ibid.

39. Ibid.

40. F. Rosenzweig, *The Star of Redemption*, trans. from the 2d edition by W. Hallo (Notre Dame: Notre Dame Press, 1985), 199ff.

41. Levinas, *Humanisme de l'autre homme*, 81.

42. V. Grossman, *Life and Fate*, trans. R. Chandler (London: Harrill, 1985), 410.

43. Levinas, *Humanisme de l'autre homme*, 82.

44. E. Levinas, *Dieu, la mort, le temps*, ed. J. Rolland (Paris: Grasset, Biblio-essais, 1993), 77. See also chap. 7 below.

1. I. Kant, "Idea for a Universal History from a Cosmopolitan Point of View" (1784), trans. L. W. Beck, in I. Kant, *On History* (Indianapolis: Bobbs-Merrill, 1963), 17.

2. I. Kant, *Groundwork of the Metaphysics of Morals* (1785), in I. Kant, *Practical Philosophy*, trans. and ed. M. J. Gregor (Cambridge: Cambridge University Press, 1996), 105–6, my emphasis [translation modified].

3. Ibid., 92.

4. H. E. Allison, *Kant's Theory of Freedom* (Cambridge: Cambridge University Press, 1990), 100.

5. Kant, *Groundwork of the Metaphysics of Morals*, 89.

6. I. Kant, *Critique of Practical Reason* (1788), in *Practical Philosophy*, 165.

7. See P. Ricoeur, *Le volontaire et l'involontaire* (Paris: Aubier, 1967), 125.

8. Kant, *Groundwork of the Metaphysics of Morals*, 105–6 [translation modified].

9. See H. Bergson, *Les deux sources de la morale et de la religion* (1932) (Paris: PUF, Quadrige, 1995), 98.

10. Kant, *Groundwork of the Metaphysics of Morals*, 108.

11. Kant, *Critique of Practical Reason*, 166.

12. Ricoeur, *Le volontaire et l'involontaire*, 127.

13. Kant, *Groundwork of the Metaphysics of Morals*, 80.

14. [*Esse* is Latin for "being"; *intéressement* is French for "self-interestedness"—trans.]

15. E. Levinas, *Autrement qu'être ou au-delà de l'essence* (The Hague: M. Nijhoff, 1974), 4–5.

16. E. Levinas, *Dieu, la mort, le temps*, ed. J. Rolland (Paris: Grasset), 71, 78.

17. See chaps. 7 and 8 for the other expressions of the Kantian return to ontology.

18. Kant, *Critique of Practical Reason*, 204.

19. Ibid., 202.

20. Ricoeur, *Le volontaire et l'involontaire*, 126.

21. E. Levinas, *De Dieu qui vient à l'idée* (Paris: Vrin, 1982), 37.

22. Levinas adds: "Unless they suggested it both in Socrates's Demon and in the agent-intellect's entrance *through the door* in Aristotle" (ibid., 48, note 19).

23. J.-J. Rousseau, *Le contrat social* (1762) (Paris: Garnier-Flammarion, 1966), vol. 1, pt. 2, p. 43.

24. Ibid., vol. 1, pt. 8, p. 56.

25. Ibid.

26. G. W. F. Hegel, *The Phenomenology of Spirit* (1807), trans. A. V. Miller (Oxford: Oxford University Press, 1977), 359, 361.

27. See Kant, *Critique of Practical Reason*, 203.

28. Rousseau, *Le contrat social*, vol. 1, pt. 8, p. 54: "Whosoever shall refuse to obey the general will shall be obliged to do so by the entire body; which means nothing other than that he shall be compelled to be free."

29. Kant, *Critique of Practical Reason*, 204, 206.

30. H. d'Aviau de Ternay, *Traces bibliques dans la loi morale de Kant* (Paris: Beauchesne, 1986), 39.

31. Kant, *Critique of Practical Reason*, 263.

32. Ibid., 243.

33. See chaps. 7 and 8.

34. Levinas, *Liberté et commandement* (1953) (Montpellier: Fata Morgana, 1994), 32.

35. Ibid., 34.

36. Ibid., 48.

37. I. Kant, "An Answer to the Question: What Is Enlightenment?" in *Practical Philosophy*, 17.

38. Ibid., 20.

39. Kant, *Groundwork of the Metaphysics of Morals*, 95.

40. Oral teachings of Rav M. Elon, Jerusalem, January 1997.

41. *Pirkei Avot* 6.2.63.

42. E. Levinas, *Humanisme de l'autre homme* (Montpellier: Fata Morgana, 1972), 97.

43. Ibid., 96: "Is to philosophize to decipher a buried writing in a palimpsest?"

44. [*Dire* is the infinitive (hence timeless) form of the verb "to say"; as a noun, it generally has the sense of "pronouncement," "assertion," or "statement." Levinas later contrasts it to *le Dit* or *les Dits*, the nominative form of the past participle of the same verb, which means "spoken words," often in the sense of "gossip." I shall translate *le Dire* as "Saying," *le Dit* and *les Dits* as "the Said." In this case, *dire* is not capitalized by Levinas.—trans.]

45. Levinas, *Humanisme de l'autre homme*, 97. The commandment to love the stranger is the most frequent of the commandments quoted from the Bible.

46. E. Levinas, *Totalité et infini* (The Hague: M. Nijhoff, 1961), 56.

47. Ibid., 57.

48. Ibid., 60.

49. See also J. L. Chrétien, *La fatigue* (Paris: Minuit, 1996), 155ff.

50. Levinas, *Humanisme de l'autre homme*, 97.

51. Levinas, *Autrement qu'être*, 73; and Levinas, *De Dieu qui vient à l'idée*, 114: "The goodness of the Good—of the Good that does not slumber or sleep . . . " See Psalm 121:4: "Behold, he that keepeth Israel shall neither slumber nor sleep."

52. J.-F. Lyotard, "Logique de Levinas," in *Textes pour Emmanuel Levinas*, ed. J. F. Laruelle (Paris: J. M. Place, 1980), 129. Quoted by Levinas in *Totalité et infini*, 192.

53. E. Levinas, *Hors sujet* (Montpellier: Fata Morgana, 1987), 83, 84. See Kant, *Critique of Practical Reason*, 207: The love of people "cannot be commanded, for it is not within the power of any human being to love someone merely on command."

54. Levinas, *Autrement qu'être*, 201.

55. Levinas, *Humanisme de l'autre homme*, 98.

Chapter 5: Sensibility and Reason

1. R. Legros, *L'idée d'humanité* (Paris: Grasset, 1990), 22.

2. E. Levinas, *Humanisme de l'autre homme* (Montpellier: Fata Morgana, 1972), 80.

3. E. Levinas, *Autrement qu'être ou au-delà de l'essence* (The Hague: M. Nijhoff, 1974), 180.

4. I. Kant, *Critique of Practical Reason* (1788), in I. Kant, *Practical Philosophy*, trans. and ed. by M.J. Gregor, general introduction by A. Wood (Cambridge: Cambridge University Press, 1996), 169.

5. I. Kant, "On a Newly Arisen Superior Tone in Philosophy" (1796), in *Raising the Tone of Philosophy: Late Essays by Immanuel Kant, Transformative Critique by Jacques Derrida*, ed. P. Fenves (Baltimore: Johns Hopkins University Press, 1993), 66.

6. Kant, *Critique of Practical Reason*, 171.

7. Ibid., 172.

8. Ibid., 199.

9. "Dreams of a Spirit-Seer Elucidated by Dreams of Metaphysics" (1766), in I. Kant, *Theoretical Philosophy, 1755–1770*, trans. and ed. D. Walford and R. Meerbote (Cambridge: Cambridge University Press, 1992), 305.

10. See J. L. Chrétien, *La voix nue* (Paris: Minuit, 1990), 171; and I. Murdoch, *Metaphysics as a Guide to Morals* (London: Penguin, 1992), 146.

11. J.-J. Rousseau, *La profession de foi du vicaire savoyard* (1762) (Paris: J. J. Pauvert, 1964), 116; and Kant, *Critique of Practical Reason*, 206.

12. I. Kant, *Groundwork of the Metaphysics of Morals* (1785), in *Practical Philosophy*, 74–75.

13. See H. E. Allison, *Kant's Theory of Freedom* (Cambridge: Cambridge University Press, 1990), 183 (a critique of Schiller's position).

14. See I. Kant, *Critique of Judgment* (1790), trans. J. H. Bernard (New York: Hafner, 1968), 55: "The faculty of desire, so far as it is determinable to act only through concepts, i.e. in conformity with the representation of a purpose, would be the will."

15. E. Levinas, *De l'existence à l'existant* (Paris: Fontaine, 1947), 163.

16. E. Levinas, *Le temps et l'autre* (1948) (Montpellier: Fata Morgana, 1979), 78: "The pathos of love consists of an insurmountable duality of beings."

17. E. Levinas, *Totalité et infini* (The Hague: M. Nijhoff, 1961), 244, my emphasis. See also 233ff.

18. Levinas, *Autrement qu'être*, 157–58.

19. Ibid., 18.

20. Ibid., 64.

21. Ibid., 139, note 2. The notion that that love can *also* exist in the erotic relationship does not seem to be taken into account by Levinas.

22. Ibid., 141.

23. Levinas, *Humanisme de l'autre homme*, 94.

24. Legros, *L'idée d'humanité*, 170.

25. Ibid., chap. 4.

26. E. Levinas, *Entre nous: Essais sur le penser-à-l'autre* (Paris: Grasset, 1991), 35, 33.

27. See chap. 4.

28. Kant, *Critique of Practical Reason*, 211.

29. Kant, *Critique of Judgment*, 96.

30. Ibid., 84.

31. Ibid., 102.

32. Ibid., 109.

33. Ibid., 111.

34. Ibid., 115 [translation modified].

35. Ibid., 116 [translation modified].

36. Kant, *Critique of Practical Reason*, 269.

37. B. Saint-Girons, *Fiat lux: Une philosophie du sublime* (Paris: Quai Voltaire, 1993), 189.

38. Levinas, *Totalité et infini*, 38.

39. Ibid., 51.

40. Ibid., 146.

41. Ibid., 51.

42. Ibid., 172.

43. Ibid., 175.

44. E. Levinas, *De Dieu qui vient à l'idée* (Paris: Vrin, 1982), 31. Regarding the verse from Ecclesiastes 1:9: "There is no new thing under the sun."

45. H. d'Aviau de Ternay, *Traces bibliques dans la loi morale chez Kant* (Paris: Beauchesne, 1986), 140.

46. I. Kant, "What Does It Mean to Orient Oneself in Thinking?" (1786), in I. Kant, *Religion and Rational Theology*, trans. and ed. A.W. Wood and G. Di Giovanni (Cambridge: Cambridge University Press, 1996), 13.

47. Kant, *Critique of Judgment*, 136–37. See above, chap. 4.

48. I. Kant, *Anthropology from a Pragmatic Point of View* (1798), trans. M. J. Gregor (The Hague: M. Nijhoff, 1974), 119.

49. Ibid., 133–34.

50. Ibid., 121–22.

51. Ibid., 132 [translation of first passage modified—trans.].

52. See B. Williams, *Ethics and the Limits of Philosophy* (London: Fontana Masterguides, 1985), 63, 55.

53. E. Levinas, *Altérité et transcendance* (Montpellier : Fata Morgana, 1995), 82.

54. Levinas, *Humanisme de l'autre homme*, 73.

55. Levinas, *Autrement qu'être*, 180, 194.

56. [See note 44 to chap. 4—trans.]

57. [The King James Version says simply: "Get thee out of thy country . . . unto a land that I will shew thee"—trans.]

58. J. L. Chrétien, *Corps à corps* (Paris: Minuit, 1997), 18: "The founding events of holy history continue to be written and perpetuated in new existences. They have so much power and sense that their date does not keep them from becoming contemporary with every present that arises. They have never finished taking place, if we offer them this place that is our life."

59. E. Levinas, *Noms propres* (Montpellier: Fata Morgana, 1976), 113.

60. Allison, *Kant's Theory of Freedom*, 51.

Chapter 6: Intelligible Character and Anarchy

1. I. Kant, *Critique of Practical Reason* (1788), in I. Kant, *Practical Philosophy*, trans. and ed. M. J. Gregor (Cambridge: Cambridge University Press, 1996), 216.

2. Ibid., 224, my emphasis.

3. Ibid., 216.

4. Ibid.

5. Ibid., my emphasis.

6. Ibid., 218.

7. Ibid.

8. I. Kant, *Critique of Pure Reason*, trans. and ed. P. Gruyer and A. W. Wood (Cambridge: Cambridge University Press, 1998), 536.

9. Ibid., 539.

10. See J. L. Chrétien, *L'inoubliable et l'inespéré* (Paris: Desclée de Brouwer, 1991), 150.

11. Ibid., 151.

12. Kant, *Critique of Practical Reason*, 218.

13. Ibid., 219.

14. See H. E. Allison, *Kant's Theory of Freedom* (Cambridge: Cambridge University Press, 1990), 32.

15. Kant, *Critique of Practical Reason*, 221.

16. See A. Philonenko in *L'oeuvre de Kant*, trans. A. Philonenko, 2 vols. (Paris: Vrin, 1993), 146: "Léon Brunschwicg declares: the intelligible character is the death of good will."

17. Ibid., 155.

18. Chrétien, *L'inoubliable et l'inespéré*, 150.

19. E. Levinas, *Humanisme de l'autre homme* (Montpellier: Fata Morgana, 1972), 75.

20. E. Amado Levy-Valensa, *La nature de la pensée inconsciente* (Paris: J. P. Delarge, 1978), 163.

21. Ibid., 164. The Hebrew letters have a numeric value: aleph has the value of one, beth of two.

22. Levinas, *Humanisme de l'autre homme*, 75, 60.

23. Ibid., 58.

24. Ibid., 63.

25. E. Levinas, *Ethique et infini* (Paris: Fayard, 1982), 125. See also E. Levinas, *Difficile liberté*, 2d ed. (Paris: Albin Michel, 1976), 183: "It is on the arid soil of the desert, where nothing is fixed, that the true spirit descended into a text to be universally fulfilled." And E. Levinas, *Noms propres* (Montpellier: Fata Morgana, 1976), 180: "Through such memories (of the war), a new access must be opened to the Jewish texts and a new privilege restored to the inner life."

26. E. Levinas, *De Dieu qui vient à l'idée* (Paris: Vrin, 1982), 48.

27. See J. L. Chrétien, *L'effroi du beau* (Paris: Cerf, 1987).

28. Levinas, *De Dieu qui vient à l'idée*, 51, note 24.

29. E. Levinas, *Autrement qu'être ou au-delà de l'essence* (The Hague: M. Nijhoff, 1974), 13.

30. E. Levinas, course on *Dieu, la mort et le temps*, 75.

31. Levinas, *Noms propres*, 123.

32. Levinas, *De Dieu qui vient à l'idée*, 36.

33. Ibid., 37.

34. Levinas, *Autrement qu'être*, 166.

35. Levinas, *De Dieu qui vient à l'idée*, 257.

36. Levinas, *Difficile liberté*, 276; and Levinas, *Autrement qu'être*, 190.

37. Levinas, *De Dieu qui vient à l'idée*, 257.

38. Levinas, *Autrement qu'être*, 157.

39. See Levinas, *Humanisme de l'autre homme*, 59: An immemorial past—"eternity, whose meaningfulness obstinately pushes us back toward the past, may be that as well."

40. Psalm 121:4: "Behold, he that keepeth Israel shall neither slumber nor sleep."

41. E. Levinas, *Entre nous* (Paris, Grasset, 1991), 214.

42. Ibid., 233.

43. Levinas, *De Dieu qui vient à l'idée*, 118, note 18: "Devotion as strong as death and, in a sense, stronger than death. In finitude, death shapes a destiny that it cuts short, whereas nothing could exempt me from the response to which I am passively obliged. The grave is not a refuge—it is not forgiveness. The debt remains."

44. Ibid., 252.

45. Levinas, *Autrement qu'être*, 67.

46. Ibid., 200.

47. Ibid., 201, 202.

48. See, in *Cahier de l'Herne/E. Levinas* (Paris: L'Herne, 1991), the essays by M. Haar and J. L. Chrétien.

49. See chap. 3.

Chapter 7: The Question of Happiness

1. Aristotle, *Nicomachean Ethics*, with English translation by H. Rackman (Cambridge: Harvard University Press, 1962), 10.6 (p. 609).

2. Ibid., 10.7 (p. 617).

3. Ra. A. Gauthier and J. Y. Jolif, *Commentaire de l'Ethique à Nicomaque* (Louvain: Nauwelaerts, 1970), 856.

4. Ibid., 856.

5. B. Spinoza, *The Ethics* (1674), book 5, proposition 42, scholia, in *The Ethics and Selected Letters*, trans. S. Shirley (Indianapolis: Hackett, 1982), 225.

6. I. Kant, *Critique of Pure Reason*, trans. and ed. P. Gruyer and A. W. Wood (Cambridge: Cambridge University Press, 1998), 117 [for "extravagant insights," the French text has *intuitions transcendantes*, i.e. "transcendental intuitions"—trans.]. See above, chap. 1, for the rupture between knowledge and virtue.

7. I. Kant, *Groundwork of the Metaphysics of Morals* (1785), in I. Kant, *Practical Philosophy*, trans. and ed. by M. J. Gregor (Cambridge: Cambridge University Press, 1996), 71.

8. I. Kant, *Critique of Practical Reason* (1788), in *Practical Philosophy*, 195 [translation slightly modified].

9. Ibid., 169.

10. Ibid., 210–11.

11. Ibid., 214.

12. Ibid. See also F. Dostoevsky, *Crime and Punishment*, trans. C. Garnett (New York: Heritage, 1938), 86–87.

13. Kant, *Critique of Practical Reason*, 208.

14. Ibid., 209.

15. I. Kant, "On a Newly Arisen Superior Tone in Philosophy" (1796), in *Raising the Tone of Philosophy: Late Essays by Immanuel Kant, Transformative Critique by Jacques Derrida*, ed. P. Fenves (Baltimore: Johns Hopkins University Press, 1993), 60n.

16. E. Levinas, *Totalité et infini* (The Hague: M. Nijhoff, 1961), 92. See also 87: "Essentially egoistic happiness."

17. Ibid., 85: "the character of fulfillment that is worth *more* than ataraxy." See also 218.

18. See E. Levinas, *De l'existence à l'existant* (Paris: Fontaine, 1947), 21, 95, 110. For the tragic side of being, see C. Chalier, *La persévérence du mal* (Paris: Cerf, 1987).

19. Levinas, *Totalité et infini*, 84.

20. Ibid., 89.

21. E. Levinas, *Noms propres* (Montpellier: Fata Morgana, 1976), 169.

22. Levinas, *Totalité et infini*, 121.

23. E. Levinas, *Difficile liberté*, 2d ed. (Paris: Albin Michel, 1976), 31.

24. E. Levinas, *Entre nous: Essais sur le penser-à-l'autre* (Paris: Grasset, 1991), 23.

25. Kant, *Critique of Practical Reason*, 228.

26. Kant, *Groundwork of the Metaphysics of Morals*, 84. [The last word of this passage in the French translation is *dignité*, which means both "dignity" and "worthiness"—trans.]

27. Ibid.

28. Ibid., 51.

29. Ibid., 97.

30. Ibid., 83, 87–88.

31. Kant, *Critique of Practical Reason*, 230.

32. See below, "Postponement and Hope."

33. Levinas, *Noms propres*, 179.

34. Levinas, *De l'existence à l'existant*, 67–68.

35. M. Blanchot, *L'écriture du désastre* (Paris: Gallimard, 1980), 40.

36. Dostoevsky, *Crime and Punishment*, 52.

37. E. Levinas, *Du sacré au saint* (Paris: Minuit, 1977), 166.

38. Kant, *Critique of Practical Reason*, 156.

39. See E. Levinas, *Liberté et commandement*, 67.

40. E. Levinas, *Autrement qu'être ou au-delà de l'essence* (The Hague: M. Nijhoff, 1974), 13.

41. E. Levinas, *De Dieu qui vient à l'idée* (Paris: Vrin, 1982), 262.

42. E. Levinas, *Humanisme de l'autre homme* (Montpellier: Fata Morgana, 1972), 63. See above, chap. 6.

43. Levinas, *De Dieu qui vient à l'idée*, 114–15.

44. Kant, *Critique of Practical Reason*, 228.

45. Ibid., 232.

46. P. Ricoeur, *Le conflit des interprétations* (Paris: Seuil, 1969), 407.

47. E. Levinas, course on *Dieu, la mort et le temps*, 71.

48. Ibid., 75.

49. Kant, *Critique of Practical Reason*, 239.

50. Levinas, course on *Dieu, la mort et le temps*, 75.

51. Kant, *Critique of Practical Reason*, 241.

52. J. L. Chrétien, *L'inoubliable, l'inespéré* (Paris: Desclée de Brouwer, 1991), 151.

53. Kant, *Critique of Practical Reason*, 243, my emphasis.

54. E. Levinas, "The Primacy of Pure Practical Reason," trans. from the Dutch by B. Billings, in *Man and the World* (Dordrecht: Kluwer, 1994), 450. See also Kant, *Critique of Practical Reason*, 247: "That there *is* such a causality [freedom] is only postulated by the moral law and for the sake of it" (my emphasis).

55. E. Levinas, *L'au-delà du verset: Lectures et discours talmudiques* (Paris: Minuit, 1982), 139.

56. E. Levinas, *De l'existence à l'existant*, 156.

57. E. Levinas, *A l'heure des nations* (Paris: Minuit, 1988), 103. See also 194: "What happened at Auschwitz seems to me to mean that the Lord demands a love that does not entail any promise on his part."

Chapter 8: Ethics and Religion

1. I. Kant, "Dreams of a Spirit-Seer Elucidated by Dreams of Metaphysics" (1766), in I. Kant, *Theoretical Philosophy, 1755–1770*, trans. and ed. D. Walford and R. Meerbote (Cambridge: Cambridge University Press, 1992), 358–59.

2. I. Kant, *The Metaphysics of Morals* (1785) in I. Kant, *Practical Philosophy*, trans. and ed. M. J. Gregor (Cambridge: Cambridge University Press, 1996), 596–97.

3. See chap. 7.

4. I. Kant, *Critique of Practical Reason* (1788), in *Practical Philosophy*, 258. After "*before our eyes,*" Kant adds in parentheses: "For what we can prove perfectly holds as much certainty for us as what we are assured of by our sight."

5. A. Philonenko, *L'oeuvre de Kant*, trans. A. Philonenko, 2 vols. (Paris: Vrin, 1993), 2:175, 176, 177.

6. E. Weil, *Problèmes kantiens* (Paris: Vrin, 1990), 24. He adds: "Even though, as theoreticians, we are obliged to *presuppose* the reasonable character of both and we do presuppose it; otherwise, we would not even ask our questions."

7. See I. Kant, *Critique of Pure Reason*, preface to the 2d edition, 109: Reason asks nature to instruct it, "not like a pupil, who has recited to him whatever the teacher wants to say, but like an appointed judge who compels witnesses to answer the questions he puts to them."

8. A. Philonenko, *La théorie kantienne de l'histoire* (Paris: Vrin, 1986), 32.

9. Kant, *Religion within the Boundaries of Mere Reason* (1793), in *Religion and Rational Theology*, trans. and ed. A. W. Wood and G. Di Giovanni (Cambridge: Cambridge University Press, 1996), 89n.

10. Ibid., 135.

11. J. Derrida, "Foi et savoir," in *La religion*, ed. J. Derrida and G. Vattimo (Paris: Seuil, 1996), 20.

12. Ibid. Derrida continues: "Judaism and Islam might therefore be the last two forms of monotheism still revolting against everything that, in the Christianization of our world, signifies the death of God, death in God."

13. G. Krüger, *Critique et morale chez Kant*, trans. M. Régnier (Paris: Bibliothèque des archives de philosophie, Beauchesne, 1960), 267.

14. Kant, *Critique of Pure Reason*, 117 [translation modified].

15. E. Levinas, *Autrement qu'être ou au-delà de l'essence* (The Hague: M. Nijhoff, 1974), 5.

16. E. Levinas, *Humanisme de l'autre homme* (Montpellier: Fata Morgana, 1972), 39.

17. Ibid., 38.

18. Ibid., 39.

19. [Like the English "sense," the French *sens* signifies both "meaning" and "direction"—trans.]

20. Levinas, *Humanisme de l'autre homme*, 41.

21. E. Levinas, *De Dieu qui vient à l'idée* (Paris: Vrin, 1982), 252, 253.

22. An idea analyzed in the chapter on Revelation in E. Levinas's *L'inspiration du philosophe* (Paris: Albin Michel, 1996).

23. Levinas, *Autrement qu'être*, 187.

24. Ibid., 188–89.

25. E. Levinas, *Dieu, la mort, le temps*, ed. J. Rolland (Paris: Grasset, Biblio-essais, 1993), 75.

26. Kant, *Religion within the Boundaries*, 57.

27. Ibid., 104.

28. Kant, *Critique of Practical Reason*, 243.

29. Letter of 4/28/1775 to Lavater, cited in Weil, *Problèmes kantiens*, 145.

30. Kant, *Religion within the Boundaries*, 119, my emphasis.

31. Philonenko, *La théorie kantienne de l'histoire*, 194.

32. Kant, *Religion within the Boundaries*, 156, 154, 146: "the faith of a religion of service is, on the contrary, a *slavish* and *mercenary* faith . . . and cannot be considered as saving, because it is not moral." See also above, chap. 2, "Morality and Legality."

33. Ibid., 155.

34. Ibid., 187.

35. Ibid., 200.

36. Letter to Lavater of 4/28/1775 in Kant, *Lettres sur la morale et la religion*, 25.

37. See chap. 3.

38. E. Levinas, *Difficile liberté*, 2d ed. (Paris: Albin Michel, 1976), 13. Quotation from Rashi on Leviticus 10:2, epigraph to the chapter "Au-delà du pathétique."

39. Ibid., 35.

40. E. Levinas, *Quatre lectures talmudiques* (Paris: Minuit, 1968), 178. Matthew 5:17: "Think not that I am come to destroy the law, or the prophets: I am not come to destroy, but to fulfil."

41. E. Levinas, *Hors sujet* (Montpellier: Fata Morgana, 1987), 83–84 (regarding F. Rosenzweig).

42. Ibid.: "And even from assimilated Judaism, which does not know how Christianized its reflexes have become, even though its reflective thought considers itself free thought."

43. H. Cohen, *L'éthique du judaïsme*, trans. M. R. Hayoun (Paris: Cerf, 1994), 350.

44. Levinas, *Dieu, la mort, le temps*, 75.

45. Levinas, *De Dieu qui vient à l'idée*, 51, 60.

46. Kant, *Critique of Practical Reason*, 243.

47. Kant, *The Metaphysics of Morals*, 567.

48. Kant, *Religion within the Boundaries*, 104.

49. Philonenko, *La théorie kantienne de l'histoire*, 226. The image of the bent is Lutheran. See also 100: "Man is egoistic insofar as he is bent."

50. Kant, *Critique of Practical Reason*, 239.

51. Kant, *Religion within the Boundaries*, 108, 109.

52. Kant, *The Metaphysics of Morals*, 567.

53. H. E. Allison, *Kant's Theory of Freedom* (Cambridge: Cambridge University Press, 1990), 175.

54. Kant, *Critique of Pratical Reason*, 208.

55. Ibid., 210.

56. E. Levinas, *Entre nous*, 234, 194, my emphasis.

57. Levinas, *De Dieu qui vient à l'idée*, 113.

58. E. Levinas, *Entre nous: Essais sur le penser-à-l'autre* (Paris: Grasset, 1991), 258.

59. In *Adieu* (Paris: Galilée, 1997), J. Derrida quotes a conversation with Levinas: "You know, people often speak of ethics to describe what I do, but what interests me when all is said and done is not ethics, not only ethics, but the saint, the holiness of the saint" (15).

60. E. Levinas, *A l'heure des nations* (Paris: Minuit, 1988), 14.

61. Kant, *Critique of Practical Reason*, 237 [translation modified].

62. Levinas, *Du sacré au saint* (Paris: Minuit, 1977), 121.

63. P. Levi, *Survival in Auschwitz* (New York: Touchstone, 1996), 106–7.

64. Philonenko, *La théorie kantienne de l'histoire*, 143.

65. I. Kant, "Idea of a Universal History from a Cosmopolitan Point of View," trans. L. W. Beck, in I. Kant, *On History* (Indianapolis: Bobbs-Merrill, 1963),22.

66. V. Grossman, *Forever Flowing*, trans. T. P. Whitney (New York: Harper & Row, 1970), 242 [the French version says: "His goodness, his mind, *his freedom*, are immovable"—trans.].

67. V. Grossman, *Life and Fate*, trans. R. Chandler (London: Harrill, 1985), 410.

68. E. Levinas, *L'au-delà du verset: Lectures et discours talmudiques* (Paris: Minuit, 1982), 21.

index

Autonomy (*continued*)
  and the sensible world, 105; and the
  tyrant, 60–61; and unique singularity, 83;
  and universality, 85–86; and the will,
  63–65; and violence, 74
Awakening, ethical: and the Book, 150; and
  the face, 37–38; and happiness, 150–51;
  and heteronomy, 78; and the ingratitude
  of God, 163; and perseverance in being,
  163; and rationality, 97; and the right to
  being, 126

Bad start, 48–54
Baptism, 104, 114–15
Barbarism, 5–6, 9–14, 43, 150, 152
Beauty, 20, 55–56, 122
Being, 55–56, 67, 125–26, 137–43. *See
  also* Perseverance in Being
Being unto death, 147, 163
Benevolence, 15–16
Bent, 169, 190n. 49
Bereshit, 119
Bergson, Henri, 64
Beth, 186n. 21
Bible, 45, 77–78, 87, 108, 119. *See also* the
  Book; *specific books*
Birkenau, 11–12
Blanchot, Maurice, 143
Bliss, 133
Böhme, Jakob, 155
Book, the, 86–87, 121–22, 150
Boundlessness, 89, 97, 99, 124
Brit, 57

Camps, Nazi death, 9–12, 142, 188n. 57
Casuistry, 29–31
Catechism, 154
Categorical imperative, 62–64, 126
Causality, 2, 110–16
Character, 114–18, 123, 126
Christianity: and ethics, 157; and good
  will, 35, 165–66; and holiness, 169; and
  intention, 35–36; versus Judaism, 8,
  165–66; and the kingdom of God, 148;
  and moral faith, 154, 164–66; and
  original sin, 50; and transcendence, 163
Cohen, H., 168
Concupiscence, 92–93, 129
Conscience, 12–14, 18–23, 26, 39–43,
  46–47, 157

Constant, Benjamin, 28
Contract, the, 56–57, 95
Critique of Judgment (Kant), 97
Critique of Pure Reason (Kant), 23–24, 62,
  68, 133

Death, 54–55, 98, 128, 129, 147, 157–59,
  163, 186n. 43
Debt: and death, 186n. 43; and election,
  127; and evil, 48, 51–53; and happiness,
  143; and the immemorial, 130; and the
  infinite, 152; to be oneself, 126
Decalogue, 35–36, 165
Descartes, René, 1, 5, 20–21
Descent of the word, 162–63
Desire, 38–39, 92–93, 118, 135,
  144–45, 149
Determinism, 2–3, 110–16, 155
Diabolical, the, 49–50
Dignity, 15–18, 33, 65–66, 86, 114,
  128–29, 187n. 26
Dire, 58, 77, 87, 183n. 44
Disinterestedness, 66–67, 97–98,
  101–103, 149
Dit, 107, 121, 183n. 44
Dostoevsky, Fyodor, 143
"Dreams of a Spirit-Seer" (Kant), 89
Duty: and the absence of God, 157;
  "adamant voice" of, 30; and autonomy,
  65; and the debt, 127; and evil, 48; and
  good will, 27–28; and happiness, 135,
  141; and intention, 28, 35; and legalism,
  38; and moral feeling, 88–89; and predisposition toward the good, 44–45; and
  self-love, 93–94; to singularities, 40;
  toward humanity in oneself, 91; universality of, 32

Ecclesiastes, 103, 133
Education, 9–16
Egoism: and awakening, 150; and evil, 58;
  and happiness, 136–37, 139, 142–44;
  and mortal destiny, 54–55; and propensity for evil, 52–54; and pure self-
  interest, 66–67; and suffering, 80
Egypt, return to, 74–78, 81, 95–96, 108
Election: and alterity, 127; and anarchy,
  124; anteriority of, 80; and the appeal,
  78–81, 94–95, 108, 127; and the debt,
  127; and freedom, 6–7, 128; and happi-

ness, 144, 149; and heteronomy, 79; and
the immemorial, 130, 143; and passivity,
107; and respect, 95; and Saying, 107;
and the to-God, 161–62; and unique-
ness, 78–79, 127–28; and the wound, 82
Elijah, 43
Emotion, 104–6
Empirical character, 114, 116
Empiricism, 111
Enlightenment, 10–11, 13, 75
Enlightenment, age of, 5, 50, 65, 104
Enthusiasm, 20, 89, 105, 146
Epicureanism, 142, 146
Erotic love, 92–93, 129, 184n. 21
Ethics (Spinoza), 25–26
Eudaemonism, 8, 136, 165
Evil, 10, 13–14, 42–54, 57–58, 181n. 6
Exodus: and the appeal, 123; and the
descent of the word, 162; on freedom,
76; on the graven image, 99; on leaving
Egypt, 76, 95–96; and moral law, 80; on
Moses, 123, 145; on slavery, 73; on the
stranger, 77; and the trace of God, 121;
and the voice of conscience, 21–23
Exteriority: and the alliance with the good,
56; and biblical teachings, 45; differing
views of, 6–7; and the face, 55; and
Judaism, 167–68; and sense of one's
being, 1–2; and the source of ethics,
6, 26

Face, the: and the Absent One, 120, 144;
appeal of, 6, 53, 80, 108, 145; and the
awakening, 37–38; and the existence of
God, 159; and for-the-other, 161; and
happiness, 142–45, 151; and heteronomy, 80–82, 124; and holiness, 172;
and the infinite, 37–40, 47, 151–52;
loftiness of, 101–102; and the loss of
being, 39; and responsibility, 94; and
shame, 46–47; shock of, 55; and the
source of ethics, 6, 26, 37–40; versus the
starry heaven, 103; and the stranger, 77;
and suffering, 39, 55, 79; and the third
party, 34; and the voice of conscience,
47; weakness of, 155–52
Fear, 98–99
Feelings, 14–17. *See also* Sensibility
Finitude: and the absence of God, 156; and
autonomy, 61; and the consciousness of

limits, 124; and the crisis of the subject,
1; and the encounter with the other, 69;
and ethics, 24; and good will, 37; inade-
quacy of, 46; and the moral subject, 5;
and the pathological, 86; and the predisposition toward the good, 47; and respect, 67; and the sublime, 99–100
For-the-other, 80, 127
Freedom: and anteriority, 109, 112; as
autonomy, 114–15; and the crisis of the
subject, 2; and determinism, 111–14,
155; and election, 6–7, 128; and evil,
50–51; and God's law, 76; and graven
images, 76; and heteronomy, 77–78; and
intelligible character, 114–17; and the
moral subject, 2–4; and passion, 106;
and submission, 69; and suffering, 80;
and the slave, 73; transcendental, 116;
and violence, 75; and the will, 116
Fruits of the earth, 137–38

General will, 69–70, 74
Genesis, 108, 144, 168
God: absence of, 155–63; and the alliance,
57; and atheism, 139, 175; and the crisis
of the subject, 4; death of, 157–59; and
deliverance from Egypt, 96; desire for,
149; differing views of, 8; and the face,
101; and freedom, 78, 116; glory of,
162–63; and happiness, 133–34,
147–52, 163; and heteronomy, 72,
154–55; and the highest good, 148; and
holiness, 174; and the immemorial, 121,
130; kingdom of, 148, 151; ingratitude
of, 160–63; Levinas's use of term, 123;
and the other, 130; proof of the existence
of, 148–49, 161; Son of, 164–65; and
the voice of conscience, 20–23
Good, the: alliance with the, 22, 56–62,
130; and anarchy, 22, 56–58; anteriority
of, 6, 22–23, 43–52, 56, 181n.6; and the
appeal, 77, 80–81, 102, 128; and election, 127; and the emotions, 106; highest, 145–46, 163; and knowledge, 13;
and passivity, 109; in Plato, 55–56
Good will: and the absence of God, 157;
and autonomy, 6, 64–65; and Christianity, 35, 165–66; failure of, 42; and
finitude, 37; and intelligible character,
117; and morality of action, 26–27;

and evil, 50; as fact of reason, 85; and good will, 31; and heteronomy, 83–84; and holiness, 174; and the moral imperative, 28; of principles, 26, 28–31; and self-interest, 31, 64; and singularities, 12, 17–18, 34, 36–37, 83, 175; and uniqueness, 32–35; and violence, 74

Unrepresentable, the, 127, 130

Virtue: and Aristotle, 21; and the death of God, 159; and happiness, 8, 134, 140–47; and holiness, 169–71; and obedience, 153; source of, 14–16, 21

Voice: and Abraham, 109; and the appeal of the face, 174; of conscience, 18–23, 26, 42–47; of duty, 48, 51; of reason, 117, 157; singular, 84

War, 98

Weakness, 81–84, 122–23, 150–51

White Rose group, 12

Will, the, 63–65, 71–72, 91, 104, 116

Word, descent of the, 162–63

Works, 160

Worthiness, 8, 134, 139–52, 187n. 26

Wound, 82, 93, 96, 102

Yohanan, Rabbi, 40

Zohar, 150